Through the Minefield

Through the Minefield

AN AUTOBIOGRAPHY

Constantine FitzGibbon

THE BODLEY HEAD

LONDON · SYDNEY

TORONTO

For Nanny Lucas from us both

Part One

Part One

I

FOR MANY YEARS I carried in my wallet a newspaper clipping. It was an extract from the report of a trial, a trial with which neither I, nor anyone known to me, was in any way connected. A young woman was giving evidence, though the nature of her testimony I also do not know. What I had clipped from that newspaper a quarter of a century ago, and what I carried with me for almost ten years until an acquaintance on Capri to whom I had shown it asked to be allowed to add it to his collection, was a very simple and intensely complicated statement. Called upon to tell the truth, the whole truth and nothing but the truth, she had said:

'I often imagine things which I subsequently believe to be true.'

Why had I cut this out? Or, rather, why had it given me such pleasure when first I had seen it, while reading the *News of the World* in 1941, after breakfast, in some forgotten officers' mess? I was sufficiently well informed even then to know that old Freud and his colleagues had let this particular cat out of its bag many long years before, while a whole host of writers had, in varying measure and degree, anticipated and succeeded them. I knew that Goethe had entitled his autobiography *Dichtung und Wahrheit*, and I had read it. *Wahrheit* means *truth*, but there exists no perfectly elegant translation for the word *Dichtung*. Perhaps the closest rendering is the distasteful phrase, then unknown to us, *creative writing*. Nor at that time could I have known, though I might have suspected, that Goethe when writing about the past was not always quite certain whether he was the chronicler of 'fact' or the creator of 'fiction'. Now I realise that Goethe probably, at least in his autobiography, cared little about such trivial distinctions. And it may have been some dim appreciation of such good sense that led me then to tuck the scrap of paper away in my wallet. The young woman's statement was an innocent testimonial of the existence of poetic truth.

9

It was more. I had not then ever been inside a court of law, but I knew enough about the pretentious mumbo-jumbo and play-acting of these gatherings from the films ('Perhaps *this* will refresh your memory!') and the newspaper reports ('With due respect, m'lud, I would suggest that my learned friend has been led by his client's brogue into confusing a point with a pint.' *Laughter.*) to delight in the honesty of this young woman. Her remark, made under oath to a god in which perhaps neither she nor most of those foolishly bewigged law officers believed, was refreshing. It, at least, was true. And therefore it also seemed to me funny, a matter of laughter, a banana-skin on which an entire begowned, self-important, double-firsted, dinner-eating, hypocritical and platitudinous inn of court slithered—or should have slithered—arms waving and faces twisted with the anguish of uncertainty, towards a gigantic judicial prat-fall.

But of course they did not, nor could they afford to slither. Their fat livelihood, material and mental and, so help us, spiritual, would have come crashing down upon hard ground like a shopping basket stuffed with fake antique china and imitation crystal. Voices went on and on until somebody was convicted or acquitted: justice had or had not been done, but at least had been *seen* to be done: the young woman, who had dropped the banana-skin, had returned to her private life in which, I hope, pleasurable fantasy more than compensated for a certain inevitable bewilderment.

Other, and very much larger and more slippery, banana-skins have been dropped over the past century or so. Our whole society seemed, at one time, in danger of breaking its back over Karl Marx's, as it slithered, lurched and teetered until Keynes firmly seized it by the arm and restored it, for the moment at least, to an upright posture. Hitler put the skids under a Europe which fractured almost every bone in its body but somehow survived. Freud—enough of bananas—opened a door, a bedroom door, but when the man, woman and child emerged, blinking in a new, and therefore unaccustomed, light, they did not realise that during their long incarceration a large part of the landing

had rotted away; it was a long, nasty drop before their feet
were again on firm ground, a drop from which many never
quite recovered.

That there were similar *bouleversements* in the other sciences
and, in appearance at least, in the arts is a truism, though
with the passage of even a generation or two what were once
regarded as artistic revolutions (twelve-tonal music or
abstract painting, for example) have taken a more modest
place between the banks of our ever-flowing culture. Poetic
truth has to be expressed anew as man's perception of the
world alters: the truth itself cannot be ravaged by artists,
and though it seemed some years ago that it could be
physically destroyed by politicians and semi-scientists
('social engineering' has not always been, and is not now
everywhere, a term of abuse) the lessons of Germany and
Russia show that our culture is much tougher, much more
capable of surviving rape and mutilation and perversion,
than many of us once thought.

This is not true of other forms of human endeavour and
human existence. Man's relationships with woman, with
parents and children, with his environment, with God and
perhaps above all with himself can be altered and have been
altered drastically in the last century. Such changes can be
gradual, as with the erosion of a desire to believe in God (how
many people actually *did* believe in past centuries is an
unanswerable question; the strenuous determination that
they *should* believe, and the horror that outspoken agnosti-
cism evoked in allegedly religious societies, would indicate
that it was perhaps not as many as was once assumed: on the
other hand even the desire, which must once have been
very vivid, has now become vestigial); or the change can
come almost overnight and be the work of almost a single
man, as with Darwinism and the vulgar acceptance for
several generations that man was only another sort of
animal; or it can involve a total re-assessment of the material
world as brought about by the physicists, which yet really
affects no one at all directly, except when the nuclear bombs
go off or the Strontium-90 drops from heaven in the rainy
season; or it affects everyone in a particular society, as was

11

the case with the emancipation of women, but in ways so subtle that the cause for an increased sense of well-being or a growing malaise are seldom correctly ascribed; or, as with industrialisation, it can be believed to produce one result, namely general betterment and thus increased happiness, while in fact creating the precise opposite.

Now all such drastic changes, when recognised as the work of man and not simply accepted as the tides of time, are initially resented by the overwhelming mass of any society. The men responsible are usually, though not of course by everybody, hated, cursed and, if the circumstances are propitious, persecuted and even executed. This is quite natural and quite correct. Love of order, if that order be tolerable and sometimes even if it is not, is an essential human characteristic. The man who questions his society's order, or the beliefs and values upon which it is based, is an enemy of his society as it then exists. Society therefore expels him, mocks him, crucifies him with such means as it has at its disposal. It must frequently succeed in its attempt, laudable or not according to one's point of view, to impose silence upon the would-be innovator, to stamp out the possibility of change. Everyone knows the story of the Roman who invented unbreakable glass. When that cheerful technologist showed his invention to the Emperor, and informed him proudly that he alone possessed the secret, the Divine Monarch ordered his guards that the monster be strangled forthwith. In one form or another his fate must have been that of innumerable other clever men: it must, indeed, be happening today. Not all those books and magazines, published every day and read by almost no one, can be totally devoid of new ideas.

But when society is not personified in a single emperor, nor the new creation or interpretation the possession of a single man, then some of these revolutionary concepts will be transformed into practice. And at some point during the transitional phase, society will accept them and incorporate them into its way of life or thought—and soon wonder what all the fuss was once about: how could the previous generation have been so hysterically opposed to the self-evident?—

or it will fight them. Or it can exclude them and their advocates: but then it is a counter-society, a social heresy, that is being created. During the past couple of centuries, when 'progress' has been fashionable (a Belgian idea, according to Baudelaire) and has been frequently confused with mere change, our most sophisticated Western societies have almost invariably accepted these heresies even at the cost of great modification for their own cherished orthodoxies. True, some eccentric re-interpretations of the world, such as that propounded by Ouspensky and his people, have never really caught on. Others, at least equally illogical, such as historical materialism or racism, have achieved, at some times and in some places, all the respectability of accepted dogma. And once this happens they often become closed systems of thought, their truth self-evident, and any opposition is, in its turn, a heresy to be stamped out. If they achieve political dominance, they like to assume totalitarian form. The old modification to accepted belief, the old-new thought, even the crackpot idea, then become 'the truth'.

'I often imagine things which I subsequently believe to be true.' She did not mean all that I have written in the last few pages: I did not grasp it when I read my *News of the World* in 1941: but its appeal was obviously great for me to have cut it out. I suspect now that that appeal was not only to the nihilism of my banana-skin-loving nature, but also to an unformulated appreciation of the world into which I was growing up.

A few years later, in March of 1946 to be precise, I went for a walk that took me out of Le Havre. I was then a tall, thin twenty-six-year-old officer in the United States Army, a major on his way back to America to be demobilised. Le Havre was mostly in ruins. When the Allied armies broke out of Normandy in August of 1944, the Germans had clung to the ports of Northern France from which they had only been finally ejected some months later after severe fighting, bombing, bombardment and to the final accompaniment of their own demolitions. Not much of Le Havre had been left.

After six years of military service, I was on my way out, leaving the Europe of my later childhood and my youth behind me, I was, as I then thought, about to start a new life, my real life, on the other side of the Atlantic. Meanwhile the Liberty ship, *Sea Sturgeon*, which had brought me and some others, in a more or less intoxicated state, from Southampton was tied up here before proceeding across the ocean, and we awaited her pleasure in a transit officers' camp. *The virgin sturgeon needs no urgin'* we had sung as we drank our way cross-Channel. The transit officers' mess was dry, dreary and cold. The cool, watery spring sunshine invited me to clear my head of fumes in the morning country outside Le Havre.

I walked the suburban streets, between the ruined houses. The pocked and cratered roadway managed to be both dusty and muddy, as is possible at that season of the year. There were few people about, and those were bowed, elderly figures, many of whom were carrying heavy, shapeless bundles or pulling handcarts. The work of salvage and reconstruction was going on, but at a very slow tempo. This human ant-heap had been kicked over long ago. Most of the ants who had survived had gone elsewhere, but a few still lingered about the rubble and the stagnant pools, and evidently some of the ruins were still inhabited. (When high-minded aesthetes dilate upon the pleasure of ruins, I wonder if they ever stop to think of what once must have happened to provide them with their pleasure.) I passed a group of ragged German prisoners moving heavy stones in slow motion under the bored eye of an almost equally ragged, though better fed, French soldier. A partly reconstructed ground floor, with three-ply or cardboard windows, bore the sign: BAR.

I stepped down into a single, dark room. Behind the bar was a swarthy man in shirt-sleeves and waistcoat, with the coarse and cynical features of a Pierre Laval. The only other customer was a thin-chested old man in workman's blue. I asked for a glass of wine, but there was none. There was, I was told, almost nothing. '*Ils ont tout pris,*' though who 'they' were I did not care to ask. At last, and for an exhorbitant price, I was given a glass of very raw Calvados. The bar smelt of charred wood and of urine. My attempts to engage the two men in conversation—and I speak good French—were rebuffed. They had no wish to talk to another foreign soldier. Who can blame them? I certainly did not. But that smell and that semi-hostile atmosphere have remained with me. I can recognise them instantly, as, for example, when I open the pages of a certain famous French Existentialist.

I went out again into the pale spring sunshine. And now I was in the very outermost outskirts of Le Havre and quite near the coastal cliffs. Here the devastation was much less and there were many houses, of the bungalow variety, which had not been damaged at all. Not even the windows were broken. Indeed, some of them looked brand-new, but whether they were the last of the pre-war or the first of the post-war houses, I could not tell. Yet rather to my surprise there were even fewer people about here than among the ruins. Indeed there were none at all. These houses were all empty and uncurtained. And then I noticed that across their windows there was written, in soap it appeared, the words: RESERVE AUX SINISTRES.

What did it mean? Who were these sinister beings for whom habitable houses were reserved while others were left to pick about among rubble? Or was there perhaps some political implication? I knew the meaning of the Italian word, *sinistra*. Were only persons of proven left-wing views, perhaps former members of the Communist resistance, to be allowed? If so, why had none of them yet arrived, for nearly a year had passed since the end of the war? Or did sinister mean something closer to the English? Were these rather ugly little houses in these utterly deserted little streets reserved solely for ghouls and ghosts? There must, I thought, be enough ghosts looking for a place to haunt, thousands of French ghosts, millions of European ghosts, the ghosts of an industrialised society that had spilled out beyond its city boundaries in great rings of bungaloid development, and which had then methodically smashed the centres of its towns and cities. I hastened through that ghostly ring, and was soon out in the countryside proper.

(Later, I discovered that *sinistré* means bombed-out. Presumably when writing, in soap and French, upon a window-pane, one does not bother with accents. 'Bombed-out' was not a word that I was likely to have heard in French during my comfortable, Parisian childhood, nor even at the senior military headquarters where I had passed the French campaign. Yet it still mystifies me why all those habitable houses should have been empty. Bureaucracy, I suppose.)

Now I was walking along a paved country road with, on my left and a couple of hundred yards away, the brow of the high cliffs and, beyond, the invisible but just audible sea. The grass between the road and the clifftops was quite long and the brisk March wind caused it to ripple and shine like the waves I could not see.

The road turned as the cliff turned, and Le Havre was out of sight. It was all country now, empty country beneath a blue sky and small, swift, very white clouds. There was not a soul in sight, no traffic upon the road and no one working upon the rolling fields and downland to my right. But on my left I could see, by the edge of the cliff, the entrance to what was obviously a German strongpoint. I stepped over a single strand of wire and made my way across the long grass towards it.

I had, as I say, spent most of the second half of the war at various very senior headquarters, and though as an intelligence officer I had had much to do with Hitler's Atlantic Wall, I had seen nothing of it. My curiosity was thus, in part, technical. In part, it was merely that feeling which makes us all examine any man-made object, any artifact that we may find washed up, among seashells and seaweed, upon a deserted shore.

A great rusty steel door hung ajar. With difficulty I pulled it open, just wide enough for me to pass through. I was in a concrete room, empty save for some mechanism which I believed to be connected with range-finding. There was also a desk and chair, and a telephone. All was neat and clean, and lit by a slit in the concrete which faced the sea. The white concrete must have been several yards thick.

The view through the slit was astonishing. The Channel,

far below, glittered in the sun, spread out like a quilt of the finest silk. Miles out, a small ship went about its business. My eyes could travel from left to right in an arc of almost one hundred and eighty degrees above the murmuring sea. I was, of course, aware of the reason for this tremendous panorama.

I turned away and found a small noticeboard, to which was pinned a single notice, dating from the autumn of 1944. It was slightly yellow and its edges were not at all ragged, for it had been most neatly fixed to the board with four drawing-pins.

The Atlantic Wall had been largely manned by Russians. Taken prisoner by the Germans in the great encirclements of 1941 and 1942, some had volunteered for the German Army because they were anti-Communist, but most in order to avoid death by starvation in the Nazi prison camps. Their fate had been pathetic. Taken prisoner once again in the West, most of them had been handed back to the Russians, who had immediately executed them. Many had been shot within the hearing of the Americans who delivered them to their executioners. Some, it is said, had been hanged from the trees within sight of the Americans. The British had been more humane, at least so far as the Ukrainians were concerned: many of these were officially designated 'Polish' and were allowed to settle in Britain.

And now here, outside Le Havre, were their names upon the German noticeboard. It was some sort of guard or duty roster: Andreiev S., Chernikovski K., Antonov V., Vladim A., and so on, with, at the bottom, Weber K., *Feldwebel*.

I returned to the casement. I shrugged my shoulders, irritated by my own sentimentality as I then called it, by my pity for those disembodied names. What did it matter? I told myself. It was all over and done with. The war was finished, we had won and they had lost, we were alive and they were dead. Let the dead bury their dead. This was a time to think of the future, not of the past. I imagine that I lit a cigarette.

Yes, the past, thank God, was over. In a few weeks' time I would be a civilian again, in another country, my own country but yet a strange one. Six years I had wasted in Europe's war. At last, at long last, I could begin my life. Let the dead bury their dead. . . .

Let the past be abolished. I was now where I should have been just six years ago, ready to create my own life and not to lose it for the sake of political and moral abstractions and under the pressure of mass emotions. Why should I spare a thought for unknown Russians?

In six weeks my wife would have joined me in New York and we would be on our way to Bermuda. At last I would be able to do what I had always wanted to do, write in freedom, live as I wished, love as I desired. . . .

Love? . . . I felt a sudden, sickening spasm of jealousy Where was she at this very minute? Forty-eight hours ago she had kissed me good-bye at Southampton. She had promised that she would never see him again, that if he telephoned her before she left for New York she would tell him that she had no *wish* to see him again. With all my being I wanted to believe her, and yet I could not. Where was she now? I knew, for certain, that she was with him, laughing with him, touching and being touched by him. It was intolerable.

I could not pretend to be twenty, when I was twenty-six and had already lived, perhaps, as much as most men do by the time they are forty. And yet, somehow, I must begin again.

In the corner of that queer, concrete room there were stairs, leading down. I took them, and was in an identical but smaller chamber. A large gun, pointing seawards, almost filled it. I glanced at the gun, bored by it or rather so pre-occupied with myself, my own nature and my past, and with the problems which these must pose for the blank piece of paper that was the non-existent future, that I scarcely saw it. I noticed, though, that it shone and seemed to be com-pletely undamaged. There was a curious smell, though so faint was it that despite its familiarity I failed at first to identify it.

I walked around to the other side of the great shiny gun. Since its muzzle filled a part of the aperture, it was slightly darker down here than it had been upstairs, and I did not immediately recognise the object on the ground. When I did, my reaction was one of astonishment, followed closely by fear.

Nothing of the corpse was left, save the skeleton within the German uniform, which itself was largely rotted away but still recognisable. He had not sprawled as he fell but lay, as they say, to attention, on his back, his finger-bones beside his decomposing trousers. The skull was still encased in its green steel helmet, and had there been eyes in the empty sockets, they would have been fixed on mine. For a long moment I looked at him. It was almost as if he looked back.

I hurried through the long grass towards the road. I would have run, had I not seen a man walking along that road: I was obscurely and for reasons connected with my upbringing afraid that to run would be undignified, would involve me in a loss of face. And, as if to smother the more pressing anxieties within me, I asked myself, over and over again, why no one had come and taken him away, why nobody had buried him. It seemed dreadful to him and, of course, dreadful to me. Why had no one come? Was I the first, in all that time, in the time it takes for a face to become a skull?

The man on the road had seen me. He was waving at me, and I knew that he was shouting, but his words were carried away by the wind. I walked towards him, somewhat more slowly, and when I was within quite a few yards, I could hear what he was shouting. '*Vous êtes fou!*' he was saying. '*Vous êtes fou!*' And then he began to walk rapidly away.

At last I stepped over the strand of wire. He had been watching me over his shoulder. Now he too stopped, and walked towards me. He was a middle-aged man, a farm labourer perhaps.

'*Vous êtes fou,*' he repeated, but with less certainty.

'*Mais non,*' I replied. '*Je ne suis pas fou.*'

'*Regardez!*' he said, and pointed.

The little signs were half covered by the long grass, but even so I should have seen them, for they were bright red and yellow. The older ones said ACHTUNG MINEN! the newer

UNCLEARED MINEFIELD. They also bore a skull and crossbones.

So I knew why nobody had come to take Antonov or Vladim away. The war might be over, but its minefields still threatened the future and guarded the past. It might be years, maybe a lifetime, before the last of those mines could be cautiously lifted.

2

IT WAS NOT just one war that had sown its minefields across my life, but two: at least two, probably three, and perhaps more. To a greater or lesser degree all my generation was affected by the twentieth-century wars, but since every individual is unique, so were the wars' effects upon each of us.

I have heard old men, who were involved in the affair of 1914–1918, refer to 'my war' and 'your war', in a tone of proprietary affection as one might say 'my poodle' or 'your uncle'. I make no such claim for the events of 1939–1945. On the other hand that other war was certainly, so far as I am concerned, my father's war. For, to the best of my knowledge, it deprived me of a father altogether.

Not that he was killed in it, as were the fathers of several among my friends. Had he been killed, then I would still have had a father, though a dead father, to be proud of and to emulate as best I could.

It did not kill him, but it ruined him. It had killed his brother, Beau, in Mesopotamia, but my father had lived on, until 1954, and towards the end of his life he used to say:

'Beau was the lucky one.'

And when at last he was on his deathbed, in a Salisbury nursing-home, the priest who had given him Extreme Unction said to me, before putting on his crash helmet, his skid-lid, and mounting his clerical motorbike:

'Your father was as surely a casualty of the First War as if he had been killed in the trenches.'

But he was never in the trenches. Even had he been a soldier and not a sailor, he would have had to run it pretty fine to be killed and also to be my father, for I was born in June of 1919. So I had a live father in theory, and also one who was a war casualty, also in theory: but in practice I had no father at all, neither alive nor dead. It is about this vacuum in my childhood that I would, briefly, write.

His story is not fully known to me, nor, I think, to anyone else. He himself I only knew slightly, during the last ten years or so of his life, a time when I was fully occupied with my own. Besides, a certain reticence would have held me back from asking questions.

He was born in the mid-1880s, and his father, Louis, was of the last generation of FitzGibbons to have lived in the great house in Ireland. Of those people I have written at some length elsewhere. Poor and proud, witty and given to the bottle, my grandfather had married a Scottish lady, a Miss Maxwell, whose mother was a Forbes and whose brother was a soldier: he rose to be Sirdar of Egypt and sank to being commander of British troops in Ireland in 1916 and thus the executioner though, let it be said, the unwilling executioner, of Pearse and Connolly and the other men of Easter Week. If any man can be said to have caused, albeit unwittingly, the Irish Revolution, it is my great-uncle, Jack Maxwell. My father said of him:

'At the age of seventeen my Uncle Jack was so stupid that they put him in the Army: fifty years later he was still so stupid that they kicked him out again.'

My father was no respecter of persons and no more, I gather, was his father. In the nineties Louis had withdrawn, with his Scottish wife and his three children, to Dinard, then a fashionable English resort on the coast of Normandy. (There is a plaque to my Uncle Beau, who was also called Constantine, in the English church there.) His motives, I am told, were to escape his creditors and to enjoy the lower cost of French living. He appears to have done nothing at all, and to have lived a somewhat eccentric life, getting up in the late afternoon and drinking, alone, until dawn. There was very little money. Mrs FitzGibbon made and sold lampshades. What did Louis think about, alone there all night, year after year, in the drawing-room of his very modest villa? Once, at least, he ventured out. He walked into the Dinard Club, of which he was not a member, with his hat on. He looked at the fashionable Englishmen there assembled and remarked in a loud voice:

'The members of this club would not be allowed in my club in London as waiters.'

He then turned upon his heel and walked out again. And he had no club in London. I have heard that as a young man he had been blackballed from White's because *his* father, who was a member, used to read the newspaper aloud there. It might have been hereditary.

Later he became amiably vague. His daughter married a rich Bostonian who lived at the Ritz in Paris. My grandfather visited the young couple there. On his return to Dinard he was asked if he had a good time.

'Excellent,' he replied. 'My son-in-law has quite a large house and a most excellently trained staff of servants. You simply ring the bell and they bring you anything you ask for.'

I wish I had known him, but he died long before my time.

It was in such an atmosphere, which to the outsider in time and space must seem essentially one of farce, that my father grew up. It can scarcely have seemed farcical to my grandmother, as she made her lampshades and sold them to her richer friends and acquaintances. On the other hand, the children presumably took it, as children take almost all the adult world, for granted. Somehow or other the boys were educated, though at the minimum expense consistent with their position in society. (And even so one may assume that some of the grander and richer relations helped out: my father, as a boy, was very close to his cousins, the Grenfell twins, one of whom won the Victoria Cross and both of whom were killed in 'his' war.) My father went to the Royal Naval Training College, Britannia, later named Dartmouth, and was commissioned early in this century.

22

Among his friends and contemporaries were the two men who gave their names to Mrs Patrick Campbell and to Lady Patricia Ramsay. If Mr Pat Campbell was one of the more obscure figures of his generation there was nothing insignificant about 'Black' Ramsay. Later, Admiral Ramsay was to play a very minor part in my own life story.

My father only served for a short time as an officer in the Navy. He had already met my mother, when her family were living briefly in Dinard. He met her again in America. They fell in love and were secretly married, for my American grandfather had refused his permission that she marry a man with no means beyond a junior officer's miserable pay. My father therefore left the Navy, and obtained a job on the New York Cotton Exchange, a type of work for which he rapidly showed a very considerable ability. My grandfather Folsom thereupon relented, and the young couple were married all over again in the American Cathedral, Paris. I believe—my father had a tendency to excess—that they even went through a third wedding ceremony, this time in London. Till the day he died, my grandfather Folsom never knew of the secret marriage in New York.

They were good years for my parents, the years just before the First World War. My father was making a great deal of money as a cotton broker. They lived in Tuxedo, among other places, and with the combination of my mother's social background (of which she has always been pleasantly unaware) and of my father's very considerable charm and gaiety they could choose their friends as they wished. The children, my sisters, were beginning to arrive. Their life was a happy one. They moved in a rather fast, but not a dissolute, set. There was a certain amount of gambling and drinking, heavy perhaps by Folsom New England standards, normal by those of the Irish FitzGibbons. My father liked their life and his work. He had, in those days, a most sunny disposition.

My mother has told me that she never saw my father affected in any way by drink. Furthermore—and this may well be significant in view of what was to happen—she said that men of their circle had then told her that they were amazed at how strong his head was. They were referring to bibulous, Edwardian evenings when the women were not present. And these friends were not negligible drinkers themselves.

Then came the war, and my father rejoined the Navy. My mother and her two little girls came back to England, where my third and youngest sister was born in 1915. And it was now that my father began to behave in a somewhat eccentric fashion. In 1916, after the Battle of Jutland, he presented the White Ensign of the destroyer in which he served, and which had taken part in the battle, to the church of the Oxfordshire village where my mother was then living. When pressed by the clergyman, he even treated the congregation to an address on that battle, and on his own part in it. This was a story he was fond of telling and which he once repeated to me, many years later, during 'my' war.

'I was officer of the watch. As dawn broke I could see, beyond the horizon, the smoke rising from the funnels of the still invisible High Seas Fleet. My destroyer was in the van, and I was well aware that a single shell from one of those great German battleships was enough to blow us out of the water. We were steaming towards them, full speed ahead, and soon enough they began to appear above the horizon, first one, then another, the whole huge High Seas Fleet. And from where I was standing I could not see a single British ship. I have never felt so lonely nor so frightened in my life.'

And then, with a characteristic chuckle, he added, to me:

'My boy, you are quite right to have joined the Army. In the Army at least you can run away. In the Navy, you are carried towards the enemy.'

It was a good story; only my mother told me later that he had spent the day of Jutland with her, in London. He was always, she said, very good at telling stories. The essence of telling a good story is the desire to please, interest or amuse. He had wished to interest that congregation in Spelsbury in 1916. There was, my mother said, no malice in him, ever. I believe her.

He said that it was during the First World War that he

24

began to take dope. The extreme boredom and strain of endless North Sea patrols in rolling, pitching destroyers were too much for him. Another officer had introduced him to narcotics, and, perhaps because he could find no relief from tension in alcohol, he had rapidly become an addict. Whether he had experimented with drugs before the war, I do not know, but it is probable. If so, they had certainly not affected him to any perceptible degree. On the other hand, by the time the war was over, he was a confirmed case, and was living with a woman in Marseilles who was also an addict.

My mother knew about the mistress, but not about the addiction. She probably would not have understood, even if she had been told, for women of her class were kept in innocence of such matters. As for his French mistress, well, these things happen. She did not quarrel with my father: indeed, she has told me that they never once quarelled. But she was lonely in England, and was expecting another baby, and my father was sending her no money. Her eldest sister (she had six sisters, all but one older than herself) sent her the necessary fares, and she took her three daughters back to America. I was thus born in my grandfather's house, in Lenox, Massachusetts, and this explains why I am an American citizen.

When my father came to America, a year or so later, my mother was delighted to see him, even though she had had to pay his passage. (She had inherited a share in two trusts, after her father's death.) When he had cabled her asking that she also pay Yvonne's passage, my mother was almost tempted to agree, but she drew the line at his further request that she buy a ticket for Yvonne's mother as well. So Yvonne remained in Marseilles.

And now my father became almost totally irresponsible so far as money was concerned. Arriving in New York without the price of a railroad ticket, he cabled from the ship for a private train to meet him. You are not expected to pay cash for private trains. He borrowed money from all his friends. He returned to London. A business venture connected with cotton, on which he embarked with Lord

Pembroke, failed. Lord Pembroke lost some £100,000 and, to his chagrin, was forced to sell the armour from Wilton. My father's English friends were constantly urging him to try his luck in America again, and paid his passage. His American friends were equally anxious that he try London, and sent him back. I believe that he was shuttled back and forth across the Atlantic in this fashion for quite some time.

By now my mother knew all, or at least enough, about his doping. It distressed her, as a hideous skin disease might distress a woman in the man she loved. But it was the financial dishonesty, which seems to be inherent in that condition, which made their marriage impossible for her. She had four children, and a small private income on which he had already made considerable inroads. She was prepared to work in order to support us, but she feared that he would somehow ruin any such venture of hers, or take her money from her as she made it. Reluctantly, and after asking the advice of friends whom she trusted, she decided that she must divorce him.

She did so, in New York. My father was there and did not contest it. After the dreary ceremony was over, he asked her to lunch at the Colony. It was a mournful meal, and by the time it was over they were both very close to tears. My father summoned the waiter.

'Send a boy out to buy two large cambric handkerchiefs.'

I was then about three years old. I have no childhood memory of him. I had no father, either to emulate or against whom to rebel. I had to find other objects for my normal, male, revolutionary instincts.

Not only had I no father and no grandfathers, but also no brother (a half-brother, my father's son by his second marriage, cannot count, since I scarcely met him before we were grown up), and no uncles save uncles-by-marriage, that is to say the husbands of my aunts. Later there was my stepfather, Bertram, or 'poor Bertram' as he was usually called. He did not last long, being quite rapidly expelled from the female colony into which he had so rashly ventured. As a substitute father, poor Bertram never had a chance.

26

This overwhelming preponderance of women during my early childhood can be explained by a sad sequence of events in the middle of the last century. My grandfather Folsom had married my grandmother, Frances Hastings Fuller, shortly after the American Civil War. She came of an old, and poor, New England family. The Fullers had come over from Essex in the middle of the seventeenth century. I once owned a letter, written by the first American Fuller, which became lost during the Second World War. That he could write, and easily, is of some interest. They became small farmers in, I think, Vermont. Doubtless many of them moved westwards. My grandmother's family stayed in New England. They were in some measure intellectuals: Margaret Fuller, the celebrated blue-stocking and liberal feminist, was my grandmother's aunt, and the blue-stocking's father, Timothy, also achieved some renown. They also remained extremely Low Church. My grandmother was Unitarian. Spiritual self-assurance—I hesitate to use the word pride—combined with material humility and contempt for display lingered on in New England until quite recently: the contribution that these qualities made to American civilisation was surely once very great.

My grandmother had them in full measure. When she visited Europe, in the 1880s and 1890s, she kept a journal. What she then wrote shows her to have been interested by the very different attitude of the European aristocracies, and delighted by an elegance of manner that scarcely existed then in the United States, but not particularly impressed. Certainly she had no wish to ape the manners, or adopt the outlook, of her English or European friends.

I remember her, just, a very small old lady with white hair, usually in bed, crocheting a series of simple, warm, practical and pretty open-work counterpanes, each square a different but symmetrical arrangement of coloured wools. I remember that we would choose the colours together from the lovely heap of skeins.

Her personality must have been a strong one, stronger, I imagine, than her husband's, though she seems to have been vague and not at all domineering. She did not, however, tolerate impertinence, either from her children, her grand-children or anybody else. There is a story that on one occasion, when some of her numerous daughters were young, a busybody clergyman, doubtless an Episcopalian, called on her and said:

'I think I should tell you, Mrs Folsom, that they are talking about your daughters in the village.'

To which my grandmother replied:

'I regard it as our duty, Rector, to give the people in the village something to talk about.'

My grandfather's background was rather different and, from a worldly point of view, grander. George Folsom was a New Yorker, who numbered among his ancestors such distinguished early Americans as Pieter Stuyvesant, who invented New York, and John Winthrop, who perhaps invented the Massachusetts of which he was the first Governor. My grandfather's father had been American Minister at the Hague, as I believe had his father before him. From Holland they had brought back pictures and, I have heard, one of the finest collections of Elzevirs in the world. My grandfather's cultural horizons were thus far wider than his wife's. He was also a rich man, with extensive property holdings in New York. He had some interest in politics— Grover Cleveland was a friend—though he himself never ran for office, but preferred to carry out his duties as a citizen and a patriot by giving financial and other support to the policies and the politicians of whom he approved. He was widely read and numbered writers among his friends (my mother was named Georgette, not after him, but after her godfather, George Berry, Edith Wharton's close friend). He painted with more talent than is usual among amateurs, and his knowledge of painting was considerable, though his taste conventional. He was an indefatigable traveller, and an enthusiastic photographer from a very early date.

Such English blood as I have derives from my mother's family, an inheritance coloured by two and a half centuries of American life. If my American grandmother's family had about them something very close to the old England of the Puritans and the Quakers, of the Foxes and the Wilberforces, my grandfather's attitude towards the world was, perhaps, closer to that of the English Whig tradition than anything which exists in America, or perhaps even in England, today.

Even in his time this was a moribund tradition. Just too young for the Civil War, my grandfather attempted to manage his properties and his fortune during the rough age of American economic explosion. He sold much of his New York property to the new rich of the Astor and the Vanderbilt period, and invested his money as wisely as he could. He had a partner, a Mr Weekes, who looked after his affairs when my grandfather was on his travels. Alas, Mr Weekes belonged to an altogether different tradition. When his own speculations went astray, he neither blew out his brains nor rolled up his sleeves, but took the easier course of absconding to the Caribbean with such of his partner's, my grandfather's, assets as he could rapidly realise. This amounted to a large sum of money, and my grandfather, though he continued to be a rich man, regarded himself as ruined. He worried about money for the rest of his life. He sold his house in Washington and his house in New York, closed up his house at Lenox, and moved, with all his daughters, dogs, cats, canaries, servants and steamer trunks, to Europe to economise. This was in the 1890s, and of the many houses that he rented one was the Villa Nahant at Dinard. But long before then an atrocious series of domestic tragedies had afflicted my grandparents, and it is this that explains, in part, the absence of men in my own childhood.

My grandparents were married when she was seventeen and he only a few years older. (There is a family legend that at the wedding breakfast she ate five helpings of Brown Betty, her favourite pudding.) After a protracted honeymoon in Egypt and the Middle East, they returned to my grandfather's house in New York, on Gramercy Park. It was there that their first child, a boy, was born, followed by another son the next year. They spent the summers at Sunnyridge, their large house with the lovely garden outside Lenox, and the winters in New York. The third child was a girl, my

Aunt Lelly. That winter they left the new baby in the country, but took the two little boys to the house on Gramercy Park, where the children sickened, became feverish and, despite the best doctors' advice, died, one after the other, in their nursery. What cause of death was then given, I do not know. The word diphtheria did not figure in the vocabularies of even the best doctors a century ago.

My grandmother was pregnant again, and again it was a boy, and again they returned to New York for the winter. The big, almost empty house on Gramercy Park had become understandably hateful to my grandmother. And, because the cause of death of the other boys had not been correctly ascribed to the condition of the drains, the new baby sickened almost at once. A sister of my grandfather's, a spinster who later went mad and who was even then, it seems, a religious maniac of very High Church views, lived with them and compelled my poor grandmother to pray with her endlessly, and in a fashion unacceptable to her Unitarian upbringing, for the life of the baby boy. The baby died. My grandmother bore my grandfather six more children and they were all girls, Lelly, Ettie, Marguerite, Maude, Wyn, my mother and Constance, a garland of Victorian names, a crowd of girls, most of them beauties (Helleu drew them all), all save one to become wives, and mothers, and grandmothers.

So there was no heir. Trusts were formed, and on my grandfather's death the inheritance was divided among the seven girls, and as, one by one, they died, it passed, shrunken and diminished during the years when there was no man to tend it, to the twenty-one grandchildren. And now the trusts have at last been wound up and dusty legal formalities have marked the end of a family which might still exist, but which died because it had no focus once my grandparents had both gone. New York had created a fortune, as it has made so many. The New York drains had poisoned and killed it. That is not poetic justice.

My mother had great affection and great respect for her father. She never ceased to regret her deception of him in the matter of her secret marriage. But she hardly knew him. How could she, a member of a crowd as she was?

(Once when she was playing with her younger sisters in the drawing-room, Mrs Wharton came to call. An older 'grown-up' sister said:

'Run along up to the nursery now. Mrs Wharton doesn't wish to be bothered with a lot of little girls.')

Only towards the very end of his life, when she herself was married, did my mother ever have any real conversations with him. Those gave her, she has told me, an almost tantalising glimpse of how much she missed in never having shared his thoughts and interests and tastes.

Indeed she had almost no formal education at all. A French governess gave the girls lessons of a sort, mostly concerned with French history, but since there was a new little girl arriving in the schoolroom each year, even these did not make much progress. My mother maintains that they never really got beyond a memorable character called *Clovis roi des Huns*, which implies a remarkably confused picture even of that chaotic period.

She grew up, in fact, into an almost purely feminine world, with feminine standards and, if such exist, feminine values. Perhaps if my grandfather had been a more forceful character he could have established a close relationship with each of his daughters, though this would surely have been an immense labour. As little girl after little girl was added to his family, he seems to have withdrawn more and more into his library and dark-room. He gave his companionship to his elder daughters, in the museums and beauty spots of Europe, and they in turn, almost like the prefects in some permanent, and permanently perambulating, boarding school, showed their younger sisters Munich and Betws-y-Coed and Rome and the Isle of Wight, when they could spare the time.

The home was where the women were. This is perhaps the normal arrangement so far as very young children go, but usually there is a man, about whom—in his opinion at least—it all revolves. In this case he was quite simply outnumbered. Had there been a boy or two among them, he

31

would presumably have formed a link with the head of the household. As it was, and particularly for the younger daughters, although Papa was around, their world was complete without him.

And this, I think, may have unconsciously influenced my mother when she decided to divorce my father. She was no sort of feminist, but feminism was very much in the air. Men were necessary for many purposes, from love to the explanation of company reports, but they were not really essential in the home, and now he was a menace which might smash up the one she had kept, with such difficulty, together. Who can blame her that she decided to divorce him before he could do any further damage to her life and her daughters' and that of the baby, who happened to be male and myself?

Thus did it come about that I spent my earliest years in what might be described as a second-generation matriarchy, though this is not quite the correct word, for neither my mother nor my grandmother were matriarchs. But it can certainly be said that in my emotionally most formative years I had little reason to believe in the concept that man is the Lord of the Universe.

In the matter of my sex I was outnumbered about six to one (that is including my nurse or governess and the cook). I suppose I might have become a queer, but this I have not done. On the other hand, and at most periods of my life, the ratio has remained fairly constant.

3

OF MY EARLIEST childhood homes, Bermuda, Concord, old Sunnyridge, New Canaan, I have almost no memories or none. Sunnyridge had burned, and with it most of the Elzivirs, when I was four. Of the old house I recall the front door and the portico under which the car that had brought us from Pittsfield station pulled up. It was after dark, Christmastime perhaps, and Jack jumped down to deal with the suitcases, while the front door was the entrance to a cave of light with Amanda's beaming face to greet us, ready to give me a great, warm hug to her broad bosom.

More vaguely, I recall the library, shelf after shelf of dark brown books from floor to ceiling, and leather armchairs to hide behind, and above all the library steps to push about and to climb. Did they run on little lines, like railway trains, or was that some other library in another house? The smell, though, was unforgettable. Whenever now I enter a library of that sort I am instantly, if only for a second, back in old Sunnyridge, before the fire.

The fire had started when the house was empty. Workmen had been busy indoors, and they were inevitably blamed for it. The blame, in fact, was pinned down to one specific misdemeanour, though not to any one workman. It was said, by the grown-ups, that one of the men must have dropped a burning cigarette-end among paint-rags. I do not see how they could have been so certain. In any event, that night it began to burn, and because the house was empty and scarcely visible from the road, it was hours before the blaze was seen. By the time the fire brigade arrived, there was little that could be saved. The house itself was completely destroyed. And when it came to claiming insurance, it was discovered that neither the value of the house nor of its contents had been re-assessed for over forty years. I believe that the sum collected was in the nature of $10,000. Several of the pictures that had burned were each worth more than that.

A smaller Sunnyridge was built on the site of the old house, and it is this that I really remember.

When we lived in New Canaan, my mother commuted to work in New York. She was nearly forty when first she got a job, and the job she took was as a saleswoman in the store that bore the name of Harry Collins and which sold women's clothes. Nowadays one or other of her numerous friends would have found her work in an office or as a personal assistant, even though she had no secretarial training. In those days ladies did not take jobs—I believe women in offices were still called typewriters—and there were therefore no jobs for them. A lady might still open a shop, and this my mother eventually intended to do (and did: a hat shop). But first she must learn something of the trade, and earn a little money while so doing. She therefore took this job with Harry Collins, whose name had been Kolinsky. She was the only employee who was not Jewish, and the other female employees soon ferreted out her background, which did not endear her to them any the more. Much has been written, and usually with a justified sob in the throat, about the persecution of a Jew or Jewess in a non-Jewish American environment. Little has been written about the spiteful and cruel things that can happen when the situation is reversed. Nor will it be written by me, for my mother never complained, though she was bitterly unhappy in that store. She stuck it for a year and easily resisted the greasy blandishments of her boss, before she opened her own hat shop.

I can scarcely have seen her, except on Sundays, during that year. Certainly my memories of New Canaan are limited to two blurred snapshots: a creeper with blue berries or flowers growing up the front of our yellow-washed house, and a brand-new scooter that glittered and shone upon the morning of my birthday, my fourth. Otherwise nothing. I do not even remember who looked after me, though it was probably Miss Wright.

Memories really begin after we had moved to New York, to an apartment on the fourth floor at 186 East 75th Street, between Park and Lexington Avenues, where the landing and the stairs were great black and white checker-boards. For four years or so a pattern was established: New York in the winter, Lenox in the summer and sometimes for Christmas. A friend of mine once remarked to me that when asked the tedious American question as to where his grassroots lay, he could only reply: 'The steam room of the Yale Club.' I must say that mine are divided between those two addresses, the one precise, the other necessarily vague, for Lenox in those days was more than a house, was more than the new

Sunnyridge, was rather a whole collection of homes. Indeed almost the entire place was home.

New York was our apartment, and Central Park, and very little else. I do remember playing hopscotch on the sidewalk with strange children, though I imagine this was not allowed. If so it was my youngest sister, Mimi, a great one for getting herself, and me, into trouble, who was responsible. It was Mimi, four years my senior, who introduced me to another of the immemorial, vile pleasures of city children. We would tie a purse to the end of a length of cotton and lower it out of the window. Then, when a passerby stooped down to pick it up, we would jerk it into the air to the bewilderment, as we assumed, of the passerby. This, too, was strictly illegal, since it involved leaning far out of fourth-floor windows as well as the destruction of a whole reel of cotton.

In Central Park there was an old and hollow tree, bent to an angle of forty-five degrees and filled with concrete. I loved it. When other children had written words, which fortunately perhaps I could not read, in chalk upon my tree's concrete flank, I would erase them with water from the nearby pond. I was a very tidy child, nor would I have my favourite tree misused. It was not a blackboard.

Other children sailed boats upon the pond. I was given a succession of boats, with various means of propulsion from sail to clockwork, but somehow I never took to this sport. Other children's boats might skim, with light elegance, across our ocean-pond. Mine resolutely clung to the near shore and, when pushed out with a stick, would return at once to their point of non-departure with all the stubbornness of a horse that will not leave its stable. Or if, by some chance, they did set off they would, without fail, become becalmed, or their motors would break down, precisely in the middle of the pond, far out of reach of myself and my governess. I do not believe that this was in any way my fault. Nor do I think that I am to blame for the fact that throughout my life cars, and indeed all other mechanical objects, have treated me with the same stubborn contempt.

Fishing in the pond, with worm, pin and string, was more

35

my style. There were probably no fish in it: at least I never caught one. I did, however, catch a splendid, imaginary goldfish when no one was looking, which I threw back 'because it was so beautiful'. I talked about my goldfish for days on end, amidst waning interest, until at last everyone was heartily sick of it, and Mimi told me firmly to shut up.

On Sundays throughout at least one whole winter I used to go, alone, to lunch with an old lady called Mrs Gardener who lived in a large house on Riverside Drive. I think it was a house, because I remember going upstairs to lie down after these tête-à-tête luncheons. Mrs Gardener, whose daughter was a friend of one of my aunts, lived there on her own. She would send her car to fetch me, and I sat in the back, unaccompanied, with a glass partition between her chauffeur and myself. The floor of her house, I remember, consisted mostly of beautifully polished wood, dark as horse-chestnuts which have just split their green outer shells. Mrs Gardener treated me with grave courtesy, and we discussed this and that while the butler passed us the dishes. Always there were Japanese flowers to drop into the finger-bowls, little screwed-up balls of paper that magically un-folded to become brilliant, exotic water-lilies and heaven knows what else. Sometimes Mrs Gardener would play to me, on her concert grand, after first removing her heavy rings with which I was allowed to amuse myself. There were no other toys, just the conversation of two old friends, excellent food, perhaps a little music, and then her chauffeur would drive me home again. I must have then been about five, and I loved her.

My Aunt Wyn lived in New York, the only one of my aunts who did, in a very much larger apartment than ours because her husband was a millionaire, my governess said, whatever that meant. Her four daughters were all older than I and I have only vague recollections of vanilla ice-cream with hot chocolate sauce. She died before I was six.

Indeed I have almost no recollection of children what-soever in New York, though there must have been some with whom I played. My two elder sisters were away at boarding school most of the time, and though Mimi and I used to walk to school—or rather she to school and I to the kinder-garten—I do not remember anything about the children there either. But then urban children, unless they are allowed to live the life of the streets, are essentially lonely. It is all too dangerous and ugly. Cities are for grown-ups.

Some have to live there, because of their work or their studies, though this is less and less the case, which is why their centres are slowly dying. (In Europe they have recovered from the recent attempts to murder them, but fewer and fewer people live in their centres, increasingly given over to office work and what passes for entertainment.) Some go there to study or to make money quickly: some because they actually like the noise and the crowds and the smells exuded by massed internal combustion engines: some to meet as many persons of the opposite sex as possible, for purposes of marriage or of mere copulation. None of these motives is likely to appeal to a normal child. The place for children is the country, and Lenox was the place for me.

We spent one summer in my Aunt Lelly's house there, Syringa Cottage, and for two we rented a house of our own, Newton Cottage, inextricably and inevitably confused in my memory with a delicious sticky kind of biscuit called a Fig Newton.

I have not looked up the facts about Lenox, and though I have been there since I grew up I shall try to eliminate these more recent memories, for it is the child's Lenox of forty years ago that I would here attempt to re-create, a place where the sun was always shining or the snow was six feet deep, the temperature ninety in the shade or thirty below, and no half-measures.

The centre of Lenox-the-town was the corner where stood Haggard's drugstore, with its ice-cream sodas and O'Henrys and the ice-cream sundaes, so oddly spelt, with their liquid caramel turning solid as it met the ice-cream, and their grated nuts or candied fruits, almost always too expensive for the likes of me. Behind the drugstore were two quarters of the town. First was what might be called the adminis-trative or monumental area, streets lined with trees, chest-nuts I think, the town hall, the library, a statue, the church

37

to which we went on Sundays, correctly spelt. The rector was called Latter Griswold, a name which even then sounded most curious in my ears, and he parted his hair in the middle. He once bought a new car and drove it all the way to Boston with the handbrake on. After that, I supposed, he had to throw it away. I did not care, because I did not like the way he patted the top of my head and called me Sonny. It was not my name, nobody else called me Sonny, and I saw no reason why he should. In retrospect I still think I was quite right not to mourn his brand-new Chrysler.

In another part of the little town were the shops which we seldom used—we went shopping in Pittsfield—and where people lived, including the Portuguese and the coloured people, of whom I shall have more to say. It never occurred to me to wonder what those people did, in Lenox. I have a vague memory of vegetable gardens. And that, so far as I was concerned, was the town.

For me the real centre of Lenox was Sunnyridge, a mile or more outside. Presumably the new house was being built during the first summer we spent there, in my aunt's house or in Newton Cottage, both of which were on the other side of the main road and only a few hundred yards away. If so, it is curious that I should have no recollection of gorgeous goings-on—wheel-barrows on planks, hods of bricks, concrete-mixers—that must have been utterly fascinating. The garden, however, I remember vividly. It was immense, and in the very middle of the universe.

In front of the house was a huge lawn, where grown-ups played croquet beneath great trees and where the grass was cut by a donkey, who wore leather boots and pulled a mower. The lawn sloped. It was a great place for a sledge in the wintertime, and once I broke a front tooth when mine collided with a hidden rock or tree-stump. It was only one of my baby teeth, but nevertheless they all made a great fuss of me, and told me I was very brave. In fact it had hardly hurt at all, and it was only when the fuss was made that I realised I was expected to cry. Naturally, I obliged.

Behind the house the garden went on downhill, lawns, flowerbeds, a little pond with a dribbling *putto* in the middle

38

who surveyed, at the proper season, a whole empire of tadpoles waiting to be caught, on through more flower gardens, past a vegetable garden off to one side, until the grass became rougher and then, without any wall or hedge or ditch, one was in the Wolsey Woods, a place of utter mystery, full of wild beasts and Red Indians and sandstones that could be crumbled between finger and thumb. And beyond the Wolsey Woods there loomed the Berkshire Hills, covered in gorse and scrub and, again at the proper season, the colour of the blueberries that abounded there. A blueberry picnic on Old Bald Top meant a feast, a glut, sometimes even a surfeit of sweet blueberries before ever one was picked and put in the little baskets that we carried. And how the sun beat down!

Lenox was ringed both with hills and with large or very large houses, most of them built towards the end of the last century by rich men from New York. The rich men, being doubtless worn out by strain and overwork, had usually, in those days, been survived by rich widows, living in solitary Victorian splendour, though nowadays I understand that most of their mansions are schools or institutions. At that time, though, the widows still surveyed the monuments to their late husbands' industry. One indeed actually surveyed her late husband, whom she had had embalmed before this fate overtook Lenin, and buried beneath a glass slab immediately outside her bedroom door, so that she stepped over him each night as she retired. On the rare occasion when we children visited her house, our one ambition was somehow to sneak upstairs and have a peek at him. He wore striped trousers and a black coat, and his eyes were closed. He would have been even more impressive, I thought, had he possessed shiny great brown marbles for eyes, like the head of the polar bear attached to the rug in the front hall at Sunnyridge.

In some of these houses there lived cousins, real cousins such as the Voorhees family in their lovely, rather ramshackle, clapboard house among the pines called Merrywood (my uncle Clark Voorhees was a painter, and a good one, the first artist I ever met), and the Channings, who were second cousins and were frequently at Valley Head, a big place with a fine view, and my great-aunt Florrie Whistler, who was my grandmother's sister and whose husband had been the brother of the painter. She had emeralds and poodles and once took a bus to Constantinople. It was also said that she used to have two very small poodles who sat motionless at either end of the dining-room table throughout her dinner parties. There was no telling what grown-ups would think of next.

Then there were honorary cousins, such as Cousin Emily, who had been married to my godfather and who was now married to Hal Lindsley, who therefore became Cousin Hal. There was something mysterious about him. He had apparently spent some time in China and I once heard someone firmly advance the thesis that persons who lived in the Orient invariably came to look Chinese, to acquire an Oriental inscrutability. I heard someone else say that he was likely to 'catch some of the steam out of the Teapot Dome'—an oil scandal of the time—though I found it hard to envisage him near a teapot. There was also talk about Canadian goldmines, most romantic. Children hear a lot more than is supposed. For me he is seated for ever on his terrace, dressed in a white suit with a cigar between his fingers and a drink at his elbow, far from the underground sources of his wealth.

He was himself a source of wealth to us. Presumably he entertained a great deal. (His daughter has told me that he once had a party of rather rough mining engineers to stay. Lenox looked down its nose at them, and even barred them from the Lenox Club until the snobs discovered that the mining engineers were even richer than themselves. In New England, too, John O'Hara's world was replacing Edith Wharton's.) In any event, his lawn tended to be scattered with cigarette-ends, cigar-butts and burned matches. This was a trouble that apparently afflicted the lawns of no other big houses, nor can I believe that their owners would not have cared if it had. Still it was only Cousin Hal who employed us children to pick them up.

He had a daughter of my age, Lenora, who was killed in

the war. (We used to climb into a great fig tree full of ripe fruit and eat ourselves silly.) There were the Clucas children, who numbered among them the first little girl with whom I fell in love. (I fear I was soon unfaithful to her, and took up with a Portuguese five-year-old named Geraldine with whom I even went through a form of marriage: the ring was two daisies which she had skilfully knotted together, their two flowers forming the very precious stone.) There was my cousin Billy Channing, the nearest I ever had to a brother: we had been born within a few days of one another. (Once we discovered a dead bat in my sand-pit, and bore this treasure in triumph to the mothers and aunts and cousins and governesses who were having an enormous tea-party on their own.) There were others, and at times some or all of us were scouring Cousin Hal's lawn for butts.

The pay was for piece-work, ten matches one cent, ten cigarette-ends five cents, cigar-butts, which were rare, five cents apiece. A fair income could be made in this fashion, particularly on the day after a party. The debris having been counted and paid for was then deposited, well out of sight, behind some bushes where no one ever went.

It was a little girl called Betty, though, who had the real money-making mind. She appreciated that one cigarette-end, whether lipsticked or not, looks remarkably like another. If the weather had remained fine for several days, as it always did, there seemed to her no reason why they should not be disinterred—indeed they were not even buried— from what was intended to be their final resting place, and presented to Cousin Hal all over again, five cents for ten. Like baby Burkes and Hares we would grow rich from their graveyard. The woman tempted me. . . . Poor Betty, pretty as she was naughty, was killed in a car smash before she was twenty.

The Lenox Club, of which my grandfather had been president for many years and whose picture therefore hung, and presumably still hangs, in its hall, was not the place for small children. Bridge was played there, and tennis, and there were dances. I did go there occasionally, though. Yet another honorary cousin was usually to be found in a leather armchair with a whisky-and-soda. (This was the age of Prohibition, though no one would have guessed it, in Lenox.) I heard it said of him that he had been 'pickled for twenty years'. Close examination of his mahogany-coloured features failed to explain this judgment to my satisfaction. I had seen pickled things in jars, in the New York Natural History Museum. They were white and very dead. This cousin of mine was ruddy and obviously alive. Once when I was thus examining him in the Lenox Club for evidence of his alleged condition, he suddenly roused himself and gave a stentorian roar: 'Waiter!' I had clearly been misinformed. You can't believe everything you hear. Disillusion had begun to enter my life.

Yes, Lenox was the place for me. There was no end to what a small boy could get up to there. For instance, there was Con's Candy Store. This consisted of a trestle table placed beside the road, immediately outside Newton Cottage. I had a child's bicycle, called, I think, a fairy-cycle, and a small amount of capital. This I invested in candy which I bought at Haggard's drug store and sold at a penny profit. It did well, particularly with children who had no fairy-cycles of their own. On one occasion a gentleman who had come to call on my mother, and who was delighted at so youthful a manifestation of the capitalist spirit, gave me a whole dollar bill.

I was not always this successful in business. An Englishman had given me a gold sovereign, though even then these were no longer currency and were worth more than a pound. I was very taken with the representation of St George slaying the dragon, but even so I exchanged it for a handsome glass marble, of the type called a bull's-eye, which was the property of a boy named Joe Gilmour, and which I had long coveted.

Joe Gilmour lived next door. His father, who was not a member of the Lenox Club, had some sort of trade—perhaps he was a builder—a big, red-faced man who did not hesitate to relieve his bladder in front of us boys, if the mood so took him. I admired him immensely and was determined to follow his trade when old enough to do so. His son, my age or a little older, was more knowledgeable about certain matters, country matters, than was I and most of the boys I knew. (Looking back on it, the girls were, as usual, better informed.) These matters, however, did not interest me at all, and I kept my innocence for a surprisingly long time. Perhaps it was because I was brought up in so feminine an atmosphere that the female as such did not have for me, and never has had, much mystery about her.

What did interest me was the dungheap, behind the garage in which Joe's father kept his T-model Ford. This dungheap, richly odorous, bred the biggest worms I have ever seen. I should like to say that some of them were a yard long, great, red, ringed, twisting creatures almost a match for Laocoön and his sons. In fact I suppose they were giants of six inches. Joe and I, however, were convinced that the bigger the worm the larger the fish—an early example of false logic— and we would fill our tins with the most formidable we could unearth before setting out for the lake, Stockbridge Bowl, a couple of miles away.

We were wrong, and all we ever caught were small, inedible things like catfish consisting almost entirely of needle-sharp bones and tasting only of mud. They may have been inedible, but this did not stop us from cooking and eating them, on the bank opposite the Lenox Yacht Club.

The Yacht Club had a toy cannon, which was fired to start the dinghy races—Stockbridge Bowl was perhaps half a mile wide and several miles long, quite big enough to race small boats on—and upstairs there was an almost bare room where old people of eighteen or twenty played *'Bye 'Bye, Blackbird* on the victrola and danced the Charleston or the Black Bottom. On its veranda even older people, such as the pickled cousin for example, sat and drank and watched the races and maybe eyed the young people nostalgically, as they dived in and swam out to the raft, and dived in again, and climbed ashore beneath them, breathless and laughing, and the young men pushed back their wet hair, and the girls took off their rubber caps and shook out their bobs and shingles. *Make my bed and light the light, I'll be home late tonight.* It must have been very Scott Fitzgeraldish, but all I remem-

43

ber is the toy cannon—boom! across the still water—and a smell of wet bathing suits and of pinewoods. I preferred the other, the unfashionable side, perhaps because I had not yet learned to swim.

On that side there was no clubhouse but only a single plank, such as those along which pirates used to walk their captives, leading from the shore to deep water. Big boys of eight or ten would jump off its far end, naked, holding their noses. Mothers, fatter on this side of the bowl, sat and gossiped on the pine-needles. Joe and I would fish with our monstrous worms from the bank. And then there was the pit.

The pit was deep, so deep that even on the hottest day the ice at the bottom, presumably laid there in the wintertime, never melted. Laid upon the ice to cool were cases and cases of the drinks that boys love best, fizzy raspberryade, sarsaparilla, root beer and many more. I do not think that Coca-Cola had then reached New England. I do know that the variety of choice was very great. Joe and I would spend a long, long time discussing how best to spend our nickels, though at the end my choice was always root beer. Down would go the string-and-loop of the man in charge of the pit, and up would come our bottles, almost frozen, wet with an ice-cold condensation. And one straw each the man gave us. Has any drink ever tasted quite so good? Have any fireworks ever been so wonderful as those that went off, with a whoosh and a bang and a 'Don't stand too close!' over Stockbridge Bowl on the Fourth of July, 1925 and 1926?

4

ANOTHER METHOD OF earning money, and a pleasant one, was caddying at the Lenox Golf Club. (It was not until I began writing these pages that I realised how much of my earliest youth was devoted to economic enterprises of one sort or another. Did I receive no pocket money? I must have, yet I have no recollection of ever being given it. Perhaps I was just a natural *entrepreneur*, but if so, I fear I must have exhausted my talents in this direction at an early age, for from adolescence to the present day my finances have alternated between chill penury and a foolish, Micawber-like optimism with corresponding extravagance. On the other hand it may have been the American ethos of the Coolidge period that led me, like everybody else, to look for the fast buck. The legend then was of the barefoot boy with the newspaper round who diligently and quite quickly burrows his way into the presidency of Standard Oil or Bethlehem Steel. I have never heard that whoever owns Electric Boat started with a newspaper round.)

I enjoyed being a caddy, because I liked the company of the men who played golf, though I never had the good fortune of a contemporary who, at about this same time, was caddying for Al Smith, that great politician beneath the brown derby. Smith had recently failed to get himself elected as President. He apparently had other worries, for after slicing a powerful drive far into the rough he turned to his seven-year-old caddy and remarked, with feeling:

'Boy, never shack up with a woman who has less to lose than you have.'

Who knows? I might have taken his advice, though I doubt it.

I caddied in an age when golf had not yet become an extension of the board-room, and the men who played it did so because they liked the game, not because it was good for 'getting on'. They wore plus-fours, and their clubs were wooden-shafted. Nor were there many of these, so a bag was not too heavy for a boy to carry.

They used a multitude of different tees, of varying shapes and designs. These I collected, as I collected almost everything else at this time or later, toy cars, stamps, coins, matchbox covers, birds' eggs, cigarette cards, seashells (which went dingy), never butterflies (because of the need to kill them), pictures of famous cricketers (after I had come

45

to school in England) and, later, books and, later still, girls. At Lennox I was allowed to keep lost golf-balls when I found them in the rough.

These I could have sold to the pro, whose shop was my home from home upon the links, but I preferred to use them for another purpose. I had learned about the solar system at an early age. I made a model of it, in the dark part of my Aunt Lelly's attic, by suspending the golf-balls with thumb-tacks and cotton from a Calder-like mobile of my own construction. For the sun I had a large flashlight, which I had borrowed from some other part of the house. The shadow-effect upon the inside of the sloping roof was most impressive and I was extremely proud of my solar system. Unfortunately the desire to share my private joys and creations with others—a desire which may account in part for my having become a writer—led me astray.

I was allowed to play in the attic, part of which was floored and lit by two dormer windows. It was here that I kept my toy soldiers and their fort, for which great battles were fought, beneath my sole jurisdiction, between the U.S. Marines, the Cowboys and His Majesty's Foot Guards on the one side and the Germans and Red Indians, natural but outnumbered allies, on the other. Nor had I been explicitly forbidden to go into the dark part of the attic, where there was no floor, but only beams with, between them, the ceiling of my aunt's bedroom.

My middle sister, Fanny, who is seven years older than myself, had always shown more imaginative interest in my world than had the other two. One day I told her about my solar system, and she wished to see it. Proudly, I led her to the attic. But, as is often the case with highly imaginative people, Fanny has always been somewhat clumsy, in word and deed, when dealing with the real world. (It was about this time that she remarked to one of our aunts: 'What an *ugly* hat, Aunt Ettie!') Now she put her foot straight through the ceiling of my Aunt Lelly's bedroom, and a small avalanche of plaster descended upon the bed where my aunt was enjoying a siesta. And that was the end of the solar system.

46

At the golf-club, or rather in connection with it, an incident occurred which has always remained in my memory. I am therefore inclined to give it a perhaps exaggerated importance in this attempt to evaluate the development of my own character and attitudes during my early years.

Sometimes the man for whom I had been caddying would invite me to have a soft drink at the nineteenth hole while he, no doubt, had something stronger with his friends. On this occasion they were seated on canvas chairs outside the clubhouse, in their plus-fours, relaxed and easy. One of them, the one who later became my stepfather, was sitting with his legs crossed, his right ankle resting lightly upon his left knee. I do not believe that I had seen anyone sit in this way before, and I was impressed. (Had I had a father to copy in such matters, I might have been less so.)

At home, on the lawn of Newton Cottage, I too sat in this fashion, and was immediately told by some woman that I must not. Since I was seldom spoken to sharply, for I gave little cause for reproach, I was taken aback and felt that I had been unfairly reprimanded.

'But,' I said, 'that's how the men sit at the golf-club.'

To which I received a tart and irritated reply. How the men at the golf-club might choose to sit was their concern: I was a boy, not a man, and I was certainly not going to loll about at home like that. Who it was who thus rebuked me I have forgotten, but I do not believe it was my mother. I still think it a silly snub. If boys are to become men, as they should and will, they must copy their seniors. And who else was I to imitate, if not 'the men at the golf-club'? Can it have been an unconscious realisation that there was no one else, that I had no father, which made me take this reproach so much to heart? Or is it a mere fluke of memory that I should recall it, still with an understanding of past pain, today?

There was another incident, at about the same time, which I do not remember, but have been told of by my mother. She had a friend called Mr Haynes. I remember nothing about Mr Haynes save that he had a stammer, and so had I. But whereas my stammer consisted of the involun-

47

tary repetition of certain consonants, Mr Haynes was at times reduced to total silence. Visitors to 186 East 75th Street, after pressing our bell beside the street door, had to announce themselves through some sort of speaking tube. A button was then pressed in the apartment, and the front door opened. Mr Haynes would often be struck dumb at the critical moment, the ringing of our bell dismissed upstairs as children's mischief, and Mr Haynes left to face the miserable choice of trying all over again or of going home. My sisters, who did not stammer, thought this a great joke. I felt very sorry for Mr Haynes.

One day, when he had either managed to get into the apartment or perhaps was calling upon my mother in Lenox, it seems that I remarked:

'What beautiful hands you have, Mr Haynes!'

Now I am told that he did have very well-shaped hands. So, as it happens, have I. It may be that I was expressing a genuine aesthetic pleasure: alternatively I may have been merely repeating what I had once heard, and perhaps should not have heard, said about myself. Mr Haynes was, I hope, duly gratified by the compliment. My mother was not pleased.

She had been worried about me for some time. I was, she felt, becoming altogether too delicate and sensitive, too emotional and too locked up in my private world. It was time I was thrown more with other, rougher children. At my New York kindergarten we sat quietly in rows and spent most of our schooldays gumming coloured squares on to black paper. This was clearly not the answer. My mother decided that it was time I went to a proper school, and that the place was the Lenox School, a public school that contained Portuguese and coloured children and all. I was then six, and I am sure she was quite right.

Whether I actually learned anything from my lessons at the Lenox School I do not know, but I doubt it. I could already read easily—I was well into my sixth or seventh *Doctor Dolittle* by that time: I collected them—and I remember that most of the other little boys and girls could not, for we had reading lessons in our huge classroom with the wood-

48

and-iron desks nailed to the floor. But that was not why I was sent there. I was sent there to learn to look after myself.

In retrospect, what I learned most about was racial discrimination, racial solidarity, and the rudiments of diplomatic alliances.

There were three 'races' represented among the boys and girls at the Lenox School. There were the coloured children, the Portuguese and 'us'. We were white, and I suppose that most of us were what would be called working-class. This I did not notice. Certainly I can recall nothing like the class-barrier that would have lain between myself and, say, Joe Gilmour in an equivalent English school. (I am sure that it is the Lenox School which has led me to underestimate the importance of these barriers to the English. Even in England such underestimation is usually all to the good, but not always.) 'We' were not WASPS, for some of us were Catholics and went to Mass with the Portuguese. Some may even have been Jews, but if so I did not notice this. Indeed I was to reach the age of forty before it occurred to me to notice whether or not the people I was associating with were Jewish, and I wish profoundly that I had never been forced to do so.

Relations with the coloured children were, on the whole, easy. My mother's attitude was precisely what her mother's had been. Coloured people were neither better nor worse than white people. It happened that they usually worked for white people, just as it happened that Irishmen in New York were usually policemen or kept saloons. They were not servants, but friends and members of the family. Amanda's pretty, well-dressed and much younger sister, Estelle, had passed through a broken marriage, and now that my mother's hat shop was successful and we had more money, she cooked for us and generally looked after us in New York. My mother had known Estelle almost all her life, and it was quite natural that she became a member of our family when her own broke up, and that she should look after one side of the home. There was no Southern old-retainer, Uncle Tom nonsense about this relationship. We were Yankees, and Southern sentimentality was as remote in our relationship

D 49

with the Estelles and the Amandas as was the European middle-class attitude of the day towards 'servants' and the 'servant problem'. All that, I am told, has changed, and obviously for the worse, at least so far as a small minority of the Negro population in the Northern States is concerned. We were not frightened of coloured people, nor, I think, they of us. The tedious question, which may be relevant in Alabama, about one's daughter marrying a coloured man, was almost as meaningless to us, in the 1920s in Massachusetts, as the question about the number of angels that can dance on the head of a pin. But if pressed, and the pressure could only then have existed in the form of abstract argument, I suspect that many intelligent New Englanders might have said that theoretically at least they had no objection, even to that. However, I was too young to pontificate on this subject now. I can only say what I felt.

Still, I learned something else as well, and this is a direct memory. It was a Lenox summer's day and Estelle's son, Henry, had come to see her. He was a boy of about fourteen, who worked in Pittsfield, and a good friend of mine despite the difference in our ages. Estelle and Amanda were pale, but Amanda's husband, Jack, and Henry were very much darker. Henry had bicycled out from Pittsfield, and we were in the back-yard of Newton Cottage, he on his bicycle turning very small circles, I leaning against the wall.

A problem occurred to me, and I asked him:

'Henry, why are you black and me white?'

Immediately he got off his bicycle. His face was angry, and I knew he was hurt, though I did not know why. He said:

'You must never, never, never, never ask that question again.'

I never have. I do not ask it now.

Who precisely the 'Portuguese' were, I do not know. Perhaps their parents really had come from Portugal or the Azores or Puerto Rico a few years ago, before the recent clamp-down on immigration. Or perhaps it was a generic term used at the Lenox School to describe all immigrants of Latin or even of non-English-speaking stock. That they can only have recently arrived was certainly the case. The bigger ones were quite unassimilated, as I recall, though the smaller, like the little girl with whom I fell in love and 'married', were already becoming Americans. The bigger ones spoke to each other in a language we did not understand. They were stupid, too, or more probably held back in school by language difficulties. In any event, they were titans in the school's lowest grades, huge creatures who had almost grown out of their short pants among the six- and seven- and eight-year-olds. In retrospect, some of these giants even had broken voices. In our classes only an occasional coloured boy was as big and strong as they. And the Portuguese set out to terrorise us, methodically.

They had two opportunities for the implementation of their policy of *Schrecklichkeit*. One was during the breaks between lessons and in the lunch hour, the other when we were on our way home from school. During the breaks, however, they did not have full freedom of action. We poured out, as I recall, into a great asphalt cage surrounded by high wire netting where we smaller children skipped and hopped and played with balls, while our seniors engaged in more manly activities such as pitching baseballs to one another or having formal fist-fights. Then a ring was made and we all watched until one of the fighters gave in, or a teacher arrived to stop it. Here, among the crowd, our tormentors did their best in the way of pinching, punching and arm-twisting, but it was usually possible to slip away. And on occasion other big boys, big brothers or sometimes the big coloured boys who were also in our grades and whom we knew, would intervene on our behalf.

On our way home it was another story. As we streamed out of the school gate, we would divide and divide again at every crossroads. At last it was only half a dozen of us who were making our way across the fields towards that part of Lenox where I and they lived. Nor were there any big boys among us, for our seniors either stayed in school longer or remained behind to play games.

This they soon discovered. Agile and fleet of foot, they would dash away ahead of us and lie in wait. As we reached their ambush they would open the attack with a volley of stones and small rocks. Then they would be among us, hitting us, forcing us to the ground, tearing our clothes and, when they could, stealing our satchels, the whole accompanied by blood-curdling yells and outlandish cries in their native tongue.

For us it could only be a question of flight, of every boy for himself, *sauve qui peut*. Every day most of us escaped, but one or two of us would be caught and tortured and arrive at their homes cut and bruised and torn and tearful, while the loss of satchel and schoolbooks was indeed a disaster which led to further punishment, in school, next day. I do not know how often they caught me, but it was more than once. And from lunchtime the inevitable walk home, and the inevitable ambush, cast a terrifying, inexorable and growing shadow across the summer afternoons.

For reasons with which all who were once boys will sympathise, we never told our parents about the terror beneath which we lived. Perhaps it was because we always ran away and thus felt secretly humiliated. Little boys like to boast, and we had nothing to boast about in our encounters with the giants. Certainly we would even less have dreamed of telling our teachers. Indeed when we arrived at our homes all tattered and torn, and our tears not yet dry upon our cheeks, we would even lie about the cause of our pitiful condition.

'What *have* you been doing? You're all dirty.'
'Fighting.'
'Fighting who?'
'A friend.'
'And where's your satchel?'
'Lost it.'

'I've told you again and again, you mustn't fight and tear your clothes. You'll have no ice-creams. *And* go to bed early for losing your satchel.'

No, there was no justice to be found in the adult world when children fought, just as there is no looking for justice in the courts when grown-ups fall out. For what are the courts supposed to be save super-adults in the adult world? Oh, parents could say that the toy in question was, in fact, the property of little Tommy, just as a court of law can rule that the property in question belongs to Mr Smith and not to Mr Brown. Apart from questions of property there can only be parodies of justice, such as the Communist 'legal' systems or the Spanish Inquisition or the New England witchcraft trials. This is equally true of personal relations. The violent, if brief, mutual antipathy that had brought Tommy and Teddy to fight is far beyond adult jurisdiction, as are the matrimonial causes that lead Mr or Mrs Smith to seek a divorce beyond that of the super-adults. The deplorable conditions of the British and American and doubtless all other divorce courts is proof enough that human emotions are not meet subjects for legal decision. And those who believe that serious international disputes, involving national emotions, can be settled 'justly' are as ignorant of the true nature of justice as are the divorce lawyers and their judges. If there are such persons as super-adults, which is doubtful, they are far more likely to be found among the saints than the solicitors. And saints judge not, that they be not judged.

Yet there was a just solution to our problem of the walk home from school, but it was a fortuitous one. Or was it?

One afternoon one of the big coloured boys happened to walk our way. When we were, as usual, set upon, he did not run, he fought. Though he fought bravely and well, he was hopelessly outnumbered, and while we escaped, he went down. However, his own interests and those of his people were now involved, for the Portuguese had been so foolish, or so ignorant, as to insult him with the unspeakable word.

The next afternoon the coloured boys were there in force, and they were looking for trouble. Our tormentors, licking their lips no doubt in anticipation of plundered satchels and blubbering little boys, had not reckoned that out of sight but within easy reach a powerful squadron was waiting to fall upon them.

It was a battle royal, and safely out of range we jumped up and down and cheered on our defenders and, I fear, finally exacted our own petty revenge on the Portuguese

53

fiends, hurling *their* satchels in a stream and piping insults after them when at last *they* ran away.

For some days the coloured boys accompanied us home. This, though, is the wrong verb. They did not come with us, and we walked across the fields, as before, on our own. But they were about, hoping for another chance to do in their enemies, who happened also to be our own. The Portuguese, however, never reappeared. And gradually the coloured boys, too, drifted off elsewhere after school was done. The war had been won.

The alliance, like many of history's best, had never been a formal one and, like all really successful alliances, had been firmly based upon the fact that we and the coloured boys were each intent on our own interests. We scarcely knew each other, and in this the difference of age was greater than the difference of colour. If we had an emotional link it may have been the fact that we and the coloured boys were Americans, while the Portuguese were not yet Americans. But one can go too far in the search for explanations. The point is that we, or rather the coloured boys, licked them. And that is justice, though it may not have seemed so to the Portuguese.

If the coloured boys were on this occasion our allies, they were not our friends. We did not play with them, not that there were any instructions spoken or tacit against so doing but because they lived their own life in their own part of Lenox just as we lived ours in our part. This gave them a mysterious, even an alluring, quality, quite apart from the mystery that was inherent in the question which I had once put to Henry. But if I did not know them, my sister Mimi, who during the last summer in Lenox was just eleven, did. Mimi, as I then thought, knew everyone and everything.

I was not far wrong, either. Mimi was what used in those days to be called a tom-boy. She was to grow up an extremely beautiful woman, but it would have been hard to guess this in 1926. Her hair was straight and cut straight across her forehead and the back of her neck. Her nose was snub and her face all freckles. She was long-legged and could run faster than most boys of her age. She could ride anything,

54

with or without a saddle. She was a good swimmer, too. And there was no nonsense about Mimi. There never was. At eleven I think that she was utterly unaware of her sex. And when she grew up, she never, like so many beautiful women, and some who are not, cashed in on it. This may, in some ways, have been one of the causes of her tragedy. I hope not, for it was an extremely attractive quality.

We had then a neighbour, an honorary cousin of Mimi's age, who was quite the reverse. Pink and white and dimpled and curled, she was very much the *petite femme*, determined never to dirty her dresses, running for protection from frogs and beetles, reading fashion magazines and spinning a parasol lest the sun damage her beautiful complexion, wide-eyed to the boys and with, as she doubtless thought, a slight, enchanting lisp, she was one of the few people whom I ever knew Mimi really dislike.

'You make me sick,' Mimi said to her once, that summer, and gave one of her perfectly braided pigtails a vicious tug. The *petite femme* burst into noisy tears and immediately ran to tell her mother. Mimi was quite rightly punished, but she did not care, and she never cried.

I have not seen the *petite femme* for many years. She too grew up to be a very beautiful woman and married three very rich husbands, whom she proceeded to divorce to her own very considerable financial advantage. I am told that she is as hard as a woman can be, and there is nothing harder than that. I am also told that she is extremely pleased with herself and with the furs and precious stones that she hangs about her money-making body and with her friends of the 'smart, international set'.

She has caused much unhappiness and will doubtless cause more before she is done. Mimi, on the other hand, who never wittingly caused unhappiness to anyone—and this again may have been one of the causes of her tragedy—has been dead for nearly ten years. Nor am I the only one still to miss and to mourn her.

During that last Lenox summer Mimi had set herself up as a sort of one-girl Society for the Prevention of Cruelty to Animals. It had started with a litter of kittens which, she had heard to her distress, were to be drowned. It was extended to stray dogs. There was a pet fox of which somebody had tired. Soon she was patrolling the town looking for animals which she might succour, and since there was insufficient room for her menagerie at Newton Cottage, the stables at Sunnyridge, which had survived the fire, were commandeered. The climax was reached when she found an old horse; she thought it looked ill-treated and underfed between the shafts of its cart. She unloosed it and led it to Sunnyridge. By the time its owner discovered where it was, he was very angry indeed. He even threatened legal action.

Now as a result of these missionary activities, Mimi knew all Lenox well and all Lenox knew her. She therefore had friends among the coloured children. And it was she who took me out one night, and one only, to play with them.

It was high summer, dusk came late, and I had a hard time staying awake until it was dark. Somehow I managed it, and I was not asleep when Mimi came into my room and told me all was clear, the grown-ups safely behind closed doors downstairs. I dressed silently, we hung by our hands from the ledge of the bathroom window and dropped on to the flower-bed below—her normal nocturnal exit, she explained to me while we made our way across the darkened garden and out through the wicket gate into the fields. There was no moon.

We skirted Lenox, a half circle, and then we were there. It was an open patch of hard, bare earth, within the centre two trees. Near the trees there was a small bonfire, which cast a flickering light upon the trees and upon the old tin bucket that hung, from a rope stretched between them, a few inches above the ground. There were figures silhouetted against the firelight and others, invisible but talking in low voices, in the deeper darkness. Never had I been in such exciting surroundings.

At once, though, all seemed doomed. A big coloured boy lounged towards us from the fire, greeted Mimi in nonchalant fashion, and then looked at me.

'What's he doing here?' the boy asked. 'He's too small.'

'He's my brother,' said Mimi, with a note of defiance.

'Yeah? We don't want no kids here.'

I looked from one to the other, fearful that I must be expelled from this magical place for the crime of being only seven. Other boys and girls of Mimi's age had strolled over towards us and were watching. I looked at Mimi. She said:

'I tell you, he's my kid brother.' This, for her, was enough. The boy looked doubtful. At this point another coloured boy pushed his way forward, looked at me in the half-light, and said lazily:

'I know him. He's okay.'

I recognised one of the heroes of the battle with the Portuguese. So I was allowed to stay and play the game of Kick-the-Bucket. (We formed two teams. One team guarded the bucket. The members of the other team had to break through their defences and kick it.) I even kicked it once, with a marvellous clang. And then there were things to roast on the fire. And bottles of beer were passed round, from which I drank bravely. And the fire glowed low, and we sat around it while the big boys and girls told ghost stories. Then Mimi and I walked home. Somehow we got in. She told me it was midnight. And that was the most exciting night that I had ever spent.

That was Lenox.

5

IT HAD NOT been my mother's intention, when sending me to the Lenox School, to turn me into an all-American boy. Though she had for practical reasons resumed her American citizenship after her divorce (and had been somewhat taken aback when the official had first asked her if she understood English, and had then told her to kiss the flag), she always took the matter of nationality rather lightly. Besides, it was assumed at that time, and indeed for many years to come, that I was English. My father, after all, had a British passport. And though my relationship with him was merely that of paternity, my mother certainly had no wish to make it in any way more tenuous than it already was. She was never possessive in the sterile, spiteful manner of some divorced mothers. At no time did she say anything to me that might have lowered my father in my eyes. She did not clutch me either to herself or to her country.

(When at the age of fifteen I went to apply for a passport in London, I was given a British one on a temporary basis; for it was discovered that my father had been born in the Argentine, on a hacienda belonging to cousins, while his father, the one who stayed up all night, happened to have been born in France. A new law had been passed, at the time of the 1914–1918 war, whereby British citizenship could not be claimed for a child born abroad, through his great-grandfather, unless that child were registered with a British consulate within a given period. My mother had been, quite understandably, unaware of this new regulation, and I was not registered. I had therefore no right to a British passport. On the other hand, and by reason of my place of birth, I am a natural-born American citizen. The temporary British passport was therefore taken away, and I acquired an American one. I have, in fact, always been a citizen of the United States. I could run for President, should I so choose. Whether I would be elected is another matter.)

In addition to my assumed, if erroneously assumed, nationality, there were other forces at work during this early period of my childhood which pulled me towards the Union Jack or, more exactly, towards the White Ensign. The most important of these was Miss Wright, my governess.

Miss Wright was never so aggressive a member of the Bulldog Breed as had been a nurse of my sisters' by the name of Spinks. Once at Dover, during the War, she had been asked by the immigration official whether she and her little charges were British. Although only two of them in fact were, Spinks had replied, in withering tones:

'Don't we look it?'

Spinks had also a sound English contempt for the French. She had once remarked to my mother, in a Paris park where some Frenchmen were animatedly talking together:

'When these Frenchmen get a drop of drink in them, they behave just like marionettes.'

Miss Wright came of a very different background, but if her patriotism was more tactfully expressed—as indeed it had to be in America—it was no less firm and just as deeply anchored. That anchor was supplied by the Royal Navy, never the British Navy nor just the Navy, but the Royal Navy.

This was indeed a bond between Miss Wright and myself. The only pictures of my father that I had seen showed him in naval uniform, perhaps I should say Royal Naval uniform, with his hat worn rather over one eye, in the slightly rakish manner made popular by Admiral Beatty, one of Miss Wright's favourite heroes. Miss Wright, for her part, had a brother who had also been a naval officer. He had recently been 'axed', most unfairly I was led to believe, by something called 'the Geddes axe'. I was not at all certain what this meant, though I associated it with the fate that had befallen Anne Boleyn and Charles I and other famous Englishmen, and I agreed enthusiastically that it was grossly unfair. I was secretly glad that my father, despite being in the Royal Navy, had not also been axed.

As a result of Miss Wright's and my close links with the Royal Navy, the White Ensign, which I still consider the most elegant and emotional of flags, played a great part in my early life. It flew proudly from all the little boats that bobbed up and down in my bath. It should have cracked its defiance at the winds of Central Park, if only my boats would have behaved there in a less unsatisfactory manner. The White Ensign, far more than the Stars and Stripes or even the Union Jack (both of which, if I may venture to say so *sotto voce*, seem to me of poor and even of vulgar design), was the flag of my childhood.

Our great hero was Nelson. Of George Washington I knew little save that he never told a lie (which I did not believe), threw a silver dollar across the Delaware (which seemed to me an odd thing to do), and filled his own teeth (which is untrue). Despite the familiarity from the postage stamps of his rather florid features, I never really believed in him. I suspect that I was not alone in such incredulity, and that many American children shared and share a certain scepticism about our first President. That ridiculous tale about the cherry tree for instance! I knew all about cherry trees. It would be quite impossible to cut one down, for it would take a very long time and one would surely be noticed. And where did he get an axe of suitable size? I knew all about axes, Geddes and other sorts, and they were invariably too heavy, almost, for boys to lift, let alone to cut down trees with. Such a lack of verisimilitude is perhaps the fate of national heroes when they are transported, too quickly and too crudely, to the national Olympus.

Nelson, on the other hand, was entirely credible, clapping the telescope to his blind eye, asking his friend to kiss him, being sea-sick whenever he put to sea, and invariably licking the French. No nonsense here about Victorian morality. Nelson, I suspected, lied like a trooper when it was in his interest to do so and he thought he could get away with it. He would have been unnatural not to. The names of his great victories, Copenhagen, the Nile, Trafalgar, rolled round in my imagination like the towering seas off Ushant. Miss Wright showed me a picture of H.M.S. *Victory*, and by her manner I knew that this was a very special ship indeed, the ship of ships, the Platonic man o' war. Furthermore, it was all connected with Beatty and Jellicoe and Jutland, with Miss Wright's brother and my father, with Miss Wright and with me. Nelson and the Royal Navy were real.

Miss Wright had first come when I was very small, too small to remember her. After a while she had gone away and there had been others, a Swiss woman called Alice and a Miss Oliphant. Alice was a knobbly, red-faced woman who tried to teach me how to yodel, to the annoyance of the household's other members. She also wore straw hats surmounted with artificial fruit, which my female relatives professed to find funny, though I saw nothing wrong with them. Miss Wright must already have planted a seed, for I remember asking Alice about the Swiss Navy and refusing to take no for an answer. She also made delicious cakes, and despite the fact that she suffered from bunions—her bunions were one of her more boring subjects of conversation—she won my general approval. But she never got on with Mimi, who technically at least also fell beneath her jurisdiction. Mimi flatly refused to obey poor Alice, whose only method of enforcing discipline was to lock Mimi in the bathroom for hours on end. Since there was only one bathroom at 186 East 75th Street, this was a cause of considerable inconvenience both to myself and, I imagine, to Alice. My mother also disapproved of this form of punishment, and when she returned from the hat shop one evening to find Mimi yet again incarcerated, Alice went.

For a happy period Estelle looked after us. Estelle was no disciplinarian. And then a new governess arrived, another Englishwoman named Miss Oliphant. Her name caused us to double up with mirth and bounce up and down on our beds before ever we saw her. ('Has she got a trunk?' 'Does she weigh two tons?') But when we did see her it was a sad disillusionment. Indeed she was a sad woman. She did not have bunions but she was bilious. And one day, when left alone in the apartment with Mimi and myself for a long weekend, she retired groaning to her bed. She remained there, in obvious agony, for two days, and quite refused to see a doctor, while Mimi fed me as best she could on the contents of the ice-box. (Cold beets, which I could not stomach, she covered with sugar to render them more palatable. I forced the dish down, but have preserved a marked aversion to beetroot ever since.) When my mother returned and found Miss Oliphant still groaning in her bed, she sent for a doctor, who dealt with the after-effects of a miscarriage, though of course we children knew nothing about it.

For a while Estelle was once again in charge, but my mother had sent a cable to Miss Wright—who was somewhere very remote, like Australia—and she came back as quickly as she could to resume what she, I and everybody

61

else regarded as her right and proper position in our home. The Fleet was in.

Our memories are usually connected with our senses, and it is frequently said that the sense of smell is the most evocative of all. I have memories of at least one woman I loved which are, in the first instance, almost entirely tactile, the texture of a skin and the shape of an embrace. Certain tastes can instantly whisk us back to our childhood (those *madeleines*!) or perhaps to a restaurant upon the cobbled quayside of a foreign fishing village many summers ago, while the sound, say, of a waterfall or of curlews calling may also recreate in its entirety a place and a time that are gone. And visual memories, perhaps the most banal, are so strong and at times so inexplicable that it has proved necessary to invent the phenomenon of *déjà vu*.

There is, however, another and non-sensual form of memory which can almost blot out the others, and that is emotional memory. I have recalled Alice's straw hats, and I remember the smell of carbolic soap that hung about her hands: on the rare occasions nowadays when I eat waffles with butter and maple syrup, Estelle is once again running in from the kitchen of 186 with plate after plate of them, while the maple syrup is called Log Cabin and comes in a can shaped like a cabin which pours through its chimney: if I were a painter I could, I am sure, exactly produce the grey tones of Miss Oliphant's complexion.

Yet Miss Wright, whom I knew so very much better than all of those, I cannot describe. And this is all the more odd in that she came to stay with us in England, more than once, during my schooldays. Indeed I saw her only three or four years ago. Yet I would be most reluctant to say, under oath, whether she was tall or short, fat or thin, wore glasses or not (and there can have been no halfway measure about this). What I do remember, though, is the absolute feeling of security she gave me.

Not that I knew the meaning of the word in those days, or was even aware of the concept. I did not run to her for protection, and I did not fret if she were not present, for I knew that she would be back. I played happily alone, while she weeded the flowerbeds at Lenox or, in New York, read her book or got on with her sewing. She did not fill my world, in no wise did she circumscribe it, and she certainly did not compete in any way for the love I gave my mother. I do not ever recall doing very much with her, though I remember that she was there, in the Wolsey Woods, and she was there, in Central Park, and she was there, when I splashed in my tub or waited for sleep.

I can only compare our relationship, or at least my side of it, to that which a man feels when he has been happily married for several years. His wife may be in some altogether different part of the house, engaged upon jobs of which he knows nothing: she may be out shopping, or he may be at his place of work: she may even have gone away for a few days. But he knows she will be back, because he trusts her absolutely, and the mere fact of her existence is, for him, security. That was how I felt about Miss Wright.

Robert Louis Stevenson, in the introductory poem to *A Child's Garden of Verses*, writes of his own nurse: '. . . my second mother, my first wife.' This was not my experience, nor do I believe that it was his. If a boy's mother is with him and loves him, there can only be one. It is a foster-mother who is, in this sense, a 'second mother'. But I think that there is a truth in the second part of his statement, if the relationship is as profound and idyllic as was mine with Miss Wright. How common such happy relationships are, I do not know. They obviously require very special, and very remarkable, qualities on the part of the woman, and it may be that not all boys are capable of total trust. I have had personal knowledge of only one other such relationship, before that little boy was wantonly snatched away by a stupid legal system, at the age of four from the woman who was giving him so happy and sensible and secure a start in life. But at least she had been allowed to give him that.

My memories of my mother during the American years are in some ways more concrete. There are plenty of sensual memories: the smell of the powder she used, the sheen of her long, golden hair which I sometimes watched her brush, the softness of her voice and particularly when she was singing me to sleep (*There's a Long, Long Trail A-winding*), an evening dress of heavy silk that she sometimes wore, if she were going out, when she came to kiss me good night. (It was of an irregular black, grey and white pattern and was known as her 'camouflage' dress: further Royal Naval echoes, no doubt.)

She was not a demonstrative mother, but there was nothing chilly or remote about her. If her presence was something special and not to be taken for granted, this was perhaps because she had to spend so much time away, at the hat shop, which was soon enough expanded to include a dress shop as well. (I visited her there occasionally. The grey pile carpets felt inches thick. The triple mirrors were intriguing, and the seamstresses made much of me, allowing me even to play with the tiny reels of coloured silk that they put into their sewing machines.) When she was at home she always had time for me and for my interests, for my blue stamp-album that began with Abyssinia and ended with Zanzibar, for the tulips that I drew by the score in crayon, slightly greasy to the touch, and then cut out and arranged in vases, for the coloured paper-chains that we made together before Christmas, for my marbles and my soldiers and my cardhouses and for Doctor Dolittle, about whom we would read together, by the hour it seemed.

I do not recall her presence at mealtimes, and I suppose she lunched near her shop. Miss Wright presided at table. She taught us our manners, firmly and patriotically. Should we perform such a gross misdemeanour as hurling our food to the floor or sticking our thumbs in the peanut butter, we were always told 'not to behave like Germans'.

Inseparably connected with my mother's memory in those years were her little dogs. These were usually Pekingese and usually ended up by being run over, times of terrible tragedy. I remember the first of these dogs arriving, on my mother's birthday one April day. Messenger boys seemed to be ringing the bell all day with boxes of flowers. One long box, when opened, contained dozens of roses, long-stemmed, orangy-yellow American beauties with their heads at each end, while in the middle, seated upon their thornless stems was an orangy-yellow puppy. What excitement at 186, and what puddles!

This must have been a present from one of mother's beaux, as she called them. There were many of these and she lived a gay, though a discreetly gay, life. Of that life I saw little, for bedtime came so early, but I remember hearing in my bed the tinkle of the cocktail-shaker (at a very early age Mimi was an expert at mixing them) and the sound of laughter from the other end of our small apartment. It was a comforting, even a cosy, sound as I fell asleep.

In New York in the 1920s a woman in my mother's position could, for the first time, enjoy what an earlier generation might have called 'her freedom'. Among her friends of her own age there was no longer any stigma attached to divorce as such, and none at all in her own particular case, which explains why she counted as many women among her friends as men. There was nevertheless a certain spice to the very word divorcée, which seems fatuous enough nowadays but which, a generation ago, had led all that is implied by *Gay Divorcée* to supplant the idea of *The Merry Widow*. This attitude had not, I think, then reached Europe. It was a good decade later that a sprightly comedy on the Paris boulevards was entitled *Divorçons*!

My mother also had freedom of another, and perhaps more real, sort. Although she was worried all her life about money, a hangover of her father's perpetual worries, she had in fact complete financial independence in those days. She possessed a small income and this she supplemented, quite adequately, from her successful little business. She drew no alimony from my father and thus what she had was in every sense and absolutely her own, to do with as she pleased. She had the responsibility and the expense of four children, but her own tastes were modest. She could dress very well, and very cheaply, from her own shop. Display was never her style, nor did she wish it to be ours. We did not think of ourselves as rich, and we were not by the standards of many among my mother's friends, but we had everything we needed.

Furthermore my mother, who was thirty-six when I was

born, was of an age to appreciate and not to abuse her 'free-dom'. At first, when she had divorced my father and went to work for Harry Collins, she was unsure of herself and lonely. She was ever a shy, even in some ways a timid, woman, and neither her upbringing nor, really, her married life had equipped her for almost total independence. Indeed she has always been almost too eager to take advice and to rely on the opinion of others, even when such opinion may run counter to her own, and the persons on whom she relied were inferior to herself in intellect or in character or both. She was never, in any way, a manly woman, and she felt very unprotected when, at the age of forty, she had to sink or swim on her own in a city that is not renowned for its kindness towards the weak.

She discovered as much, I think, in Harry Collins' store as anywhere else that she was not weak. She also made the discovery, than which none is a greater reinforcement in such circumstances, that she had a great many very good friends. She has told me that when she was alone in New York, and we children were in New Canaan, she went dancing almost every night, and that it was this that kept her going, physically because it was such good exercise, mentally and morally because it did not allow her to brood upon daytime miseries and the past and her own precarious position.

By the time we came to live in New York, her situation was no longer precarious. She had proved, to her own satisfaction and to that of her friends, that she was entirely capable of dealing with circumstances for which she had never been prepared. If she remained shy, she was no longer unsure of herself, and if she did not go out every night, she could and did so as often as she pleased. Her situation was in many ways a very pleasant one. She herself was of an age to appreciate this.

Friends of mine, brought up in circumstances similar to my own, have told me that as children they resented, and sometimes suffered traumatically from, the atmosphere of latent sexuality that can surround a single and attractive mother, that they felt unduly possessive of her and jealously

66

resented her male friends, with results that often bedevilled their own adult lives. To the best of my knowledge I was not affected in this way at all. I do not recall that I ever felt neglected by my mother (though I suppose that like all children there must have been times when I did) and I certainly do not remember any atmosphere of 'latent sexuality' in her relationships with her friends, though I did become aware of such an atmosphere, at a very early age, so far as my eldest sister was concerned. I discussed this with my sister Mimi, shortly before her death, and she, being both older and a girl, would presumably have been more likely to be affected by such matters than myself. She agreed with me entirely. 'Mummy's friends,' she said, 'were Mummy's friends, and that was that.'

I may say that I most certainly do not assume that that was in fact, that. When I was almost middle-aged, and had committed some foolish matrimonial indiscretion, my mother said to me:

'In these matters you can commit murder if you set about it properly, and keep your mouth shut. I know. I have.'

I doubt if she has actually ever done anyone to death, and it is obvious what her metaphor meant. In any event, whatever she may have been up to during those years before she remarried, she saw to it that neither we children nor, I hope, anybody else not concerned was affected. After all, in these matters is not the essence of the law: do what you will, provided you are discreet and others are not hurt? If I write about this at length here, it is to prove, if that be possible, a negative: I did not know, or sense, anything I should not, and I was not hurt.

As I have said, I have only vague memories of my mother's beaux. One was a colonel, who once took Mimi and myself to see *H.M.S. Pinafore*—how the Royal Navy does recur: maybe he was an English colonel, though I believe he was a much rarer bird for that period, an American one. Afterwards he led us to the Plaza and gave us double ice-cream meringues with whipped cream: I thought him a splendid colonel, and the Plaza remains, to this day, my favourite hotel in all the world. Another had a very red face and was known, in friendly fashion, as the Setting Sun. A third was forever being pestered by Mimi to take her to the polo, which he did frequently, though I was left at home. After the first humiliation I maintained, against all argument, that I did not *want* to see the polo. There were other, even more shadowy, figures. And, as I have said, she also had many woman friends most of whom, of course, were married.

These were the years before the Great Depression, when the business of America was business. My mother was too old to be a member of the 'jazz age' and I think that on the whole her circle of friends was successfully concerned with business or the stock exchange or the law. Apart from the colonel of ill-defined nationality, I recall no soldiers and no politicians. Nor do I remember any writers or painters, and there was only one rather hectic brush with the theatre.

This was on the occasion of *Charlot's Revue* of 1926. If my memory is correct, this was surely the most star-studded revue of all time: Beatrice Lillie, Jack Buchanan, Gertrude Lawrence, Noël Coward and Tommy Mundin. It was my Aunt Wyn, a friend of Beatrice Lillie's, who introduced us to the magical cast. (Tommy Mundin gave my sister Geraldine a large and extremely heavy fountain pen, a new invention in those days, mottled red in colour and made, I should guess, of malachite: it did not work, and therefore I got it. I treasured it for years.) I used to go to the matinées of *Charlot's Revue*. In fact I went eleven times. Originally Miss Wright used to come with me, but her delight in *Limehouse Blues* and the rest was less insatiable than my own. Later I was deposited at the stage door on my own, and made my way to my usual seat, in the middle of the front row of the stalls. In the intervals I would go backstage where I often sat on Beatrice Lillie's knee. I have not seen Lady Peel since then except, whenever it is in any way possible, across the footlights. While I write these lines I have a glass beside me, and I raise it to her now.

Looking back on it, I suppose that the environment in which I was growing up in New York was one that would nowadays be priggishly called philistine. Books were read for pleasure rather than for enlightenment, pictures were supposed to be easy on the eye, classical music was something of a bore, listened to from an obscure sense of duty, while modern music (that is to say anything since and including Wagner) need not be listened to at all, poetry had to stir the emotions, as did that fine long narrative poem of the period, *John Brown's Body*, and sculpture was statues. Artists were not despised, they were indeed in some ways admired. Nor were they believed to be automatically disreputable. Clark Voorhees was actually an uncle, while Whistler had been a distant relation. Nevertheless it was rather odd, rather special, to have artists in the family. Their status was very much that described by Galsworthy in *The Forsyte Saga* (a favourite book of the period and of my mother's: I think that she identified herself, heaven knows why, with Irene, that most incredible and insufferable of heroines who, single-handed, ruins an otherwise excellent series of novels). But artists were also, and particularly for those who were not related to any, the grotesque figures of another period best-seller, *The Constant Nymph*. This may have been why, a very few years later, the American bourgeoisie accepted so readily as a culture-hero the almost equally improbable figure of D. H. Lawrence, as seen through the eyes of his women. There have been others, since.

Into this world there came, from Paris, Bertram Winthrop, a distant cousin of my mother's and a man of much sweetness. I shall write of him in the second part of this book, for it is there that he belongs. He asked her to marry him. After some hesitation, she accepted. She thought that she loved him, and she knew that she had no more interest in her New York life. Her point, there, had been made. The hat-and-dress shop had grown beyond her immediate control: it ceased to be a challenge. He was rich enough for her to get rid of it without worries. It would be a wrench to leave New York, but they would be coming to America every year. I had almost outgrown Miss Wright, and my sisters were certainly outgrowing 186 East 75th Street. And Paris was much more Paris, in 1927, than it is today.

My mother married Bertram. They were already in Paris,

when my eldest sister, in whose charge I was, set sail with me on board the Cunarder, S.S. *Carmania*, bound for Cherbourg. (For some years I collected postcards of Cunarders.) My sister spent the greater part of the voyage locked in the arms of various young men behind the lifeboats. This suited me perfectly. During that crossing I became quite a familiar figure upon the bridge, where I managed frequently to imitate Lord Nelson, and an even more familiar one in the engine-room. As for the kitchens, or galleys as I preferred to call them, I knew my way about them almost before New York had sunk out of sight over the horizon.

And that was my first America.

Part Two

Part Two

6

BERTRAM WINTHROP WAS the first adult from 'outside' to assume an important and, as it seemed, a permanent place within my world: all the other adults who then peopled my life I had known for as long as I could remember. It is therefore to be expected that I should have given him the closest inspection of which I was capable at the age of seven or eight. No doubt he examined my sisters and myself with equal care, though few adults can manage the unwinking gaze of a small child.

His first, and to me most outstanding, quality was that he was a foreigner, though the reasons for this were not immediately apparent to me. In theory he was an American. In fact, as I have subsequently learned, he was probably not the son of his putative father, Neilson Winthrop, a smart and very neat old man with a trim white imperial, but of a certain well-known French duke, who figures in the pages of Marcel Proust. It was his mother who had brought him up, principally in France, while his supposed elder brothers, the twins named Harold and Gerald, were brought up by their father, with whom, indeed, they lived until Neilson Winthrop died and they were nearly fifty. Bertram's mother I remember vaguely, a sick, tired old woman awaiting death behind closed Venetian blinds. While the twins had been to Eton, Bertram had been educated in France, at Harvard, at the Sorbonne and at the Harvard Law School. He was a lawyer, with both American and French law degrees. His English was perfect, but with a foreigner's perfection. It was, one felt, not his native language, and this led one at times to detect a very faint accent, perhaps because the English language did not perfectly fit his cast of mind. There was about him a meticulous quality, an almost fussy punctilio and a preoccupation with the *comme il faut*, which is often to be found in a certain type of bourgeois Frenchman. This was presumably accentuated by the facts of his being a lawyer and also a bachelor in his middle forties—not at all a hey-nonny-nonny, supper at Maxim's, champagne out of satin slippers type of bachelor, but rather a *vieux garçon*—when he married my mother and entered our lives. He also attached immense importance to food and wines, which had to be not only excellent but also correct. He was, in a word, a Frenchman with an American passport.

In appearance he bore a certain resemblance to Woodrow Wilson, on whose staff he had served at the time of the Paris Peace Conference. (Several volumes of manuscript in Bertram's sloping French hand, dealing with I know not what international legal problems of 1919 and bound in red leather, had a place of honour upon his bookshelves.) Indeed he may have even modelled himself upon his old boss, wearing the same type of spectacles with a similar almost mirthless smile. He dressed in dark suits, which though made for him in London did not somehow hang right from his rather narrow shoulders. His hats, too, seemed almost as though built for another man, but this may have been because he wore them dead straight, central, and pulled down rather low over his high forehead. His dark silk ties were never ruffled, for they were affixed to his white silk shirts with a pearl-headed pin. He had the French city-dweller's distrust of the weather, and when he ventured forth it was after a lengthy process of dressing up in overcoats, of varying weight according to the season, scarves of wool or silk, gloves, umbrella if there was the slightest danger of rain and, if it had been raining, galoshes. In fact he was a thoroughly urban person, and though he had seemed natural enough upon the Lenox golf links when he was Cousin Bertram, once he was back in France and had become simply Bertram he always looked out of place and faintly miserable either in the real country or by the real sea. A formal garden or the seaside terrace of a casino were as far as he could comfortably go: fields or woods or beaches made him appear definitely ill at ease.

There was a considerable favouritism in the Winthrop family. Old Mr Winthrop had a house in Paris and another near Cannes, and he would travel between his residences at the appropriate season, wintering in the South as was then still the fashion. The twins were not only favoured above

74

Bertram, for obvious reasons, in that they lived with their
father and were not expected to do any work, but were also
the objects of favouritism, in at least one matter, between
themselves. Since Harold and Gerald had nothing whatever
to do, they spent the greater part of their time, when in
Paris, at the Ritz Bar and Maxim's and when in Cannes at
the Maxim's down there. I am told that persons entering
the Ritz in the twenties and finding the twins' stools vacant
would be reminded that winter was coming and that for all
who could afford it it was time to head for the coast. They
lived, in fact, very regular lives, each with his most respectable mistress of many years' standing. (When their father
died both of them immediately married their ladies and
each bore a son within the year. These were christened
Ronald and Reginald.)

Now one and perhaps only one unusual event had occurred
in the life of these twins. When they were both Eton boys
Harold had, accidentally I am sure, poked out one of
Gerald's eyes with a cricket bat. Gerald wore a glass eye
ever after, and on the infrequent occasions of their visits to
our house, he would remove it after lunch for my entertainment. This is the only reason why I remember him; his
twin had no such trick of survival.

It was because of his glass eye that Gerald was favoured
by their father above Harold. And one form that this
favouritism took was in the travel arrangements when the
three of them went from Paris to Cannes or back again.
Gerald's mistress was then allowed to sit in the front of the
Rolls, with the chauffeur: Harold's had to go by train.

Bertram was extremely fortunate in his choice of profession. He was not, I am told, a particularly clever lawyer,
but he was one of the very few men at that time who was a
member both of the French and of the American bar.
Though he was not one of the big international lawyers,
there was still a very great deal of private litigation for
which his attainments made him an obvious choice. He had
a French partner, a highly efficient and totally colourless
man called Monsieur Landy, and an American partner in
New York, whose name I do not know but who was, no

doubt, equally capable. Bertram, if the truth were told, was little more than the figurehead or cornerstone of this transatlantic legal bridge. He went to his office in the rue de la Boétie punctually every morning, and remained there all day. If one wished to see him he was invariably in conference, but when at last one was admitted to his office, nobody else had just emerged. He did, however, have at least one client whom he saw quite regularly and whose visits invariably cheered him up. He would then come home in the evening, rubbing his hands:

'Pearl White was in today!'

Meanwhile, thanks to Monsieur Landy and his American partner he made a great deal of money.

If we looked closely at Bertram he may be assumed to have looked equally closely at us. To begin with, however, he had little opportunity and this almost certainly had unfortunate consequences.

For when Geraldine and I arrived in Paris, we had nowhere to live. Bertram and my mother had moved into his small bachelor's flat in the rue de la Baume, where for years he had been looked after by an elderly gorgon of a housekeeper who deeply resented my mother's existence and, almost equally, my own. The apartment was gloomy, heavily over-furnished and dark, for the daylight could scarcely penetrate the thick lace curtains. Bertram had always liked everything 'just so', and his housekeeper had seen that he got it. This, however, had never included a small boy with potentially muddy shoes. Even less so had it meant a woman, and an American woman at that, from whom the housekeeper was expected to take orders. She did her best to make my mother feel unwanted and unnecessary, and since my mother was shy and strange, she almost succeeded in making her miserable.

There was no room in the rue de la Baume for us children. My two younger sisters, Fanny and Mimi, had been sent to a boarding school near Bromley, in England, where they were not at all happy. It was at this time that Mimi became almost aggressively American, though in fact she was the only one of us who was technically British, having been born in

London. Geraldine was dispatched to a finishing school outside Paris, which she disliked for its convent-like nature and the shortage of hot water. I was sent to live in a hotel around the corner from the rue de la Baume, with a new governess called Mademoiselle de Condé. Our antipathy was strong, immediate, and lasted for as long as she did, which was several months.

My mother realised almost at once that her marriage was a mistake. Bertram had been a bachelor for too long and his knowledge of women was far too limited for someone of my mother's age and temperament. Furthermore, almost as soon as they were married he adopted what was then the traditional European attitude towards his wife. Not only had she lost her freedom (she had been prepared for this: but in our private as in our political worlds the immense value of freedom is seldom fully grasped until that freedom has gone), but she quite failed to gain a friend, a comrade, a man with whom she could laugh as once she had laughed with my father. The long-range prospect was bleak, but nevertheless she was determined to make the best of it.

The short-range situation was even worse. Perhaps Bertram, perhaps she too, had thought that it would be as well for them to be alone together for a while. She had underestimated how homesick she would be for America and, even more, how much she would miss her children, her daughters at schools they disliked and her son quite obviously miserable and cross. But, she told herself, as soon as they found a house all would be different. Therefore she was prepared to put up with this, too. However, her second marriage had got off to a very bad start from which it never really recovered.

(And here I would ask in parentheses how many people are in fact capable of two real marriages? Some unfortunate people are not even capable of one, though they are perhaps unaware of their own inability to love and to be lovable. For them an endless succession of temporary relationships, whether entered into in the belief that each will be permanent or not, and whether or not legalised by a registrar, may provide as good a solution as any. But can a man or woman who has ever given himself or herself entirely to another repeat the really profound act of love that should be the basis of marriage? Perhaps if death has frozen a first marriage so that it becomes untouchable and immutable in the glacier of the past, then another, different love is possible. Perhaps, though, even then there can never be a second, true, high summer in a single lifetime. Of course the 'real' marriage need not necessarily be the first one.)

To return to myself in 1927, I loathed France, the French language and Mademoiselle de Condé, who personified them both. She wore black and she smelt wrong. I missed America, I missed my mother—though I saw her every day, that is not at all the same—and perhaps above all I missed Miss Wright. Instead of Nelson I now had anecdotes, in French, about a character called *le grand Condé*. Although I rapidly learned to understand French, *le grand Condé* remained to me a most unsympathetic character, not least because he was related to my loathed governess, this impostor who had stolen Miss Wright's place. I fear I must have given the poor woman a quite dreadful time. I learned to have tantrums, I refused to eat the strange food, I was forever pestering her to know when I would see my mother and when I could go back to America. And she would burst into tears and slap me and, forgetting her aristocratic connections in her distraction, would at last shout at me the only phrase of hers that I can now recall:

'*Fiche-moi la paix!*'

After a little while she went. There was still no house (though there was a rented one, early Charles Addams in design, at Trouville during the summer) and Bertram's step-children were not becoming any easier a responsibility for him. Geraldine had left the finishing school and was spending her time with assorted, and invariably unsuitable, men, alcoholics and the like, in Montparnasse. She was sent to Oxford, in the hope that she might there learn some-thing better. Whether she did, I would not profess to say.

But for me, my Russian period was about to begin, and a very happy one it proved to be.

It was Mademoiselle de Révoutsky who led me into the Russian world. She had taken over from the unspeakable Mademoiselle de Condé, and no two women could have been more different. The relative of *le grand Condé* was short and fat, in creaking stays, a cross little pouter-pigeon with a voice as sharp and penetrating as the yap of a Pomeranian. Mademoiselle Révoutsky, for reasons unknown to me but which may well have been very sad, never spoke of her family. She was a rather tall, quiet woman who had to go upstairs slowly because of a bad heart. She was gentle and as patient as the steppes of her native land are long. Her clothes were greyish in hue, and hung rather loosely about her—no doubt they were old, and she had grown thin—the reverse of the stiff black serge into which the Frenchwoman had squeezed her plump shape.

We can love in one person what would be most unattractive in another. I remember Mademoiselle de Révoutsky's spectacles, which were cheap, thin, steel pince-nez of the type often seen in pre-Revolutionary Russian photographs. Chekov wore such spectacles, and so did Trotsky, and it would seem likely that Mademoiselle de Révoutsky had brought hers with her from Russia. Although I imagine that such spectacles are more convenient for reading than for normal use, she wore hers all the time, because she was extremely short-sighted. When she did take them off, her expression was even more vague than usual. And it is then that I remember a minute detail. She would rub the bridge of her nose between finger and thumb, as though to relieve a small headache, and where the spectacles had pinched her skin were two grey marks with red centres. In someone I disliked such a strange disfiguration would have been unattractive. In her it aroused within myself an emotion which I then could certainly not have identified but which today I should describe as tenderness. That is perhaps an odd emotion for a boy of eight to experience, yet I think it sums up, better than any other single word, the feelings I had for her. I would have done anything rather than hurt her, perhaps because I sensed that she had been hurt too much already.

She was the vaguest person I have ever known. During the month of January any of us may date his letters by the previous year. It is even possible to get the decade wrong. Mademoiselle de Révoutsky is the only person I have met actually to confuse her centuries, and when I went to school letters from her would reach me written in 1828 or 1829.

Once she lost me in the rue de Rivoli. We had been to Brentano's bookshop together, I to buy the English comics, *Tiger Tim* and so on, which I regarded as infinitely inferior to American funnies, but which were still better than similar French productions. We were walking along the crowded street, towards the Place de la Concorde, I with my nose in my newspaper, when she realised that she had lost me. In her anxiety she dropped her spectacles, which broke, and then she could see nothing at all. It was a little time before I realised that I was lost. This did not perturb me. When I could not find Mademoiselle de Révoutsky, I simply hailed a cab and had myself driven to the rue de la Baume. By the time my mother had been found and had taken me back to Passy, where I was then living, poor Mademoiselle de Révoutsky had had a heart attack. She cried bitter tears, but soon enough she recovered.

My mother and Bertram had found a house, but it was not yet habitable, which was why I was in Passy. Our home-to-be was just off the Champs Elysées, near the Etoile, and had been the stables of a large town house, or *hôtel privé*, at No. 1 rue Lord Byron. The main house flanked the street and a *porte-cochère* led through a dark archway into the garden, our garden, at the back. Beyond were the stables and the coach-houses, one of which became our garage. It was all neatly tucked away, very quiet and safe for children. But the conversion of these heterogeneous buildings into a single house, and then the decorating and the furnishing took a long time. (Both the main *hôtel* and our house were pulled down just before the war, and a cinema run up in their stead. I believe that this, too, has now gone.) Therefore while No. 1 rue Lord Byron was being got ready, Bertram and my mother continued to live in the rue de la Baume, while I spent the better part of a year with Mademoiselle de

Révoutsky in Passy, interrupted for the girls' Christmas holidays, which we spent at Chamonix.

Poor Bertram! Chamonix was surely his idea, reeking as it did of an out-of-date fashionableness (and that as a summer resort, what is more), and so no doubt was the brand-new hotel, reeking of new paint, in which we were installed. Chamonix at Christmastime is, as I recall, a most gloomy place. The sun rose above the Alps shortly before noon and set behind another range of Alps a few minutes later. There was no snow within reach. In fact there was nothing to do in Chamonix at all. In the hotel I was reprimanded for running along corridors: Mimi maintained that the smell of paint made her feel sick: Geraldine, that the wine waiter blew down the back of her neck: Fanny frequently burst into tears during meals, for reasons unknown to me, and had to flee the hotel's huge and almost empty restaurant.

Poor Bertram! It was not a successful holiday. He would take the girls on excursions, trudging across the Mer de Glace while the ice gradually froze their feet, or to other French and Swiss provincial towns as dismal as Chamonix itself. I walked around the place with my mother or with Mademoiselle de Révoutsky and we visited steamy cafés where I managed to get through a great many cakes washed down with bowls of hot chocolate. That was all right. So too were the evenings, though these were somewhat protracted, for they began almost immediately after lunch. Then I played cards with my mother and Mimi, and occasionally with the older girls and with Mademoiselle Révoutsky too. As a child I always played a lot of games, and particularly cards, with my mother. When we were alone together we played a game called Russian Bank, a sort of double solitaire. When we were more, we played Hearts, a primitive and simplified form of Whist. At Chamonix, perhaps in desperation for ways to pass the time, she taught Mimi and myself to play Bridge. (Auction Bridge, of course: Contract was only just coming in and was regarded as a rather fast gambling game: Bertram and his French friends played their own variety, unknown to us and called *Plafond*.) It was not in Chamonix but only a little later that my mother taught us

F

to play Poker. She herself played that most fascinating of card games better than any other woman I have ever known, nor did she talk while playing it. I am grateful to her not only for the pleasures these games and these lessons gave me when small, but also for having taught me about card sense and card manners at so early an age. In later years I would have lost more money, and more friends, had she not.

Back in Paris after this rather gloomy holiday my sisters returned to what passed for their studies, and I to Passy. The flat in which I lived belonged to Madame de Carrière. Despite her late husband's name, he and she were Russian, his forebears having been driven from France by one gang of revolutionary assassins, his widow driven back again by another. (Though much can be—and it all has been—said in favour of the spirit of 1792 and even of 1917, nothing can excuse terrorism, even though the terrorists claim to be acting on our behalf, to be on our side. Whatever they may allege, and whatever may be later alleged in their favour, terrorists are always and only on their own side.)

Madame de Carrière lived there with her daughter, Myra. Mademoiselle de Révoutsky and I were 'paying guests', a bleak phrase and one quite unsuitable to the circumstance, for we were entirely members of the family. It was a very large family or clan with other Russians for ever dropping in, cooking meals, drinking tea, making music, playing games or telling stories. There was always something going on in the de Carrière household, which I remember as crammed with furniture and people, windows hermetically sealed as if it were the Nevski Prospekt in December and not the rue Lyautey outside, a great fug and a smell of incense, and of oil lamps glimmering beneath ikons, and in the middle of it all fat, jolly old Madame de Carrière, in her ancient armchair with her two sticks beside her, and on the mantelpiece a tinted photograph of Myra in the court dress which she had worn when presented in 1912, its train studded with sequins, and beside it the rather dirty cardboard pill-box in which the diamonds were kept. I was allowed to play with the pretty, winking stones, and as the time came when one more must be sold, the intensely animated conversation would touch on how and where this could most advantageously be done. Myra, who worked as a seamstress, would then have to sacrifice her lunch hour in order to visit the jeweller reported at the time to give the best prices.

This was the apogee of the White Russian emigration in Paris, of which the cliché symbol is the Russian nobleman driving the French taxi. But it should not be seen either in terms of farce or of a patronising, sentimental comedy. Those former officers of the Imperial army did not drive cabs because it amused them, but because it was the only way that they could earn a living. Few had been trained to any profession, and even when they had it was not easy to get a job or a labour permit in France. As for learning a profession, many of them in the late twenties believed—as refugees always begin by believing and usually wrongly—that it was only a matter of time, even of months, before they would be returning to their own country. They knew how extremely shaky was the Bolshevik regime, with Stalin and Trotsky fighting for mastery while the people starved. Unlike certain Western progressives, they could only regard the miseries that had befallen the country they loved as an atrocious disaster. Most of the young men had fought until quite recently with Wrangel or Denikin, and though they had suffered the bitterness of defeat, in 1928 they did not yet accept this defeat as absolute and final. They were prepared to fight again, if the opportunity arose—which they believed it must. Meanwhile they must find a leader and agree upon a cause. The opportunity never arose. Had it done so, would it have produced the leader whom they never found? Nor did they ever reach agreement as to what their positive policy must be should they return to Russia.

Their struggle was not imaginary. A Russian grand-duke who lived, I think, in the apartment below Madame de Carrière's, was murdered by Bolshevik agents while I was in the house. This, however, was kept from me for many years, and I am therefore not sure of the details.

I remember them as immensely gay and uncomplaining. I loved their language, which to their delight I learned to speak quite quickly—alas! I have forgotten every word of it—and I recall dimly stories of wolves and bears and white foxes. I do not believe that they talked to me about the revolution through which they had lived, or if so it passed above my head. I do, however, recollect one very frequent visitor who became a close friend of mine. She had contracted spotted typhus in a Bolshevik prison, and had lost all her hair. She therefore wore a wig, a bright red wig which did not look at all like human hair, and this she would tip over one eye, with an immensely comical wink, so that I laughed until the tears poured down my cheeks and had to beg her to stop.

They had a panache, in those days, the White Russians, a style that was quite lacking in Europe's next great flood of refugees. The Germans, whether Jewish or not, who were driven abroad by Nazi gangs of revolutionary assassins, were certainly cleverer and more valuable additions to their new societies than the White Russians. Many of them, however, demanded as a right the pity that they undoubtedly deserved. Nor was this, I think, primarily a matter of class. From all I have heard those poor Russians, whose names I was to see years later upon the noticeboard outside Le Havre, never complained, never whined. It is a sad quality of many Germans that when they cannot utter sneers or shout orders, they will whine, three most unattractive sounds. The Germans have many talents and many virtues, but these do not include style. The Russians have style, and none more than those White Russians in Paris, many years ago.

As the years passed they grew older and poorer. For those who were almost utterly destitute, the late Dorothy Paget founded the Maison Russe, some miles from Paris. Madame de Carrière went there and so at last did dear Mademoiselle Révoutsky. I visited them several times before the war. It was quieter, of course, than the rue Lyautey had been a decade earlier. They knew that they would now never go home, and very few even of the younger ones in Paris still hoped for a reversal of history. In the Maison Russe, where the old gentlemen addressed the old ladies with the same courtly deference, while they themselves remained excellencies and imperial highnesses and the rest of it, they had at least one another, and shared memories. And there Madame de Carrière died, and later Mademoiselle de Révoutsky faded quite out of life, as happy, I believe, as Europe's awful circumstances allowed.

If Dorothy Paget is remembered in England beyond the circle of her family, it is because she once won the Derby. The Maison Russe was no more lasting a monument—the war swept it away almost without trace—but it is one that I, at least, prefer to appreciate.

With Mademoiselle Révoutsky I began to appreciate Paris or rather to lose my antipathy for all things French (which, in reality, was nothing but homesickness for America). We would go to the Tuileries together, where there was a merry-go-round. The wooden horses rose and fell in time to the music and each child was given an instrument like a large screwdriver, or perhaps a minute lance, with which to spear metal rings the size of curtain rings, as he rode past the box from which they were suspended one by one. A certain number of rings, three I think, won a small and brightly coloured sugar stick, none the less delicious for being almost tasteless.

The place for exploring was the Bois, and for sailing boats the Luxembourg, though mine behaved as dismally here as they had in Central Park. Occasionally I played with other children in the parks, though attempts—usually of grown-up origin—to create friendships with French boys or girls of my own age were seldom successful. Even though there was soon no language barrier, there were others. Not unnaturally the French children preferred to play with one another rather than with a foreign boy who did not know their games. The children with whom it was arranged that I should play were almost inevitably of bourgeois origin. In those days the Parisian bourgeoise still put their sons and daughters into most elaborate clothes, velvet suits or dresses with lace collars and often with hats. The cult of childishness had not then reached France, and they were expected to be miniature adults, grave and, if possible, self-possessed. I thought them an awful bore, and overdressed into the bargain. I remember none of them. And though I saw a certain number of American and English children, and particularly my cousin, Billy Channing, whose parents were also living in Paris, these meetings, too, had to be arranged, were therefore lacking in spontaneity and were scarcely more memorable. In fact in Paris, as in New York, I was once again a solitary child.

Nevertheless I grew fond of Paris, and later came to love the place. If I never had the passion for that city that many foreigners have felt and described, often in moving terms, this may have been because of my youth when first I went there. It became my home and as such I took it increasingly for granted, though when I went to school in England I felt for it all the emotions implied in that word. Indeed to this day there are certain Parisian sensations which, when I experience them, make me know that I am home again. Some of these are so obvious as to be quite hackneyed: the mixed early morning smells of good coffee, fresh bread and clean linen; the mauve light that often fills the Place de la Concorde at dusk and, a few hours later, the moving chain of lights cast by the cars in the Champs Elysées, seen from the Etoile or from the Louvre; an elderly, aproned waiter, flicking a fly from a deserted café table with his napkin; the smell of a really good restaurant at lunchtime or of a really ripe métro during the rush hour; above all, perhaps, Parisian voices, never silent, speaking that most civilised and delicious of languages with every accent from the Académie Française to les Halles.

There are other, smaller, more personal and less easily explicable emotional responses: a certain street corner; the Ripolin advertisement; the dustiness of the Bois; the hum in a French theatre before the curtain rises, which is quite different from the hum in an English or American theatre; the chestnut braziers in the wintertime and the bookshops; the arrogant young men of the Latin Quarter, and the friendly tarts in the bars of Montparnasse; the barges shooting the Seine bridges, and the eternal lovers, young as 1937 was young, young as Eloise, young as tomorrow, sauntering along the *quais*. During the war, when the

86

Germans were in Paris and I was on leave in London, I put on a suit I had not worn for years. In a pocket I found a Paris bus-ticket, two or three strips from the conductor's little roll that he stamps with a quite particular rattling noise as he reels them off his small metal drum. Immediately it was all back, and my eyes, of course, were filled with tears.

Oh, I can be as sentimental as the next writer about Paris, but yet, but yet. . . . When I go there now, indeed whenever I have been there since the war, the magic has worked only fitfully. Whether this is my doing or the city's, I neither know nor care. Although I did not then realise it, something died at about the time of my visit to that half-ruined bar in Le Havre in 1946. My love affair with Paris had been a real one, but it was never a *grande passion*, and it is over, perhaps because she or I or both of us have changed. She has gone her way and I mine. Nowadays when I visit her my emotions are those of great affection, combined with a certain irritation at her decline in manners, and gratitude for past favours. So far as I can tell on these occasions, her reactions to my presence are absolutely non-existent. This is not altogether unusual among women who have been much loved and the objects of endless attention. On the other hand I am told that she remains more considerate to those who have ever completely lost their hearts to her.

In Paris I attended for a term a small international day-school for the sons of foreigners, businessmen, diplomatists, and such. My cousin Bill was also there, and so too were the more distant cousins of my old enemies, the Portuguese. When we were wolf-cubs in the afternoons, their games took a form which I am sure was never intended by the first Chief Scout. Among their less repulsive amusements was the insertion of smaller boys, such as Bill or myself, into empty lime barrels which were then sent rolling down a steep and bumpy hill.

Lessons were in French and punishments were frequent. These included slaps from the schoolmistresses, rappings over the knuckles with rulers, and standing in the corner for hours wearing a dunce's pointed hat. There was one dunce's hat per classroom. If another boy was already wearing it, the second dunce had to put on the waste-paper basket. This contained ink-sodden pieces of blotting paper, pencil shavings, apple cores and plum stones, which used to descend slowly and squishily about the new dunce's ears and even down his neck.

It was a dreadful school, but fortunately the headmaster was quite soon convicted of some heinous crime, dope-peddling or white slavery or, more probably, the *détournement de mineurs*. So Bill and I were taken away, and in September of 1928 were sent to boarding school in England. By the time I came home for the Christmas holidays, my mother and Bertram had moved into the rue Lord Byron. We had a home at last, and my formal education had begun.

7

THE FIRST BOARDING school that I attended (in the English usage of the period, a preparatory, private or prep school) was called the New Beacon and was near Sevenoaks, in Kent. Such schools, as their name implies, were intended to prepare boys between the ages of eight and twelve for entry into the so-called public schools where in those days some five per cent of Britain's youths were educated until the age of eighteen. From there the boys went to a university, one of the military academies or straight into business. This process provided and provides far the easiest, though a rather expensive, method of progression from the nursery into the professions, the armed forces and the socially more acceptable forms of commerce. The public schools were really invented by Thomas Arnold early in the nineteenth century. By the end of that century they were attended by virtually all the sons of the English upper and upper-middle class families, and the men they produced ran the British

Empire: it is frequently alleged that they were there specially trained for this job. They ossified English class distinction (the Irish, Scots and Welsh have never taken the matter of accent as a *prima facie* indication of class) and in general they also provided the best academic education available, though this varied from school to school. Apart from a few grammar schools the educational facilities provided by the rest of the system, the state schools, were deplorably low, higher perhaps than the American equivalent but far beneath what was generally available in France and Germany. This is said to have been a major contributory factor in the relative decline of British power and prestige since about 1880. The concentration of educational facilities in favour of a small élite class not only served to produce the men able to run an Empire but also contributed to that Empire's speedy demise. For if the ex-public school boys came into existence to forward the imperial idea, it soon became apparent to the rest of their compatriots, and even more so to their subjects overseas, that it was in fact the Empire which served the interests of the men who wore the old school ties. The modern equivalent of *civis romanus sum* was never created either for the English working-class, for the Irish or for the Colonial peoples. The white Dominions had, for many years, great and proved loyalty towards England, but even that is evaporating now that they are supposed to form part of a multi-racial and multi-lingual Commonwealth, a strange and clumsy organisation which is essentially a series of intermittent agreements between governments and commercial interests rather than an identity of peoples. Its name, presumably derived from the Cromwellian precedent, augurs neither a long nor a happy life.

I mention all this because, with the Empire gone, the days of the public schools and of their appendages, the prep schools, are surely numbered. Did they not still provide almost the only decent education in England, they would be quite moribund already. There will no doubt be many to regret their passing, but I must say that I shall not be among them.

So much has been written about the miseries of a public-school education during the period between the wars that I shall not add to this vast and lugubrious literature, shot-through as it often is with self-pity and a sort of unadmitted envy. Its writers, being writers, had usually been clever boys, or at least intellectually alert. But the purpose of the public schools was generally to mould character—whatever that may mean—rather than to foster intellect. With this end in view, an end that can be more accurately described as the creation of a mutually reliant élite, a quite ludicrous emphasis was placed upon the playing of team games, football and cricket being the favourites. Even here individual expertise was not encouraged. The very fast wing three-quarter or the century-making batsman might be the star of the team and the hero of his house, but the kingpin of the whole system was the unknown boy stolidly pushing his head between the buttocks of his fellows in the rugger scrum or standing motionless for hours on end in the cricket field when all the joys of a summer's afternoon should have been his for the asking. Intelligent and sensitive boys tended to despise these muddied oafs and flannelled fools.

At most schools, however, they did not get away with opting out. The clever boy who could not accept or could not be bothered to feign acceptance of these strange values was not considered of much worth by his fellows and was often the object of distrust on the part of the schoolmasters. He questioned, if only tacitly, the validity of the whole accepted order and to do this, as I suggested at the very beginning of this book, is to court unpopularity or worse. (Such is normal herd reaction. Nor is it limited to reactionaries and philistines. Progressives, whether in the world of the arts or of politics, can be at least as savage when their own, often far more doubtful, accepted absolutes, their *idées reçues* Flaubert called them, are questioned.)

Inevitably, perhaps, I eventually became a rebel and increasingly unhappy during the six and a half long years that I put up with the public-school system and that that system tolerated me. Of the unhappiness I shall have little to say—it has all been said before—but rebelliousness is a more individual, and therefore perhaps a more interesting, subject.

90

As a rebel, I really started on the wrong foot. Let me say at once that, to begin with at least, I was happy at the New Beacon. But there was one master, whom I shall call Mr Henderson, who was an unkind man. Harsh, sarcastic and cold, a very strict disciplinarian and a poor teacher, he might have done well as a recruits' sergeant in the Foot Guards or the U.S. Marines, but he should never have been allowed to vent his accumulated bitterness and presumably his own personal failure upon little boys.

It happened within a few days of my arrival at the New Beacon, before I even knew my way about the school or the names of my classmates. Mr Henderson was teaching us. I raised my hand and, using the formula that I had been taught, asked if I might go to the bathroom. Mr Henderson's rapier-like wit was ready:

'Why? Do you want to take a bath?'

So I was branded a foreigner, and Mr Henderson saw to it that I was not allowed quickly to forget this fact. But was I? At that time, as I have said, I thought I was English, as English as Miss Wright and Lord Nelson and old Don't-we-look-it. Yet I spoke with an American voice, or at least I used American phrases. I may even have had a slight French accent, for I was bilingual at that age. Certainly Mr Henderson corrected my pronunciation of French vowels, teaching me that in an English prep school the proper way to pronounce '*tu*' is 'too'. Thus from the very beginning it was made plain to me not only that I was somehow 'different' but that this was my fault and the sooner I put it right the better. (My cousin, Bill, who was much more American than I, managed to achieve this metamorphosis with complete success, remarkable speed and without apparent damage to himself: to this day he has remained, in some superficial ways, more English than the English, though he is entirely American.) This is perhaps what is meant by the moulding of character.

Yet it may be that if Mr Henderson was, as he appeared to be, a paranoid xenophobe he was right to distrust me, though I do not believe he had any justification in persecuting me as he did. (I once overheard our headmaster's gentle and sensitive younger brother, whom we called Captain Cecil, explain to Mr Henderson that I must be treated carefully as I was very highly strung. Though I did not know the meaning of the phrase, for what seemed months on end I was taunted by Mr Henderson, if I stammered or otherwise displeased him in class, with this apparent crime. More character-moulding, no doubt.) For though I considered myself English, in the land of my imagination America remained my private paradise lost. In some ways it has remained so to this day. At times of great personal stress I tend to turn, in thought if not in deed, to the land of my birth. It was this as much as any other consideration that sent me back across the Atlantic in 1946. When I was the victim of a gross injustice on the part of the British legal system, my first thought was to seek true justice in the United States, though I am of course consciously well aware that there is at least an equal amount of injustice to the west as to the east of the Atlantic. But this reaction is emotional, not intellectual. And though at the New Beacon I must soon have become, nationally at least, quite indistinguishable from the other boys, I clung to this mirage. I even clung to fragments of the childhood reality. Our jam was supplied by our parents. I asked for peanut butter, then unknown in England and only obtained, after considerable trouble and great insistence on my part, from Fortnum's.

This backward look towards America was rare in a child of that time, though it must be quite common nowadays, when so many American servicemen and civil servants live for years, with their families, abroad. In those days America, for most people in Europe who felt drawn to it, was the country of the future, perhaps of their own future if they were lucky. It was the promised land. For me it was the country of the magical happy past.

And this in turn was to affect my own 'rebelliousness' in the years to come. Since my imagination led me back, not to some corner of an English county or of a London square, but to Stockbridge Bowl and the blue Berkshire Hills, so my rebellion against those aspects of the British 'system' which have at times infuriated or distressed me is, in some measure, the rebellion of an outsider.

When Rousseau sat down to write his successful attack upon French institutions and what were then accepted French Attitudes, his opening words were: '*Moi, Jean-Jacques Rousseau, citoyen de Genève.* . . .' When, a century and more later, Jules Lemaître wrote a most violent book of sustained invective, he began it with: '*Lui, Jean-Jacques Rousseau, écrivain français.* . . .' They were both right. And in this, though I trust in this only, I perhaps resemble Jean-Jacques, for I am an American citizen but an English writer.

That I have a great affection for England and for most things English is, I hope, proved by the fact that for the past fifteen years I have lived, voluntarily, in England, though by the nature of my work I have had absolutely no need to do so. Yet there are many qualities of the English which remain to this day quite incomprehensible to me. To give but one very minor example, I, like, I think, all people who are not English, find their attitude towards their monarch totally beyond me. I cannot understand either why most of them regard the Queen as an almost semi-divine object of adulation, nor why others froth at the mouth with rage at the very concept of their impotent monarchy. That one can love a king or queen, or hate a tyrant, is straightforward enough. But the emotions that are expressed about Queen Elizabeth II seem to me just rum. When uttered by Socialist cabinet ministers, they sound rummer than ever. As for the notorious hypocrisy of the English, this has long ceased to surprise me, for I do not believe that they are, in fact, much if any, more hypocritical than the Americans or the members of other nations. But what does set them apart, and is doubtless a great source of strength to them, is that unlike other peoples they appear to be blithely unaware that they are ever hypocritical at all. For anyone who would put this rather wild generalisation to the test, I would recommend a brief chat with an educated Englishman on the subject of Ireland's history.

This condition of not being English has had its effect upon the form that my personal rebellion has taken. In the 1930s

I accepted as my allies and friends those English men and women of my age or a little older who wished, as they then thought, drastically to alter a society whose institutions seemed to them cramping, boring, frequently stupid and sometimes wicked. They have in large measure succeeded. And now we are all middle-aged. They, having modified their society from within, have been quite rightly allowed to take charge of what is in some ways their creation. They have, to use a word that is popular with them, become the Establishment, both in politics and the arts.

It is now, however, that their English quality of self-deception takes over. They pretend that there is another Establishment, connected with peripheral figures such as the Archbishop of Canterbury, Nöel Coward, the President of the Royal Academy and, of course, the Queen. Solidly installed in the seats of power, the constant guests of those society hostesses whom they once professed to despise, rich and honoured in their own land and even, occasionally, abroad, they pretend that they are still busily fighting another and totally imaginary power complex which has long vanished. They throw their whole weight against doors that have been wide open for years. They do not even tilt at windmills, for they themselves pulled down the windmills long ago. They speak with fury of the standardised, commercial theatre, and apparently cannot see or hear that their own favourite plays are even more standard and even more successfully commercialised. They maintain that were it not for them privilege would still be favoured above talent, and they appoint Frank Cousins to their Cabinet. The list is endless. That they have done much good is not here in dispute. But what they have also done is to create, *Mutatis mutandis* (and even so not all the changes were necessary), an only slightly distorted mirror-image of the society that they were once so anxious to pull down. What else could they do? That was the society which produced them. But to the semi-outsider all the sound-and-fury nowadays has a curiously hollow, unreal and, at times, hypocritical ring to it. A speech by the Duke of Edinburgh urging shorter luncheon hours upon industrialists sounds, in my ears at least, remarkably like Mr Henderson ordering us to push harder in the scrum. Why, I have always wanted to ask, with what object? To win, comes the sharp response. To win what? But that is not an English question. The answer is detention, or a bad review in the Sunday papers.

I have said that I was happy at the New Beacon to begin with and despite Mr Henderson. The food was good and plentiful, the buildings large and airy, and all the other members of the staff kind and agreeable. The headmaster, whom we called Major Frank, was a shrewd fat man, a man who clearly enjoyed the good things of life. When we were very small he used to enliven his classes with jolly jingles:

Charlie the troubadour ran round the waterbutt.

Suddenly a brickbat hit him on the coconut.

As we grew older he told us enthralling and improbable stories about his wartime experiences. ('The Great War was a *picnic* compared to the Boer War. I remember . . .') In his classes we were always attentive, because we never knew what was coming next. He, too, babbled of green fields. ('I remember once, one winter when I was a boy, it was so cold the stoats hunted in packs!')

Although the games bored me, I was tall and strong and was able to put up a performance which was adequate, if nothing more. We played soccer in the autumn, rugger in the spring term and cricket in the summer. Of these rugger was the game I liked least, because it was muddy and at times painful, besides being played in the coldest months. It did not, however, go on for very long, since the last weeks of that term were given over to sports, running, jumping and so on, which I liked and was good at. Boxing, which was compulsory and over which Mr Henderson presided, I did not like at all. Not only was it more painful than rugger but it also necessitated the infliction of pain on others. I was prepared, though always rather reluctantly, to fight another boy when the need arose, but these formal bouts of fisticuffs seemed to me as pointless as they were unpleasant. (I must have talked about this aversion at home, and was presumably misunderstood. During one or two holidays I was given extra boxing tuition in, of all places, the crypt of the

American Cathedral on the Avenue Georges V. It did no good. I continued to dread the boxing and to lose.)

Lessons, on the other hand, I enjoyed. In the first place I liked learning new facts, and did so quickly and easily. In some subjects, such as elementary mathematics or the parsing of sentences, it was possible to find the one correct answer, to achieve a perfect score. From so doing, and from an almost exaggerated neatness and tidiness which I cultivated, I derived a pleasure which was in some ways aesthetic. History and geography interested me, and I enjoyed drawing maps of Africa or genealogical tables proving why Edward III was really King of France. And language fascinated me. I had long been intrigued by the differences and the resemblances between English and French. Now I had all the strange, stiff and improbable Latin words with which to play. The unravelling of awkward sentences, the extraction of clauses, the recognition of subjunctives and spotting the elegant ablative absolute, all this was a game to me. I was also fortunate to possess a quick and retentive memory, so that the learning of dates, declensions and the rest of it came very easily. I was not a 'swot'. I did not need to be, even had I so wished, because I could do it all so quickly and, since I enjoyed it, with very little effort, I was almost invariably top of my class. Nor did examinations worry me at all. As a result, I moved up the school as fast as my age would allow. Furthermore, since academic prowess was not regarded as particularly praiseworthy, this was not a matter to cause resentment or envy among the other boys. At the New Beacon I learned as much as I could: learning there was essentially a private game that I played with, and against, myself. As a solitary child the games I most enjoyed had always been that way. A minor contributory factor may have been my stammer, which was now at its worst and which was not to vanish completely until I was nearly twenty. Learning, like writing, generally takes place in silence and without the need to talk.

There was very little bullying at the New Beacon. Certainly I myself was not bullied, but there was one very fat boy who had a bad time. Fat boys are notoriously unpopular, though whether this is because their physique is displeasing or whether the fatness is a symptom of some psychosomatic maladjustment, I do not know. Our fat boy was a pitiful creature. There are some people who go through life with an invisible but unmistakable placard that shouts KICK ME! pinned to their backsides. They are very dangerous, for even if treated with extreme kindness their gratitude can quickly change into a vicious and unsatisfied masochism, and they will then frequently pretend that they have been kicked even when they have not. In adult life they are not so readily identifiable, but when recognised it is possible, indeed highly advisable, to flee them at once. At school it is another story. Our fat boy used to be wedged into desks, crammed into cupboards, punched and generally tormented. The poor fellow was permanently on the verge of tears, and his trembling lower lip only increased the fury of his tormentors. He is now a Member of Parliament, and nothing would induce me to say which party he represents. When I read his name in the papers, I cannot help wondering what happens when the Speaker's eye is averted. A sharp pinch? And in their lobbies and smoking-rooms do the beastlier ones jam him underneath leather sofas or snatch his whisky-and-soda from the bar before ever he has had a chance to taste it? And then the tears and that extraordinary bawling noise reminiscent of a cow suffering acutely from bloat?

The only subject that I really took against at my prep school was one that I might have been expected to like best of all, Greek. Indeed, to begin with I did enjoy it. *First Steps in Greek* was a small red book, given to me when I was ten. Its format and lay-out were identical to the blue *First Steps in Latin*, which I had outgrown, and this symmetry pleased me. I liked learning and writing the elegant new alphabet, while the mysteries of the middle voice and of the periphrastic subjective were right up my street.

However, we did not have many Greek lessons, and when it was decided that I should sit for a scholarship, it was also thought that I needed extra tuition if Greek were to be one of my subjects. This tuition took two forms. Twice a week I

G

would go across, in the evening, to the house beyond the football fields where lived Captain Cecil with his wife and the baby boy who is now headmaster of the New Beacon. In his comfortable drawing-room, lying on my stomach in front of his coal fire while he sat in his armchair, I would read Xenophon with him, and later be given milk and ginger snaps. I loved those evenings.

There was another form of extra tuition which I certainly did not enjoy. I wonder if others experience the same bleak despair as myself at the mere mention of Greek irregular verbs?

I could learn them well enough, but because of my stammer I could not speak them. Since my teacher in Greek by this time was Mr Henderson, who mocked my stammer, I preferred to pretend that I had not learned them rather than that I could not speak them. For this I was punished, and the punishment took the form of a special session each day with Mr Henderson, before breakfast, during which I was supposed to recite a score or more of the filthy verbs.

Imagine me cold and hungry, standing before a man I both feared and hated, and expected, despite a stammer to recite βαλο, βαλλο, εβαλλου, βεβλοωκα or μεμνισγο, μεμνειμι. As a result of these awful sessions, I developed a mental bloc, a resistance to the Greek language which continued for as long as I was expected to study it. It would be absurd to pretend that this has caused me a great deal of anguish in later years, but I suspect that it may have deprived me of a fairly considerable source of pleasure. After all, nobody in his right mind wants to read many of the Latin poets and historians and dramatists once he has grown up: the Greeks are another story and their great plays and poems were, save in translation, closed to me for ever as I tried and failed to stammer forth their irregular verbs, near Sevenoaks, in 1932, before breakfast.

There was one other experience at the New Beacon which may have had an effect, even a traumatic effect, upon me that I myself cannot recognise but which would, I suspect, be revealed were I ever so rash as to consult a psychoanalyst. I have described the incident in fictional form in one of my novels, but it also belongs here.

Friendships between boys who have not yet reached adolescence can be passionate affairs, even though there is no, or no apparent, sexual content. At the New Beacon I had, in succession, three or four 'best friends'. They were all, in their different ways, extremely handsome boys. Whether I am more or less susceptible to physical beauty than most, I do not know. Certainly ugly people do not distress me, as I have heard that they distress others. On the other hand almost all my friends of either sex—and I do not here speak of mistresses—have been remarkably good-looking.

It was always so. My first 'best friend' at the New Beacon was a tall, dreamy, blond boy, with skin the colour of a bleached almond, golden hair and jet-black eyes. Unfortunately he was rather dull, and also he came down with appendicitis, which meant a term's absence from school, so our friendship lapsed. His successor in my affections was a Scots boy whom I shall call Colquhoun. He was what used to be called in Ireland a 'black Gael' with an olive skin and an absolutely straight and bridgeless nose like the archaic Greek sculptures. We were the two cleverest boys of our age, and if I was not top of the form or at the head of the examination list, then I knew that the name in first place would be his. This did not involve any sort of rivalry or self-satisfaction on our part: it was the accepted order of affairs. For a year and more we did everything together. Together we amassed huge balls of silver paper which were despatched at last to hospitals for reasons I now forget. We swapped stamps so assiduously and so generously that our two albums seemed but one. I read no novel by Henty or Rider Haggard which he had not read immediately before or would not read immediately after. Together we found a nightingale's nest, and took one egg each. When we learned about David and Jonathan or of Achilles and Patroclus it was of myself and of Colquhoun that I thought.

Now the sleeping arrangements at the New Beacon were by class—roughly speaking, as we moved up a class we also moved into a new dormitory—but the hours of bedtime were according to age. Since Colquhoun and I were academically ahead of our contemporaries, this meant that we went to bed half an hour before the other inhabitants of our dormitory, when we were allowed to read, or finish our prep, until the other boys came up and, finally, Major Frank made his rounds, wished us all good night and switched off the lights, leaving a pleasant smell of very good pipe tobacco behind him.

One cold winter's night, when we were in our beds in the otherwise empty dormitory, and I was having a last look at the conjugation of the past subjunctive of *s'apercevoir*, which I must recite in the morning, I suggested to Colquhoun, who was similarly engaged, that I get into his bed for warmth. As I have said, I was sexually entirely innocent and uninterested until a comparatively late age, nor was I ever aware of any homosexual activity among the older boys at the New Beacon. Colquhoun, I know, was in an equal state of innocence. So I could not understand why the matron, who happened to enter the dormitory, spoke in tones of such horror when she ordered me back to my own bed and assured us that we had not heard the last of this. I was equally surprised by the grim expression of Major Frank's usually benign, red face when he wished the dormitory an unusually curt good night. Still, I thought no more about it, and fell placidly asleep.

Next morning, at the daily inspection before breakfast in the gym, Major Frank still looked as angry as ever. Furthermore the entire staff were present, which was unusual except on the first or last days of term. Then, the inspection completed, he addressed us.

Only gradually did it dawn upon me that the two boys 'whose names he preferred not to mention' were Colquhoun and myself. Our crime was apparently of an enormity such as to demand our immediate expulsion. Only our youth prevented him from taking such drastic steps. Our fathers, he said and I remember his queer choice of words, would rather 'see us screwed down in our coffins', and so on. If there were to be any repetition of this crime, between those two boys or any others, his rage would be awful and the punishment instant and Draconic. We were dismissed. My face was scarlet.

I did not know what I had done wrong, but I never spoke to Colquhoun again. For days I was utterly miserable, and there was no one to whom I could talk, of whom I could ask enlightenment. All I understood was that it had been wicked of me to love Colquhoun, to build balls of silver paper with him, to share our stamps. Very well then, I would hate him. Whether or not he felt the same way about me I do not know, for we have never spoken since.

And then came the boxing. Mr Henderson arranged this. He saw to it that I fought Colquhoun in the first heat. I did my best to murder him. It was the only 'arranged' fight that I ever won.

A year later I sat for a scholarship to Wellington College. This was intended as training, for I was expected to win an Eton scholarship in the following term. As it happened, I was awarded a minor one to Wellington. Major Frank advised my mother not to accept it and to await the Eton examination, but I begged to be taken away from the New Beacon just as soon as possible. I went to Wellington in January, 1933, within a few days of Hitler being appointed Chancellor of Germany and Roosevelt's inauguration as President of the United States.

Wellington was one of the larger public schools, with some six hundred boys. It was also among the dozen or so most famous, but it lacked the social splendour of Eton and the intellectual distinction of Winchester. In these as in other respects it was probably much on a par with Harrow, Rugby, Marlborough, Charterhouse, Uppingham and one or two more. If it had one distinguishing characteristic, this was undoubtedly its strong military connection.

It had been founded, early in the second half of the nineteenth century, as a memorial to the Iron Duke. It provided a free, or almost free, education for a number of boys whose fathers had been army officers and who had died on active service. Its explicit aim was also to produce future army officers and in addition to the normal sixth, or top, forms—the Classical Sixth, the History Sixth, the

Science Sixth and so on—it had its 'Army Sixth' for boys destined to go on to Sandhurst or Woolwich. These academies drew only a minority of their cadets from Wellington—the flashy, expensive regiments such as the Brigade of Guards or the Cavalry were largely officered by Old Etonians, while technical branches such as the Engineers or the Tank Corps were beginning to accept as future officers men who had not been to a public school at all. Nor did a majority of the boys at Wellington go into the Army: I do not know the figure, but I should guess about one in three. Nevertheless the connection was a very real one and influenced the school.

This influence, in my time at least, took the form of a strongly anti-intellectual bias. Among army officers of that period cleverness was not only regarded as unnecessary but was deemed, in general, potentially harmful. Brains had not distinguished the generals who had 'won' the First World War. A 'brainy' officer might doubt the wisdom of his superiors, might advocate innovations, might even undermine unquestioning obedience. Now since the senior officers between the wars were, with few exceptions, men who believed that the horse was more than a match for the tank, that infantry was the queen of battle, that air power was of only limited value, and that the essence of military training was close-order drill, a man did not have to be particularly brilliant in order to win the opprobrious epithet of 'brainy'. And this attitude was inevitably reflected in the atmosphere at Wellington, though there were a few among the younger masters and older boys who did not at all agree. This distrust of brains may well explain why Wellington, despite its avowed purpose, has produced so very few generals who have made great names for themselves in war, Lord Auchinleck being the only one who immediately comes to mind. It is fairly safe to assume that it could never have produced the Duke of Wellington.

Thus, while at the New Beacon it had not mattered one way or the other whether a boy was good at his lessons, at Wellington this aroused suspicion among many of the masters—including the master of my house, a remarkably dim and depressed chemist—and distrust among the future officer cadets.

It was they who really ran the school in those days. (I am told, incidentally, that it has much improved in all respects in the last thirty years.) They controlled us rather on the lines of the concentration camps that Hitler was setting up in Germany, and the future cadets were privileged, rather as the criminal Capos in many Nazi camps were privileged above the political prisoners. Like them they hung together and shared out among themselves such spoils of office as there were. The masters liked to say that 'the boys impose their own discipline' and only occasionally did they intervene directly, usually to inflict some even more savage punishment upon a rebel against this perverted form of democracy. No different was the attitude of the headmaster, or Master, who snuffled out interminable and almost inaudible sermons in the cold, ugly Gothic chapel and who only very rarely knew any boy by his name.

Nor is the comparison to a concentration camp quite as far-fetched as it seems. Thus the first way of 'breaking' a concentration camp inmate—apart from physical brutality and an enforced shortage of sleep: we had plenty of the first and far too little of the second—was to make him perform obviously meaningless tasks, such as carrying heavy stones up and down hill, or digging holes only to fill them in again. Similarly the better part of a new boy's first term at Wellington was devoted to learning by heart a mass of pointless and useless information, such as the names of all the games captains in all the houses, and to being trained in an elaborate and grotesque etiquette such as which button of one's jacket might be undone where and when. This moulding of character—in the German camps it was more bluntly called the breaking of character—continued in varying ways throughout the whole of a boy's time there, sport being the principal means of implementing the policy. To give but one example, boys who were no good at cricket and who may therefore be presumed to have disliked it were given extra training in the game, training which was not only tedious and disagreeable but also purely wasteful. The pressure to conform, to become exactly like everybody else, was in fact enormous. If a boy simply could not conform, he was lucky if he was not smashed. This took some extremely unpleasant forms. In my house, for instance, there were two or three Jewish boys and it was then that I learned to hate anti-Semitism. There were other positive lessons to be learned at Wellington, though I have found few of these to be of any lasting value. How to avoid being buggered by prefects in the Army Sixth is, for example, a talent which was once invaluable but for which I find really no use at all nowadays.

For over a year I made myself as inconspicuous as possible, though I could not help being top of my class and therefore moving rather rapidly up the school. I was thus the object of suspicion. We were allowed gramophones and I had at that time a passion for what was then called 'hot jazz', spending almost all my pocket money on records by Duke Ellington, Louis Armstrong, Coleman Hawkins and the rest of that glittering generation. The dim chemist disapproved. It was, he informed me, 'decadent nigger music' and why could I not enjoy nice English dance tunes like anybody else? But I remained firm, and this may have been another and belated example of my clinging to my American paradise lost, though I think not. I really liked that sort of music, and still do. (It is perhaps not altogether fortuitous that my house-master's musical prejudices should have closely resembled those of the Nazis.)

Books, of course, were a more serious matter. Reading for pleasure was in itself frowned on, and a strict censorship was carried out. I read a great deal, and precociously. I was somewhat taken aback when I was informed that the novels of Aldous Huxley were obscene. As for D. H. Lawrence, there was a terrible row, but that came later. . . .

The summer of 1934 was the turning point. I was fifteen in June of that year, and beginning to weary of playing the fieldmouse. And then, to my delight, the great Romilly scandal broke over the school's head.

Esmond, the younger but more dominant of the Romilly brothers, was then sixteen. He was in another house, and I only knew him slightly, but he was a charismatic figure. He ran away from Wellington, announced that he was a Communist, and proceeded to publish a magazine called *Out of Bounds*, the avowed purpose of which was to raise the red flag of revolution throughout the public schools of England. Philip Toynbee, who became a close friend of his and who has painted an excellent portrait of him in *Friends Apart*, took up the cause at Rugby. It spread to other schools, but it was Wellington which enjoyed the publicity. This was considerable because Esmond Romilly's uncle by marriage was Winston Churchill. One of the contributors to *Out of Bounds* (which was of course immediately banned) was Gavin Ewart, the poet, who was actually in my house. I therefore felt that I had a direct link with the very centre of the revolutionary movement which was established in David Archer's bookshop in Bloomsbury. (Archer was himself an Old Wellingtonian.) I became an enthusiastic partisan, bought all the extreme left-wing publications that I could find, and announced that I too was a Communist.

In that same term I sat, at a rather young age, for my school certificate examination. I passed with eight credits, including Greek, which was exceptionally good. Since this meant that I had achieved the equivalent of matriculation, one result was that the school authorities would have no alternative but to put me into the Upper School in the autumn. This in turn meant a number of pointless privileges involving buttons, and also a certain increase in personal freedom.

And finally I went to America, to Lenox, for the summer holidays. (It was now that I found that I was a United States citizen.)

I returned a confirmed and active rebel. I was against everything that the school valued. A Communist, a pacifist, an atheist, a partisan of free love, alcoholism, surrealism, free verse, *New Verse*, James Joyce, Epstein and Picasso, my enthusiasms were as vast as they were violent, though had they been analysed by some super-computer I suspect that the machine would have needed to stamp out only one word: 'Freedom'.

Henceforth, my career at Wellington was devoted to a

single cause, the flouting of authority. Inspired by Esmond Romilly's example, there was nothing I would not do.

I had reached the age for joining the Officers' Training Corps. This, technically at least, was voluntary. I refused to join. It was pointed out to me that no boy had ever refused to join. I replied that I was an American and therefore could not serve in the British 'armed forces'. They had to give in. A few weeks later it was the matter of being confirmed. I produced the same argument: as an American I could hardly accept confirmation by an Anglican bishop. Rather to my surprise they gave in again, and I felt that I would soon have them on the run. I must have been becoming quite insufferable.

In my school certificate examinations I had done exceptionally well in mathematics getting, if I remember correctly, hundred per cent marks in both the ordinary and in the advanced papers. It would therefore have been logical for me to pursue this subject and perhaps become, in due course, a Senior Wrangler. However, that was not the method at Wellington, as I well knew from endless hours of fielding practice on the cricket ground. I was put in the Classical Lower Sixth, presumably for the reason that Greek was my weakest subject and the one I most disliked. I fooled them here too, by sitting for, and winning, the school History Prize. This was most irregular, and they transferred me next term to the History Sixth, where I won the Classics Prize.

I also engaged in a mild homosexual experiment. In America I had become enamoured of one or two girls of my own age, about which I shall have more to say in another chapter. Back at school I transferred these new-found emotions to a rather dull boy only slightly younger than myself. Since homosexuality, though widely practised among the Capos of the Army Sixth, was a very serious offence, it was clearly my duty as a wrecker to encourage this perversion. I suggested to the boy in question that we go to bed together. This he declined, to my secret relief, for I had only the haziest idea as to how such a union, or indeed any union, could be consummated. In the Christmas holidays, however, the boy informed his father of my immoral proposition.

Whether the father would sooner have seen his son screwed down in his coffin, I cannot tell. Certainly he took rather a long time making up his mind to approach the headmaster of Wellington, and it was only towards the end of the spring term that I was sent for and interrogated. During the Easter holidays my mother received a letter. In view of the generally abominable nature of my behaviour, and of my attempts to corrupt the other boys, the school would prefer it were I not to return in the summer.

I was not expelled: I was asked to leave. This, I am told is equivalent to the difference between being cashiered from the Army and asked to resign one's commission. It is a distinction to which I have always attached the greatest possible importance.

8

IN THE MIDDLE of the six-and-a-half-year period during which I was being formally educated at English boarding schools, our home life was twice turned upside down. For little over two years we lived in Paris, in the rue Lord Byron. In 1931 my mother left, and divorced, Bertram. She then bought a house in Devon, but that too only lasted for some two and a half years. After Sandy Park House was sold, in 1934, we had no home at all. But then, however, I was nearly fifteen, and my childhood almost over.

My memories of the house behind the *hôtel* in the rue Lord Byron are fragmentary. Although I can recall most vividly the atmosphere of the place, which I loved, very few incidents or pictures come to mind. This is perhaps hardly surprising, since I now realise that in fact I only spent two Christmas and two Easter holidays there. And this in turn explains why for me there is for ever a lighted Christmas tree, as spangled and decorated as a field-marshal, in the front hall, that reached the height of the house, with the stairs curving around it and the presents piled high at its foot.

As one entered the hall there were, to the left, the drawing-room and Bertram's study, to the right the dining-room, kitchen and servants' quarters. Being converted stables, the house was only one room deep, but double doors between the hall, drawing-room and dining-room could be thrown back to turn almost the whole of the ground floor into one big room. This had presumably been so arranged in anticipation of parties, receptions, maybe even balls. But there were none of these, at least not when I was at home. The drawing-room always retained its own identity, deep, dark, red silk curtains hiding the french windows at night, a cheerful wood fire hissing and crackling in the grate, with the eternal Pekingese snoring before it.

Above the drawing-room and study were my mother's and Bertram's bathroom, bedroom and dressing-room: on the other side of the house were the rooms where we children, and Mademoiselle Révoutsky, slept. There was no nursery, but there was a long, carpeted corridor, splendid for marbles and for paper aeroplanes. I remember lying in my warm bed with a feverish cold, snug as snug, sipping hot lemon and glycerine, and reading, reading, reading. Our baths were scented with pine essence. There were dark and unidentified portraits in the dining-room, stiff ladies and gentlemen in eighteenth-century costume about whom I made up stories which I told to no one, and there was Bertram's gold and silver plate in the glass-fronted cabinet which, I told myself, had sailed around Scotland with the Duke of Medina Sidonia, and had later been captured by me and David Copperfield and Robinson Crusoe from Blackbeard in the Spanish Main, and, later still, had been given to me by the Count of Monte Cristo in return for some trifling service that I had been only too glad to render him. And up in my bedroom my friends Athos, Porthos and Aramis were waiting, in their floppy boots, to spring into the saddle and take me off on strange and fine adventures. The house behind the rue Lord Byron was filled with such friends, and I was happy there with them.

I have few memories of my sisters during those holidays, nor in the summer which we passed in a rented house at the back of Dinard. (Dinard must have been my mother's choice and perhaps represented a retreat into her own past. This would indicate a discontent with her present. If so, such emotions were not shared by me. That present, whether in Paris, Dinard or at the New Beacon, was a good period.) The two eldest girls were grown up and usually gone, and though Mimi was still at school the gap between us had widened. Sisters of fourteen and fifteen have little time for brothers five years their junior, a sentiment that is usually returned. For the next few years Mimi's principal interest was horses: at no time was it books. To me the girls were shadowy figures who flitted with their friends in and out of the rue Lord Byron or the Villa Surville and who scarcely impinged upon my life.

The servants made a greater impact, but in general a fleeting one, for they seldom stayed long. There was a butler, name forgotten, who was too young. When he passed the soup, in white gloves, his thumb used to be actually in the soup, which gave him a somewhat soiled appearance throughout the rest of the meal. He had a merry, Mediterranean face and Geraldine complained that he tickled the back of her neck. So he went away to smile elsewhere.

He was succeeded by Eugène, whose wife cooked. Eugène spent the greater part of his time stoking the boiler while the silver plate grew tarnished and nothing was done. He was usually dressed as a stoker, which had perhaps been his previous and normal occupation, in rolled-up shirt sleeves, unbuttoned waistcoat, unshaven and with coal stains upon his arms and face. He was, however, most anxious to prove that he was in fact a real butler and he would hurry from the boiler-room in his usual attire and attempt to help guests on or off with their overcoats. In the dining-room he was more nervous than ever, and meals were punctuated by the crash of laden platters or the more delicate tinkle of Sèvres disintegrating upon the parquet. He and his wife departed.

There was an upstairs maid of whom I saw little, but the really permanent figure was Paul, the chauffeur. He was a stocky, red-faced man with a black moustache and a jolly manner. I spent a lot of time hanging about the garage helping him polish the two cars or hose down the floor. In retrospect I would say that he breathed the spirit of the horse rather than of the internal combustion engine, with all the individualism that this implies. He was a tough, self-assured little man who always wore a beret (to hide his bald head, as he explained to me with a wink) when not in his chauffeur's uniform. I can visualise him whipping up a team of mules under German shellfire and swinging his seventy-five into position. Indeed if I were to envisage the sort of French soldier who won the Battle of the Marne, it is of Paul that I would think. He had a wife who cooked for us after the departure of Madame Eugène, and two children. His wife was devoted to him, as well she might be, and used to bring trays out to the garage, small between-meals for Paul and for myself. With sublime self-confidence they had christened both their children after him. Little Paul was too young for me to play with, but Paulette was nearly of my age. She was a very pretty, rather shy girl who wore little gold earrings. I once kissed her quickly behind the kitchen door, and her big black eyes grew even bigger.

Instead of a butler we now had a maid. Madeleine did not drop quite as many dishes as had Eugène. All I remember of her is that she would stand behind the screen that hid the door to the kitchen, on tiptoe, and peer over its top to see if we were ready for second helpings or the next course. My mother found it unnerving to be watched in this fashion by the top half of a face; it made my sisters giggle; and Bertram maintained that it was not proper. So my mother, who always hated to reprimand or correct servants in any way, reluctantly told Madeleine that she must stop peeping over the top of the screen. From then on she peered around its edge, her head on one side. She was a jolly, milky peasant girl who had no wish to displease. After a little while she left.

What exactly caused the break-up of my mother's second marriage I do not know. But whatever the more profound causes may have been, they were superficially visible in a basic incompatibility and in very different views of life. In this respect the matter of the servants, or rather of her and Bertram's attitude towards them, was both symbolic and significant.

Bertram, as I have said, was a middle-aged bachelor when he married her. He was an extremely conventional man as only the French can be conventional, and whereas he was prepared, as a bachelor, to lead a bachelor's life and eat in restaurants, once he was married he expected a comfortable, well-run house in which he could entertain his friends in a manner becoming to his position in Parisian society. Quite apart from the fact that he was obviously and deeply in love with my mother, he must also have regarded her as an experienced and knowledgeable woman of the world who could run his household efficiently and be his hostess. He must have seen that this was not at all how she lived in America, but he could easily ascribe this to the complications of her life as a working woman with four children. People often assume that their own accepted conventions, their own cherished desires, are equally acceptable and desirable to others. He must have thought that what he was offering my mother was a great improvement on the life she was then leading. Had she not in some respects agreed with him about this, she would hardly have married him. He was prepared to accept a brood of children not his own, and not always easy, and she to take on a role she did not know. They were both of an age to think that they knew what they were doing.

Bertram was not only conventional, he was also old-fashioned. In view of the life that he had led, both with his mother and with his housekeeper, he had only a theoretical outsider's view of how a house is run. Servants, in his opinion, were obedient semi-people who did what they were told. This may have been true of the Boulevard St Germain in the 1880s, though I doubt it, but it was scarcely so in Paris forty-five years later unless perhaps those servants had been with the family for so long that they had become members of it. Certainly it would have been well-nigh impossible to produce, overnight, a staff of silent maids gliding about their business while delicious meals were being cooked and immaculately served twice a day. And even if there were women capable of arranging this, my mother was most definitely not of their number.

Furthermore, to Bertram's conventionality there was added a basic lack of self-assurance which may have been connected with his own paternity and childhood. If his house were not perfectly run, if his dinner parties were not precisely as they should be, he would construe this as a reflexion upon himself (what would they say?) and he would take it out on his wife, with tolerance at first, but with increasing impatience and at last with silent anger. Nor did it always remain silent. A fish served with a white sauce followed by a meat with a sauce of the same colour would at last lead to an outburst of temper.

My mother did her best to learn about these matters, but when it came to servants his deeply rooted prejudices— complexes might be a better word—came into direct conflict with equally deep-seated feelings of hers.

I have already described her relations with Amanda, Estelle and others who helped in the house in America— servants would here be an absolute misnomer. There can be no question that the relationship between master and man or mistress and maid has had deep and potentially dangerous overtones in American life. Since the servants have all but disappeared in any save the very richest households, and although this is grossly inconvenient and perhaps incompatible with truly civilised living in the European sense, it must be said that their disappearance has at least dispensed with a feeling of humiliation on the one side and of guilt on the other. My mother had, and always has had, a feeling of guilt that to me, having been largely brought up in Europe, is almost incomprehensible whenever she has had to ask—let alone tell—a servant to do anything for her. And for this there may have been personal, as well as inherited social, reasons.

To this attitude there must be added, in the case of my mother, certain characteristics personal to herself. She had inherited from her mother a great and admirable dislike of pretentiousness and of vulgar display. Although she liked beautiful objects, she also liked her beauty to be simple. This applied equally to food and to life in general. Heavy Victorian gold plate and elaborate, formal seven-course dinners were the precise opposite of all that she appreciated. So was the way of life that they symbolised. In those days upper-middle-class life in England and France was more artificial than it is today and than it was among her friends in America then. To this attitude she far preferred the comparative simplicity of her working-class servants. She preferred the company of Paul and his sort to that of Bertram's business friends and their sort. She has continued to do so, and has established a long chain of friendships with the men and women who have worked for her while making only a limited number of new friends, in Europe at least, among people of her own sort.

I would guess—and here I believe that I can guess with some accuracy—that there is an unconscious motive in such preference. My mother has always been a shy and reserved person. But, and again like myself, she is gregarious and enjoys company. However, she values her independence, her freedom, very highly indeed, and one of the quickest ways to lose such freedom, and particularly for a woman, is through indiscriminate intimacy with friends. One defence against this is the social artificiality which I have mentioned and which has always been distasteful to her. Another is to choose as friends persons from whom one is in some degree separated by an invisible barrier. A man may find such easy and uncomplicated relationships in his work in French bars, in English pubs. A woman who was not prepared to become *déclassée* found herself, in my mother's generation, inevitably forced to fall back on the people who worked for her. No woman was ever less of a Lady Chatterley than my mother. Precisely because intimacy was not what she desired, she could and did have real friendships with people who made few emotional demands upon her, and upon whom she made none beyond asking that they treat her with affection and as an equal. This reserve, this shyness, is also not unconnected with the great affection that she has always given to her dogs. I can fully sympathise with this too, even though my own line of retreat is in another direction, into abstract thought and the creation of fictional characters who may be demanding but are seldom impertinent towards me—though they can be impudent enough towards one another—and who never try to finger my soul or otherwise interfere with my freedom.

Now this was considered by Bertram as excessive familiarity on her part. He simply could not understand why she objected if Paul were asked to wait for two or three hours outside someone's house, just as he could not understand that at times she actually preferred a bowl of bread and milk to the best meal that the chef at the Tour d'Argent could provide. He must have been hurt that she could not feign more gratitude than she felt when he gave her diamond clips or sable coats. She liked these objects well enough, but the very fact that they were so expensive decreased her pleasure in them. He would assume on the other hand that they were not expensive enough and a holiday in St Moritz would be proffered, or a new car, but with diminishing returns. He began to feel, poor fellow, that there was nothing he could do right. For them both happiness drained away into duty.

With her children now away for the greater part of the year my mother found time hanging heavy on her hands. For years she had been an extremely active woman. Now she began to suffer from boredom. She even studied bookbinding in order to pass the time.

With me Bertram was always kind and considerate. He was a man of considerable culture, *Revue des Deux Mondes* culture, and had I been even a very few years older I believe that I would have enjoyed talking to him and would have learned from him. But I was both too young for companionship and too old for simple, physical games of the piggy-back sort. He would address me, in rather a loud voice and with well-meant laughter, and I did not understand that his was the laughter of embarrassment, nor did I know how to answer his rather clumsy questions about how I had spent my day.

He was scarcely more successful with my sisters. Visits

to the opera or the theatre were little appreciated. Only with Fanny did he have a link, for they were both really interested in painting and sculpture, which she was now studying. (She gave him a horse she had sculpted; he kept it in his office long after he and my mother were divorced.) Sometimes he would take us sightseeing, to Versailles or Provins, once on a long trip to see the battlefields of the First World War. These were particularly gruelling outings, when we were told what to admire after spending far too long in the car being told which bits of scenery to remember.

I am sure his taste in the arts was as conventional as in other matters. Religion was church, an English-speaking Protestant church, on Sunday mornings. (Beyond this, and the nightly saying of my prayers, religion played no part in my childhood whatsoever: at school, chapel was merely a part of the curriculum.) His politics were, I imagine, of an extreme conservative orthodoxy. I recall only one, rather eccentric, pronouncement.

It was in London, at the end of a school term. I was supposed to be returning to Paris with Bertram and my mother, but we were held up at Fleming's Hotel, for he was ill in bed. He was suffering from ptomaine poisoning, which he blamed on the Russian caviar that he had eaten at dinner.

'The Bolsheviks,' he announced, 'knowing that only the rich eat caviar here, deliberately stick their dirty thumbs into it, to poison us all.'

I remember him with affection, but he was no sort of father-figure to me.

How far I was aware of the deterioration in his relations with my mother it is hard to say. Consciously, not at all, and I certainly never witnessed any scenes or quarrels. I have heard that children sense these atmospheres nonetheless. If so, I fear I must have been unusually obtuse, for I remember only happy holidays until the very last, at St Moritz during the winter of 1930–1931, and then Bertram was hardly there, for he had had an accident.

Even this accident was somehow ludicrously characteristic of his ill luck. He had been lent a large châlet by a client of his, located immediately below the Suvretta House. It was luxurious and everyone was looking forward to the winter sports. The winter Olympic Games were being held at St Moritz that year and for Geraldine there were friends in the Oxford and Cambridge ice-hockey teams too. Fanny was happy in the cold clean air, and her cheeks were always scarlet. Mimi loved skiing, as she loved everything that was fast and slightly dangerous. Many of my mother's friends were spending Christmas in the mountains. It should have been a splendid holiday and we arrived in high spirits.

On the first evening that we were there Bertram and my mother had guests to dinner. Afterwards they played bridge. Bertram's foot went to sleep. When he got up, his ankle collapsed under him and he fell to the ground. His ankle was not merely strained but broken. After spending two days in considerable pain he returned to Paris for treatment, his leg in plaster. He did not return.

At St Moritz I was lonely for the first and almost for the last time in my life, lonely and bored to the extent that it made me unhappy. Why this should have been I am not quite sure. There were no children of my own age for me to play with, but this did not actually upset me. Perhaps it was the impending dissolution of my mother's marriage that I sensed. Or maybe it was the first and inexplicable pangs of adolescence. Or it may just have been the snow and the cold. Certainly the emotion was acute and it produced two para-physical manifestations which I remember clearly but which I could not understand then and cannot now. One was of a visual nature. Just before sleep my vision, behind closed lids, would be one of absolutely pure whiteness, no doubt the memory of the snow. This would then, quite slowly, break up into a mottled, clotted pattern of brown and green and yellow, entirely non-representational and quite repulsive. I would 'watch' this pattern intensify, with a great and growing disgust, until it reached a climax of foulness, after which it would, to my relief, slowly revert to perfect whiteness again. The whole process would be repeated several times before I fell asleep. This happened each night. The other phenomenon was oral, and again subjective. Just as one can get 'a tune on the brain', as the expression goes, so I could not clear my head of four Greek words. (This was before Greek had become a distasteful subject to me.) These words were ου μονον, αλλα και, which means, as I knew, 'not only, but also'. Now I would frequently think about a word, play with it, turn it inside out and juggle with it for pleasure. But there was no pleasure in these four. They would not let me go. They were the subjective equivalent of the fly that will sometimes buzz about our heads, follows us about, and quite refuses to be shooed or frightened away. Ου μονον, αλλα και were inside my head, like the mosquito inside the skull of the Emperor Titus, and the stupidity of their meaningless, repetitive presence there, day after day, almost brought tears to my eyes. I still do not understand these phenomena, neither of which has recurred since.

I was bored in St Moritz. The complicated games that I played against myself were beginning to seem childish and silly and I lacked the imagination that winter to invent new ones. I was alone a very great deal. Mimi was nearly sixteen and was at least as attractive to the young men as were my older sisters. They were off with them all day, and most evenings too. No doubt my mother was much preoccupied with her daughters, for I saw little of her, though I do remember one lovely sunny day when she and I went tobogganing together. True, I was taken to watch the Olympic Games and the ice-hockey, but with the exception of the ski-jumping I found this a chilly and uninteresting way of passing the time. Usually I was simply turned out into the snow, with my skis, and told to amuse myself. I tried to learn to ski and quite liked whizzing downhill, though climbing up again, carrying the heavy skis in frozen hands encased in wet, woollen gloves, seemed to me a most dreary business. I set about building myself a ski-jump in the garden: it collapsed. Skating I preferred, but the Suvretta rink seemed usually to be requisitioned for some Olympic event or else for an exhibition. I was not allowed on the Cresta Run, because I was too young. I fear that I never took to winter sport.

In the evenings, too, I was often alone in the châlet. The cook who went with the house was no companion, for she spoke only German, and in any case she went off after giving me my supper, I tried the books, but they were too old for me. This was the first, but not the last, occasion on which I have attempted to read *A la Recherche du Temps Perdu*. Perhaps Proust has remained too old for me. I moped about the place, played *Little White Lies* and *Twentieth-Century Blues* on the gramophone, and one night found a bottle of cherry brandy. Delicious! I drank the lot and reeled off to bed in a happy stupor. So if I learned nothing else, St Moritz did teach me that alcohol, particularly if drunk to excess, is a splendid antidote to ennui and spleen.

We spent the Easter holidays of 1931 in Devonshire. (I am well aware that the county's correct name is Devon, cream and dukes notwithstanding.) An old friend of my mother's from New York had recently opened a small hotel, called the Easton Court Hotel, a few miles from the large village, or small town, of Chagford, which is itself on the edge of Dartmoor. Caroline Cobb was her name and her guest-house then had some six or eight bedrooms. There was a lounge but no bar, and in the garden at the back crazy-paving was being laid between newly sown lawns. Attached to the establishment was a filling station, where I was allowed to work the pumps and collect the tips, and a small sweet shop where I also served behind the counter on a percentage basis. These were the first honest pennies I had earned since Lenox days, and the last for many years to come.

Fanny was there that spring and also, I think, Mimi, but not Geraldine. (My eldest sister had left Oxford after being involved in a mild scandal which Terence Rattigan, also an undergraduate, dramatised in one of his earliest plays. She already had a brief career as a painter behind her. Now, after appearing with the Oxford University Dramatic Society, she had decided to take up that lively art and was being trained at the Royal Academy of Dramatic Art. I am not sure whether it was at this time or a little later that she wrote an unpublished novel.) We were not the only guests.

Alec Waugh was there, and took me for rides on the back of his motorbike, which was much appreciated. I have a very hazy memory of his younger brother, Evelyn, who either did not have a motorbike or else preferred to ride it alone. There was a young man who had written a very modern novel entitled *Little Green Apples*, and who was himself known as 'Little Green Apples'. From this it can be seen that Caroline Cobb had connections in the world of literature which, I believe, her hotel preserves even though she has long departed. In those days Alec Waugh's motorbike meant more to me than *The Loom of Youth* and the rich smell of petrol pumps and the tart taste of unripe apples.

It was there that my mother told me we were not returning to Paris. I do not believe that this worried me at all, for I had already taken an immediate liking to Devonshire life. We went and looked at a house a couple of miles away, on the edge of a hamlet called Sandy Park. With my firm approval, and no doubt that of my sisters as well, she decided to buy it. It had a rather pompous name, such as the Manse or Glebe House, which we all agreed would not do. I remember one evening, when walking with my mother in the April dusk, discussing this matter of its name. I proposed Sandy Park House, and was proud that my suggestion was accepted. By the time I came home for the summer holidays, we were installed there.

Apart from school, which cannot count, this was the first time that I had lived in England and also the first time, since Lenox, that I had really been in the country. (Dinard was a seaside town: beaches are different.) And at the perfect age of twelve I was able truly to enjoy country life. I did, and my memories of Devonshire, or Devon, are almost all outdoor memories. Far and away the most vivid of these are the bird's-nesting seasons of 1932 and 1933.

Our cook was called Mrs Coombes. She was a most friendly woman, almost stone deaf, and a good plain cook. There was always something delicious for a hungry boy in her big, stone-flagged kitchen (across which huge armies of black beetles marched and counter-marched all night) with its great coal range almost filling one wall. Our gardener, an old man named William, was also stone deaf. When he and Mrs Coombes were enjoying a quiet cup of tea together, their thick Devonshire accents boomed throughout the house, and far up the garden too, as they exchanged the day's news and discussed the iniquities of the weather. This was in the mornings or afternoons. In the evenings Mrs Coombes went home, to her cottage in the village, where she lived with her husband and her son, Leonard.

Coombes was a mysterious, even a slightly sinister, figure, as dark as a black Romany and with a squint or a wall-eye that made it difficult to decide if he were looking at one or not. He had a reputation as a poacher, and he certainly did no regular work. (This was not unusual, even in the country, in 1932, but though he did do odd jobs for my mother—such as looking after the chickens—he refused any permanent arrangement.) In the face of local gossip, my mother always stoutly maintained that she had the utmost confidence in Coombes and would not hear a word against him. When told that Mrs Coombes fed him from our kitchen, she replied that she knew this and approved. And a regular feature of lunch at Sandy Park House was to watch Mrs Coombes two minutes after the main course had been served, hurrying down the lane towards her cottage in her white apron with a large covered dish for Coombes. She was always back in time to bring on the pudding.

Leonard was a couple of years older than I, and after a while he went away to work in Paignton, but before then he had shown me a lot of the countryside and had taught me much that he himself had perhaps learned from his father.

I remember setting out with him, early in the morning before the dew was gone, sometimes on our bicycles, sometimes on foot. If we were walking, we would cut ourselves switches from the hedgerow with our pocket knives and swing these, decapitating dandelions and cowparsley, as we sang at the top of our voices in the deserted lanes. On our bicycles we could go for miles, out on the moor or even to the seaside if we had the packets of sandwiches Mrs Coombes had made strapped on the carriers behind us. But adventure need not be far away. There were woods and gorsy hills, streams and small hidden lakes where the water tasted of peat, meadows to be crossed and drystone walls to be climbed, and everywhere birds and animals and fish. The fish were to be caught, which occasionally we did, though this was not my favourite sport. The animals were to be watched. Leonard taught me how to sit absolutely still. He knew where a litter of fox-cubs might be seen, if only briefly before the vixen scented us, playing with their mother outside their earth. He took me to the one stretch of river within our reach where the otters lived and we watched them streak away. We spent hours in the half-light watching a badger's sett, but here we were disappointed: I have never seen a badger. There were moles and snakes and squirrels, both the common grey ones and, very occasionally, a red one too. The countryside abounded in rabbits and from time to time we would put up a hare, much more rare before the rabbits died, and watch him bound away and disappear over the horizon.

It was the birds, though, that made those springtimes. The first year Leonard went with me, and showed me how to find their nests and how to blow their eggs, our only tool a pin. The next year I went out on my own, and I had soon acquired more elaborate equipment: a small metal drill for making the hole, a glass pipe for sucking out the egg's contents, a cabinet with drawers of varying sizes in which to lay them upon their cottonwool. There were exciting times. There was the buzzard's nest, high up in the crotch of a great oak. I was just reaching for one of the big, almost round, reddy-brown-speckled eggs, when the angry buzzards arrived. I jumped down twenty feet into the ferns below, the egg unbroken in my hand. There was the rookery, high in the clump of elms, and the tremendous climb until the trunk of the tree was as thin as a mainmast and swayed as if I were rounding the Horn and the egg was popped into my mouth for safety amidst a crowd of cawing birds. There was the kingfisher's nest, and, lying half underwater, my thin boy's arm just able to slip down the hole in the bank up to the shoulder, and the excitement as my fingers gently touched the warm eggs. Nor was it all egg-stealing. (I am sure it is wrong. I would never do it now. But if by some miracle I could be twelve years old again, I know how I would spend my March and April and May.) I remember once finding a wild duck's nest beside a woodland pool. There was a tapping sound from the eggs. I sat silently and watched, and soon enough a worried duck appeared a few yards away. I saw chick after damp dark-yellow chick leave its egg and take to the water and be rounded up by its mother, until all ten were swimming together, so that she could guide her little convoy around a corner out of my sight. There was a remote, sun-drenched, stone-fronted bank, where jackdaws nested by the score. There was a great raven's nest, half-way down a cliff. I could see it, but could not reach it. But by the time the Easter holidays had come, the raven chicks were hatched and almost ready to fly. In February I have no doubt that I should have reached it, somehow. There was an incredibly beautiful long-tailed tit's nest, domed over and suspended, as it seemed, by threads, in a patch of wild bamboo. There were nests in the hedgerows and nests in the gorse, nests on the ground and high in the sky, as simple as a pigeon's or as elaborate as a warbler's.

There was a pony, too, but I used to ride him more from a sense of duty than for pleasure. This may have been because my mother engaged a man, one of the many unemployed majors who were more common than missel-thrushes in those days, to teach me how to ride. I disliked him and had no interest in his lessons. Also the pony used to bite me with his long yellow teeth, and leer at me over his shoulder, and try to brush me off by suddenly veering to one side underneath low branches. We were not made for one another. As for jumping, which the major also tried to teach me, this was the one subject on which my pony and I were of a single mind: there would be no jumping.

Sandy Park House was a fine home for a boy. It was not large, but it rambled. There was an attic where I was allowed to keep mice and guinea-pigs and other malodorous beasts who used to eat their babies with depressing regularity.

When the parents died, of indigestion or guilt, there was a special part of the garden which was their cemetery and where they were buried beside the graves of dead robins and grass-snakes. Each grave was marked and tended. One mouse even had a coffin in the form of a metal box that had once held a sparking-plug. He was repeatedly dug up to see how the process of decomposition was getting on. It was getting on fine.

Alas, Sandy Park House could not go on. The economic depression grew worse and worse and my mother's dividends disappeared. She had an alimony from Bertram, but this was not large (she could have had more money from him, but had not wished for this) and when Roosevelt raised the dollar price of gold this, as well as the rest of her shrunken income, dropped by twenty per cent. Furthermore British income tax, which as a resident she had to pay, went up steeply. Money worries settled on her thick and fast.

Geraldine and Fanny were now only occasional visitors to Sandy Park. Mimi would soon be following them. There seemed little point in keeping a house she could not afford for the few weeks a year when I was home from school. Early in 1934 she sold it. Her intention then was to spend over half of each year out of England, thus avoiding British income tax. And so she went to Jersey, where I joined her for the Easter holidays. Once those were over, she took Mimi to America, where I again joined them for my summer holidays. But before describing this visit, I must mention an incident of which I have no memory whatsoever.

My father had gone from bad to worse. His second marriage had broken up. His sister, whose devotion to him throughout the years was astonishing, had paid for him to be set up in one way or another. She had even found him a job in Angola, had bought him what he needed for that climate, and had paid his fare out, but he had come straight home. He got into worse and worse trouble for bad cheques and similar offences, and soon enough was to be sent to prison. Meanwhile my uncle, his sister's husband, was becoming increasingly irked by the endless financial drain that he represented, for it was ultimately my Uncle Phil who had to pay. It was a miserable story, but one of which I knew nothing. All I did know was that my father was quite frequently in England and that I almost never saw him.

I did see him, whenever he so wished it, which was very seldom: once at my aunt's house, twice, I think, with my mother in London. (I am here referring to the years before Sandy Park.) He made very little impression on me. He was just another stranger, and not at all the man I had expected. This is hardly surprising, since the man I expected could only be the father I had invented.

Schoolboys talk about their fathers a fair amount. The father about whom I boasted at the New Beacon was immensely tall, strong, brave and with a very fine, loud singing voice. (My mother had once told me that he had had a fine singing voice, its loudness must have been my own addition.) The man I met, on the other hand, was rather short, stout, not very healthy-looking, and softly spoken. He was given no opportunity for displays of physical bravery during those encounters.

Now by the time I was twelve, although I had never heard anyone say anything against him, I must have reached the conclusion that this impostor had betrayed me and my mother and my sisters. In any event, when my mother told me that he was coming down to Devonshire to see us, I was extremely distressed. I said that I had no wish to meet him, that I regarded him as a traitor. My mother tried to calm me down, explained that he would only be there for a few hours, and did her best to dispel my anger or fears and to make me feel affectionate towards him. Such, I have no doubt, were her own feelings.

It was of no avail. When he arrived, I was not to be found. And I am told that I remained in hiding until I had seen his car drive away again, several hours later.

This incident is not perhaps very strange. Whatever my emotions may then have been, a few years later I was perfectly prepared to meet my father, for whom, indeed, I developed a measure of affection. But what surely is strange, and what would perhaps be of considerable interest to the analyst whom I do not intend to consult, is my complete and permanent black-out of memory concerning an incident which, at the time, must have been of the greatest possible emotional importance to me. My memory is in general good, but that day of painful hiding from my father has gone. It is possible that there may have been some connection between this incident and the one with the boy I have called Colquhoun, which must have happened at about the same time or slightly before. Whether this is so or not, I am quite sure that the Freudians certainly, the Adlerians probably, and perhaps even the Jungians could make a great deal out of them both.

Despite the passage of time and the arrival of the Depression, the Lenox to which I returned in the summer of 1934 was not markedly different from the Lenox of seven or so years earlier. A few of the widows in the big houses had joined their husbands, while others were complaining of poverty. This was the high tide of the New Deal, of General Johnson and the Blue Eagle, and the rich were beginning to convince themselves that it was Roosevelt's fault they were not even richer. As a recent convert to left-wing thought— the great Romilly scandal had taken place during the previous term—I was keenly in favour of the N.R.A., the P.W.A., the A.A.A. and all the rest of the Government's alphabet soup. I found that most young Americans whom I met, and who had any views about such matters at all, shared these opinions. The extreme activity of the American administration seemed to me to contrast favourably with the apparent lethargy of the National Government in England. It may seem odd that Harold Ickes could ever have been a hero to a fifteen-year-old schoolboy from England, but no doubt others have had even odder ones. My emotions were firmly enlisted on the side of the unemployed, the bonus marchers, the Negroes, the Ladies Garment Workers' Union, the pacifists and the socialists: with righteous horror I read about the iniquities of strike-breakers, corrupt bankers, stock exchange manipulators, corporate thimble-riggers, company stores and merchants of death. My newly awakened social conscience thought to find its echo in that of Roosevelt's America. If one had to choose a side—and what with Hitler and all that, it was becoming increasingly apparent that one did—then I had no doubt which side I was on. And if I now write with a certain inevitable irony about the naïve political emotions current at that time, this is not because I believe naïveté or those emotions to have been wrong. At the risk of sounding almost incredibly egocentric, I would say that I have remained on the same side: it is others who have changed their allegiance, while preserving the once honourable names and labels that they have, in too many cases, sadly devalued. (A study of the change in meaning over the last seventy years of the political label 'liberal' is most revealing, particularly in the United States.)

America that year meant to me not only the search for economic and social justice, it also, and in a quite personal sense, meant freedom. At Lenox my mother and Mimi and I lived in a flat above Aunt Maud's stables, now converted into garages. My grandmother had died some years before, and Sunnyridge was sold, but Lenox remained very much our home town, with friends and relations scattered all around it. I had, by birthright as it were, the freedom of the town. And I took it with both hands.

Oh, it was simple enough, that American adolescent freedom, and it was taken for granted by the American boys and girls of my own age. But coming from England, and above all from Wellington College, it went straight to the head, and to the heart. There were many young people in Lenox in the summertime. My age-group, my society, almost overlapped with that of Mimi and her contemporaries and our behaviour was not very different from theirs. We too drove around in cars, and played tennis at the Lenox Club, and went to a certain speakeasy on the Pittsfield Road, to drink Tom Collinses and Planter's Punches, and danced to the victrola in the barnlike room beside Stockbridge Bowl (*Moonglow* and *La Cucaracha*.) Above all we were allowed to play at falling in love, and out of it, and in again.

There was holding hands in the movies, there was canoeing miles down the lake, there was a long drive with her ash-blonde hair blown back by the wind of speed to dance to Cab Calloway's orchestra and the long drive back, there was the night when, with immense daring, half a dozen of us swam nude in somebody's private pool, there were kisses in the woods and kisses in the car, kisses by the lake and kisses on the porch. (And in my experience it stopped with kissing. Perhaps it was my innocence or ignorance that prevented further experimentation, though from remembered conversations with the other boys I am inclined to think that the more advanced forms of petting and necking were not then practised, in Lenox, by children as young as we were.)

Were there ever such delicious girls, so sweet-smelling, so tip-tilted, so smooth-skinned, so long-legged, so brown-backed in the sun, so soft-lipped in the dark, with such smiles and dimples and curls and giggles, so mysterious, so wise and so utterly desirable? Of course there are millions of them, new ones every year, fifteen-year-olds fresh as butter, from Maine to New Mexico. Yet never again will there be girls *quite* like the girls of Lenox, in 1934.

Part Three

Part Three

9

WARS DO NOT only leave their minefields to threaten the survivors and the unborn (mines waiting, overlooked and quite forgotten beneath the meadow and the sand dune, mines drifting, dark and silent off the headland by the shipping lanes, amidst the gliding, goggling fish) but they also lay their fields, sow their dragon's teeth, often among the debris of earlier wars, long before hostilities begin or ultimatums are delivered. At the age of eleven I was taken to the battlefields of the First World War where split steel helmets and dented water-bottles were still to be picked up beside burned-out tanks or in crumbling trenches and where the torn, smashed and nakedly dead trees of the old Argonne Forest still stood taller than the new, the post-war, growth. Four years later, before I left Wellington for Germany, we were living in a pre-war world.

I remember the evening well. After the meeting of the school debating society we had gone to a young master's room for coffee. He had switched on the wireless, for the news. (This, too, was symptomatic of a change. Until recently, for almost everyone, the wireless had been a harmless and rather dull purveyor of light entertainment, dance music and such, usually banished in big houses to the servants' quarters. In the years to come it was to be the announcer of doom, the voice of Adolf Hitler above all, the voice that catalogued the long series of defeats, destruction and death, the grim accents of Churchill, and at last the news of ashen victories. The servants had by then long left the servants' hall, the wireless had been moved to the drawing-room and the chimes for 'the News' were a summons to silence more peremptory than those of the Angelus in happier lands.) In March of 1935, in this young master's rooms at Wellington, we heard that conscription was to be re-introduced in Germany immediately. Mr Crawley informed us that this meant the end of Versailles and he added that war was most probably coming within a very few years. I cannot speak for the other boys who were silent for a moment, but I know that I believed him.

This belief that war was coming—a belief that overhung all my youthful years until the threat became the reality— was neither a romantic pose nor yet a cynical acceptance. Almost as much as the war itself, it conditioned the outlook of myself and my generation and perhaps continues to do so now. For the purpose of this book it is therefore important what this bare phrase—'I believed that war was coming'— meant, thirty years ago, since it had neither the meaning it bore in 1912 nor that which it bears today.

In 1935 the next war was foreseen by almost everyone as a repetition on a larger and more appalling scale of the First World War with one notable new horror added, the massive bombing and gassing of civilians. It was not only the products of the Army Sixth who were being taught to fight the last war all over again: those, like myself, who called themselves pacifists and who were determined never to fight in another one were also protesting against a war that had happened years ago.

We thought we knew all about that war. Its poets, whom we admired, were Owen and Graves, Sassoon and e. e. cummings, and the poets nearer to us in age whom we also admired had accepted their detestation of that war. From their prose works and those of other writers we thought we knew exactly what life in the trenches had been, and would be, like. The bleak realism of *All Quiet on the Western Front*, the anger of *Good-bye to All That* or of *The Enormous Room*, the honest disgust of *Le Feu* or *Quiet Flows the Don*, in fact the whole bitter tenor of First World War literature was accepted by us as a proven indictment of past and future war. We knew what had happened to the old battalion: it was hanging on the old barbed wire. That was what would happen to us, after living for a few weeks in water-logged trenches with rats the size of terriers, coughing our guts up because the gas-masks would not work, being mown down by German machine-guns and the stupidity of generals as we stumbled beneath huge packs across churned-up, lunar landscapes. Life expectancy: six weeks.

We also knew who would be responsible for this: first and

foremost, the capitalists who made money out of it all, not merely the munitions manufacturers but the Bradford wool millionaires beneath their 'silk hats', the shipping magnates growing fat as lobsters thanks to U-boats, the bankers who were behind it all and the politicians and the newspaper barons trumpeting their lies about national honour and the atrocities committed by an enemy who was an equally miserable dupe. Indeed the enemy of the last—and, by extension, of the next—war was not at all the German on the far side of no-man's-land: he, our books told us, lived and suffered and died exactly as did we. The enemy, rather, was the boss class. The fact that our fathers and uncles, and those of most of our friends, came from that class was an irrelevance. If they were good men, they were exceptions, if bad, then typical. There was a vast conspiracy on the part of these evil men with the ultimate objective of preserving or increasing their own power and wealth by killing the young, who were ourselves. We believed this naïve and pathetic rubbish with the same simple-minded acceptance that our German contemporaries granted to Nazi lies about international Jewry and the awful alliance between Wall Street and the Kremlin. Still bewildered by the unspeakable and much spoken-of horrors of the First World War, this new generation of intellectuals found an illusory refuge in mass paranoia. A conspiratorial interpretation of public ills is always sure of a hearing. This is one reason why so many clever young men were prepared to become Communists in the 'thirties: another is that a belief in conspiracy breeds conspirators: a third lay in the intellectuals' search for coherence during a period of great emotional incoherence, and for those who could swallow it whole dialectical materialism often provided an apparent solution.

Incoherence was the true climate of the period. Some, though in England not many, accepted and welcomed the nihilism of the intellect which produced Nazism elsewhere. Quite clever men not only admired D. H. Lawrence as a descriptive writer but also as a thinker. (In Germany they 'thought with the blood': in England the disciples of D. H. Lawrence seem to have advocated the use of other body fluids for this purpose.) Surrealism made a similar appeal. Others reacted in the opposite direction and embraced more or less logical closed systems of thought, such as Marxism-Leninism or the Roman Catholic Church. But the great majority of those who thought about such matters at all remained in a state of mental incoherence. Many people, of whom I was one, thought that it was logically possible to be both a pacifist and an anti-Fascist. George Orwell believed this for years and so, in his own somewhat idiosyncratic way, did W. H. Auden. Others again—Hegel has really too much to answer for, and I shall not blame him for this one—attempted a synthesis between Communism and Christianity. Middleton Murry was of their number, while Conrad Noel had a bust of Lenin in his church at Thaxted. It was a great muddle, made muddier yet by those (including almost everybody on the left except the real Communists) who cried 'Peace!' when there was no peace.

For despite the major contributory factor of economic misery caused by the Great Depression, the issue of war or peace was, for the young men of the middle class, the most directly personal. It was then believed by many that a Second World War would not only repeat all the horrors of the First but add to them greatly. (That this was true is irrelevant: envisaged horrors did not then include Auschwitz.) It was assumed, or at least frequently stated, that another war 'would mean the end of civilised society as we know it', and this prospect was deplored by many who were simultaneously and explicitly anxious to see the destruction of their society as they knew it. H. G. Wells, a characteristically bewildered period thinker, was responsible for a film about this called *The Shape of Things to Come*. The beginning, at least, was plausible enough: civilised Londoners coughing through clouds of gas while their city collapsed about them. Post-civilised England had a quaintly Luddite quality. I recall a scowling, bearded chieftain seated in an old Rolls-Royce which had to be pulled by hand—no petrol, or perhaps the disappearance of technological know-how—while the members of his harem, almost naked and rather tasty young women as I then thought, fawned and cringed around the old brute. At last it was all put right by a lot of splendid young people, technologists to a man and a woman, who arrived in flying machines and tidied the place up. They then set about creating a civilisation such as we do not know. Whether they came from another world, or merely from a remote corner of this one, I no longer remember. They were all dressed alike and resembled efficient Comsomols or keen, clean members of the Hitler Youth, as represented in the propaganda photographs of the totalitarians. H. G. Wells was, of course, an anti-Communist, an anti-Fascist, a pacifist, a humanist, a perfect progressive of the 1930s.

Now one point must be made clear immediately. There were intellectuals in the 1930s who were neither Communists nor suffered from the sort of intellectual flatulence that so distended the reputation of an H. G. Wells. But the intellectual climate into which I emerged at Wellington, which was only a clumsily constructed microcosm of that prevailing at the universities and in London, was one of intellectual and political confusion. A whole *sottisier* could be compiled from the remarks attributed to Dr Johnson, particularly from those most frequently quoted, but his remark about an impending execution clarifying the mind of the condemned is surely among the most foolish. Fear may be a fine stimulus to action: like any other primary emotion it is an almost insuperable barrier to clear thought. And between 1934 and 1939 we were increasingly fearful of a war that became ever more inevitable.

It was with the acquired left-wing beliefs or prejudices of the age, only half understood and quite unquestioned by me, that I set off for Berlin in May of 1935, shortly before my sixteenth birthday. Also in my suitcase were John Strachey's *The Coming Struggle for Power*, Lenin's *Imperialism*, *The Complete Poems of D. H. Lawrence*, 18 *Poems* by Dylan Thomas, *Those Barren Leaves* by Aldous Huxley and doubtless several other seminal and improving works. I was moderately priggish, as befitted my years, a confirmed intellectual and artistic snob, a nervous and frightened child, and intensely curious to see a country where, as I had read, they were

135

busily engaged upon 'the destruction of civilised society as we know it'. I travelled via the Hook of Holland, talked to no one, and got out at the Zoo Station.

I was in an isolation hospital, suffering from mumps, when my mother brought me the news that my presence at Wellington College was no longer desired. Mumps is a painful malady and this was aggravated in my case by incarceration in a children's ward. Its other inmates 'the sturdy, unkillable infants of the very poor', were shrill torturers. Nor was I in any state to cuff them into silence and respect. The nurse had been instructed by the doctor to give me two aspirins every four hours and proceeded to give me four every two hours. I was thus in a condition of near coma in which only the voices of the children, for ever singing *Knees Up, Mother Brown*, reached me. That deplorable Cockney folksong still brings the dreary taste of aspirin back to my mouth.

From this coma my mother roused me. When she came to see me on the following day she was more worried by my physical condition than my educational future. However, I was recovering from this rather crude over-medication—with the superior drugs available nowadays it would have presumably proved fatal—and she told me about the head-master's letter. If she was distressed or even taken aback she did not let me see this. She asked me what had happened, I told her, and that was that. Sick and weak as I was, I remember feeling gratitude mingled with surprise at her matter-of-fact attitude. We went on to discuss my immediate future.

There were three possibilities. Esmond Romilly had con-tinued his education at Bedales, a progressive school where expulsion from Wellington, if not a positive recommendation, was at least no great hindrance. But Bedales, like the other progressive schools of the period, was expensive. My Wellington scholarship was forfeited, of course, and my mother was passing through one of her periods of acute financial anxiety.

An American school was considered, but this would have

been even more expensive. Besides, I myself had had enough of schools, and had no wish to attend another.

The third possibility, and the one which was accepted, was to send me abroad to learn a language while I made up my mind what I wished to do. Since I already knew French, Germany was the obvious place for me to go. And fortunately we had a friend who could arrange this.

Nandl von Hutten's American mother was the authoress of the *Pan* novels. Nandl was then in his middle thirties, an immensely tall and somewhat eccentric figure with a pleasantly dry wit, equally at home in half a dozen languages and as many countries, a descendant of the great Renaissance scholar and a friend of Max Beerbohm, Gerhardt Hauptmann, Cunningham Graham and heaven knows who else. Although unmistakably German in appearance, there was at least one Teutonic virtue which he lacked. That quality of industriousness of which his compatriots like to make such a boast was never Nandl's style, but since his father was a miserly skinflint, who lived alone on a large Franconian estate and gave his son and heir nothing, Nandl had to work in those distant days. He had a vague job with a London publisher, lived a gay social life in the upper-class Bohemia of the time and was a friend of my sister Mimi. He knew precisely where to send me.

Dr Schackwitz was the German State Pathologist. He lived with his wife and three children in a large flat overlooking the River Spree and within easy walking distance of Berlin's great park, the Tiergarten. The youngest child was a daughter, only a year or so older than myself. Ilse was an exceptionally beautiful girl, blonde and straight as an elm, with the very slightly Slav eyes of the true Prussian. It is not surprising that Nandl should have fallen in love with her. Her father, however, had grave doubts. Not only was Ilse far too young for marriage—she was still at school, preparing for her *Abitur*—but Nandl's lack of industry and generally light-hearted attitude towards the world were no recommendation to the old Doctor. Indeed he had forbidden his daughter to correspond with Nandl at all. Thus one of Nandl's motives in introducing me into the Schackwitz

137

household was that I should act as love's messenger, passing his letters to Ilse and occasionally forwarding hers to him. This task I carried out loyally for as long as I remained in Berlin, and a year or so later they were married. I even took my responsibilities so seriously that I refrained from attempting to discover whether or not the delicious Ilse was interested in an occasional, harmless kiss from myself. In later years one is apt to regret such a foolish devotion to duty. On the other hand, Nandl and Ilse have remained my good friends to this day.

Whatever the rumblings and widening fissures in the cracks of civilised society may have been that I then expected to find in Nazi Germany, they were not visible, or certainly not immediately visible, in the Schackwitz flat on the Flotowstrasse.

The flat itself was airy and, as one might expect, scrupulously clean. There was a huge living-room, with a long dining-room table off which we ate in front of one of the french windows, and a big tiled stove at the other end. Most of the wall space was taken up by books, though I recall one or perhaps two very handsome flower pictures by Emil Nolde, a family friend. (I did not then know, nor did anyone tell me, that Nolde was forbidden by the Nazis to exhibit.) Off the living-room was Frau Schackwitz's little drawing-room, where all the furniture was Biedermeier and the water colours and miniatures were also early nineteenth-century. This room was only ever used by Frau Schackwitz when entertaining other ladies to coffee and cakes in the afternoon. No men or children were present at these functions. Next came the Doctor's study, entirely book-lined. Beyond was the sons' room, but they seldom slept there. Herbert had just got his medical degree and was studying surgery with the great Dr Sauerbruch. Gunther was still a medical student, and they shared a flat with another medical student in the suburb of Reinickendorf. Down a long, dark corridor—more books—were Ilse's room, complete with a cast of *La Noyée de la Seine*, a Bellini print and one of Franz Marc's *Blue Horses*, then her parents' bedroom which I never entered, and finally my room. My room overlooked the courtyard. When I arrived in May the court was filled with a huge chestnut tree, its eye-level blossoms salmon-pink. In the morning houseproud housewives hung their bed-linen from the windows around the yard, and all day long, it seemed, they beat their carpets down below. In the Schackwitz flat a single diminutive maid called Jenny, almost a hunchback and with an endlessly cheerful, crooked grin, worked in her spotless kitchen, or dusted or pushed a carpet-sweeper. Frau Schackwitz, too, did a lot of work about the house and Ilse was expected to give a helping hand whenever she could spare the time from her studies. The whole apartment smelt of beeswax and lavender, to which must be added good frying smells in the neighbourhood of the kitchen and cigar smoke in the living-room.

The cigars were the Doctor's, and to a lesser extent Herbert's. (Gunther smoked cigarettes, to his father's annoyance: a mild gesture of defiance. Frau Schackwitz and Ilse did not smoke.) The Doctor was a formidable figure, both as an intellect and as a paterfamilias. He had several doctorates, and had studied with Freud, among others, in the very early days of psychiatry. Externally he was a typical member of the higher German professional and official class, the *Beamtentum* whose real hour of glory had come before the First World War. Short, stocky, shaven-headed, black-suited, with a watch chain stretched across his waistcoat and an amber holder for his cigar, he left nobody in any doubt as to who was the head of the household. At table he was an autocrat. If a subject of conversation was not to his liking, it was changed. Had the food not been to his taste—but his wife always saw that it was—no doubt that would have been changed too. Lateness for meals was a grave offence. His children were not frightened of him, and indeed they tended to laugh at his old-fashioned ways behind his back, but only behind his back. His wife obviously worshipped him, and that commonplace verb is not here misused. Such a household was a revelation to me.

I spent six months with them, including a month's holiday on the Danish island of Bornholm, and I gradually came to see that Dr Schackwitz was far more than the caricature figure that he appeared at first glance. The Nolde pictures were indicative, but so was his conversation. Needless to say, he did not talk to me a great deal. He was busy and I was a child. But once I had learned to speak German fairly well—his English was adequate and rusty—he was always most courteous when I put questions to him.

I remember once asking him about Freud, inevitably a culture-hero of mine in those days, though only at second hand. He suggested that I read Freud's works and led me to the shelf where they stood, monographs and first editions, many signed by the author. I did my best, but the medical German was beyond me. Dr Schackwitz said:

'A great man, a very great man, within his own limitations. One of his limitations has been Vienna. He should have come here, to Berlin, where the climate is in every respect more bracing.'

I did not understand, and remarked that his theories were surely unacceptable in Germany nowadays. Dr Schackwitz growled:

'Yes, the Third Reich has no place for Freud. Or for Einstein.'

Because of their being Jews, I asked, or because of the nature of their writings?

Dr Schackwitz replied:

'It would please me to think that Herr Dr Goebbels and Herr General Göring have detected methodological errors in Freudian analysis and mathematical shortcomings in the theory of relativity. If so, I can only regret that they have so far failed to publish their findings.'

He was, or had been, a very senior freemason in Germany. Freemasonry was now forbidden by the Nazis. But if Dr Schackwitz was an anti-Nazi, he never said so. I remember once asking him about the Jews. Surely, I said, Germans were Germans whether of Jewish blood or not?

'Unfortunately that is not so. Some German Jews are two hundred per cent German while others, those who came from Poland after the war for instance, are only ten per cent German.'

'But will they not become as German as the others?'

'They will not be given the time.'

'Do you agree with the Nuremberg Laws, then?'

'In England, my boy, you are lucky. You do not have to try to understand such . . . such subtleties of thought as are imposed upon us by our government.'

His children were totally apolitical. I tried to talk to Herbert and Gunther about these matters and about the Marxist books that I was reading at the time. They brushed me off. Their attitude might be summed up:

'We discussed all that, *ad nauseam*, for years. Now it is all finished and done with. Have a drink.'

I did not agree with them, but it is difficult to go on reading Marxist theory at the age of sixteen if you have no one with whom to discuss it. Besides, there was so much more to read and look at and think about.

Frau Schackwitz gave me German lessons each morning and once I had mastered the rudiments of the grammar, I taught myself the language in a very simple way. I read, with a dictionary beside me, and wrote down the words I did not know. Each evening I learned fifty new words by heart. At the age I then was that is both quick and easy, and within a very few weeks I could read German. I went on with my lists of words, though, and within a few months my vocabulary was sufficiently large for me to be able to enjoy German poetry. If one can appreciate its poems, I believe that one knows a foreign language and can then begin to understand another nation.

Never again have I read as many books as during the two years after Wellington. At first, and particularly in Berlin, my reading was more or less haphazard. My mother had told me that she would give me three pounds a week until I was twenty-one, and that meanwhile I must decide what I wished to become. Three pounds a week in those days meant the essentials of life and no luxuries. Cigarettes, for instance, were a luxury, and for a long time I rationed myself to three a day. Drink, too, was usually beyond my means. (Frau Schackwitz gave me a small bottle of beer with the evening meal: at lunchtime it was fruit juice.) New books were also far too expensive. When sent them for my birthday perhaps or for Christmas, I got a positive sensual enjoyment from their smell, from their very newness, from the occasional crack! of the glue behind the spine of the binding when the book was first opened. Thus my reading was largely limited to what I could borrow and to what I could buy, very cheaply, second hand.

The Schackwitz flat was filled with books, though most of these were of a technical sort. Ilse, however, read for pleasure and it was from her that I borrowed books as soon as my German was up to it. I do not know whether she was then passing through a Russian phase, but certainly when I first began to read German fluently it was above all the Russian authors whom I devoured, in translation: Gogol and Pushkin, Tolstoi and Chekov, Gorki, with difficulty Dostoievski, and Turgenev with most enjoyment of all. I was still little more than a child, and I am sure that my absorption with nineteenth-century Russian literature was not very different in quality from the pleasure I had only recently derived from the novels of Alexandre Dumas, Dickens or even Mazo de la Roche. Old Russia became, for me, a self-enclosed and for ever mysterious land that existed only in the pages of its writers. I could not learn too much about its inhabitants and their strange lives. I would start a new story: *One fine autumn's day in the province of K——, in the year 18—, a heavily laden travelling chaise could be seen driving at speed along the unpaved main street of S——, the provincial capital,* and I was off into that land, half fact and half fantasy, where I too loved to travel at speed.

(In later years, when reading or re-reading the great Russian novelists in English, I have derived great intellectual pleasure both from the content and from the form, but the magic has almost all gone. This may be because the German language still held a certain freshness and mystery for me that corresponded with the strangeness of the Russian characters and their doings. Or it may be, as I have heard, that Russian translates better into German than into English. Certainly the old, standard English translations, and particularly those made by Constance Garnett, often lapse into a language and a prose style that tumble into the ludicrous: Raskolnikov staggers into dram-shops, and the princess's samovar begins to sing.)

Since I was reading purely for pleasure, I did not attempt many German novels, from which there is little pleasure to be had. Early Thomas Mann was the exception, and I remember a little garden, behind a small café on the island of Bornholm, where I sat at a rusty metal table beneath half-wild roses, eating strawberries, totally absorbed in *Buddenbrooks*. As a result of this I tried my hand at Schopenhauer and Nietzsche, too. And, as I have said, I was soon reading the German poets, particularly the Romantic poets and those long short stories or *novellas* that they wrote and that no one else has really emulated. But few German novelists have ever appealed to me. I gagged over a book called *Der Grüne Heinrich*, a truly rebarbative work of rustic tedium, though in fairness to German literature I must say that its author was Swiss.

Thomas Mann was the exception. Not only was he a famous and magnificent writer, but he was also unacceptable to the Nazis and therefore politically heroic in my eyes. (His brother Heinrich, being a Communist Party member, should have been even more to my taste: unfortunately I found his novels as unreadable as Gottfried Keller's Swiss classic.) Indeed the whole business of living German authors was at that time rather complicated. Jewish writers of course were banned, but so were almost all the non-Jewish ones, some because they were homosexuals but most for having expressed pacifist or left-wing views. Or if not banned, they were not being reprinted, and the German public was forced on to a very stodgy diet of right-wing writers, usually of an older generation and very often in translation. The sales of Knud Hamsun and of John Galsworthy, for example, were enormous. But of course many foreign writers too were banned, and their books burned. In fact the forest of literature, in Germany, had been felled. Scarcely one tree remained. The publishing houses went on churning out new titles, but the names of their authors have been rightly forgotten. Apart from a few very old men, such as Hauptmann, hardly one is remembered today. Ernst Jünger is the only one who immediately comes to mind, and his mental processes were so sombre as to be almost impenetrable—at least to me, and perhaps to the Nazi censors as well.

It was therefore no great hardship for a young man to be forced for financial reasons to buy his books from the second-hand shops and the barrows. There were a number of these in the neighbourhood of the Schloss and the great museum. But my favourite, because its proprietor became a friend, was at the corner of a windy street in that part of Berlin called Am Knie. It was there that I found a copy of Thomas Mann's novella, *Tonio Kröger*, a story about a young man with whom I managed to identify myself. The owner of that barrow sold me a most beautiful first edition of another Thomas Mann story, which I still have, inscribed in a round hand with my name and the date 12 Sept. '35. It cost me a few pennies. Once he had discovered my tastes and political opinions, both of which he shared, my friend found me all sorts of oddities from the Weimar period, many of which could not be sold openly and which he therefore let me have for very little or even for nothing. One was a de luxe edition of the tale attributed, falsely I am told, to Oscar Wilde and entitled *The Priest and the Acolyte* with illustrations attributed, also falsely I believe, to Aubrey Beardsley. He also gave me some anti-Nazi pamphlets printed in the very early days of the regime. No doubt he was glad to be rid of them: I wish I had them now.

Once or twice we had a coffee together, on the terrace of a nearby café. I questioned him about the Weimar period, which was already becoming legendary. He really preferred to talk about literature, for which he had both love and respect. The great writers whom he used occasionally to see in bygone days had been his film stars.

'And now they are all gone. To America, mostly. Lucky fellows. Who can blame them?'

(And this prompts yet another parenthesis. For centuries we have been told that the pen is mightier than the sword. Since the middle of the eighteenth century this dictum has been accepted, at least by most writers, almost as axiomatic.

Yet in Germany, in a free and highly literate society, almost every writer of talent had warned his compatriots, in ample time, against Nazism and the Nazis, but to no avail. In France, at the time of writing, General de Gaulle has, for years, enjoyed almost no support from his country's best and best-read writers. For forty years Russian writers of talent have been monotonously murdered or locked away. None of this has apparently had the slightest political effect, anywhere. To talk about the *trahison des clercs*—which certainly existed and exists—or the alienation of the intellectuals is only a partial explanation. Can it be that the power of the pen has been vastly overestimated by those who wield it?)

At this period of my life I was at least as interested in painting as I was in books. Before coming to Germany I had spent my last two holidays from Wellington in London, and I had there acquired the habit of visiting museums and art galleries. For this part of my education I was principally indebted to my sister Fanny and to Harold Scott, the actor, a close friend of hers for many years, and until his death in 1964 among my very closest.

After the sale of Sandy Park House, my family had drifted to Chelsea. Mimi and Geraldine already had a small flat there, at 91 Oakley Street, and when my mother was not escaping the Inland Revenue in Jersey, she was near by. Fanny had, at one time, a small studio-flat around the corner, in Oakley Crescent. It was down its narrow stairs that I was carried, on a child's stretcher, when stricken with mumps, an awkward job for the ambulance men as I was over six feet tall. Harold Scott lived in Paultons Square and there were other friends dotted about what was then a friendly, unpretentious and comparatively inexpensive borough. I was usually given a furnished room at some other Oakley Street address: almost all the houses in that street then let furnished rooms very cheaply.

However, none of these arrangements was in any way permanent. Only Geraldine, having by now run through most of the arts, actually set up house with a friend in a flat on Cheyne Walk, and since her friend moved on the fringes of the artistic world (for a few months he and she helped run a semi-artistic nightclub underneath Shaftesbury Avenue) she became a stern critic of the artistic productions of others. Later she married a painter, and was henceforth to be an even sterner critic of loose living in any form. Mimi and I found it difficult to preserve a suitably solemn expression when she held forth about the evils of sex, drink, art, smoking and the other pleasures of life. Meanwhile, however, her flat beside the Thames, though liable to flooding, provided by reason of its comparative permanence a sort of family centre, particularly as there was a spare bedroom. The price of a bed was high, in the form of extensive lectures on morals, literature (Charles Morgan was held up as a model), diet (meals were planned from a revolving chart called the Hay Diet, which was compulsory) and rapidly changing esoteric religions (only Christianity was out).

Fanny painted, and never tried to bully anyone. Mimi modelled clothes and had her photograph taken in them leaning against the bonnets of property Bentleys in Bruton Street or outside ducal homes. She was far too busy preventing highly eligible young men from marrying her to bother about other people's lives. She had no interest in the arts; *Black Beauty*, which as a child she used to read over and over again, tears streaming down her cheeks, was the high-water mark of her literary education, though I did once catch her, in bed with 'flu, frowning over *Gone with the Wind*. She was the gayest of companions, shared my passion for jazz, and quite frequently took me with her in the property Bentleys or to the parties she enlivened with her beauty and her high spirits. We had a thousand private jokes, but in public these were unnecessary, for we understood one another at a glance.

It was Fanny, and above all Harold Scott, who encouraged and gently directed my intellectual and artistic appetites which had first been awakened at Wellington. Harold was that very rare phenomenon, a highly intelligent, educated and articulate actor. That he was truly brilliant in his principal profession is, I think, admitted by anyone who was connected with the theatre in his time. He did not give a performance that was not perfect. On the other hand he never became a star, which, he told me, means that he never captured the public emotionally. And, as he explained, the reason for this was that he thought too much about acting, that he knew too much about technique, and that this created a sort of barrier between himself and the public that often prevented the direct emotional flow which is essential before an actor or actress can become an Irving or a Duse. He told me he regretted this, but that there was nothing he could do about it. The very finest actors, he said, are far more instinctive in their art than he could ever be. That is why they are, off the stage, frequently rather stupid and colourless people. Once on it, there is no intellect, no thought, to intervene between their expression of a part and the audience's reception. This, he taught me, is true in some measure of all the interpretative arts, but not at all so of the creative ones. A stupid poet or composer or sculptor is inconceivable, if he is to be any good.

'What about playwrights?' I asked.

'Playwrights,' he said, 'live in a sort of half-way house. Like novelists. They can get away with a lot. For a while, at least.'

Harold Scott deserves more than these few paragraphs. He should have written his autobiography, and indeed he toyed with this for years—as his published books show, he was an extremely accomplished writer. He was born in the early 'nineties, and had started life as a musician. During the First World War he had been a conscientious objector and in prison he had met the leading pacifists and many of the leading socialists of the time. (He once escaped from Dartmoor Prison, in order to play the piano at a concert in the Aeolian Hall. After the concert he returned to Dartmoor and climbed back in.) In the 'twenties he and Elsa Lanchester ran the Cave of Harmony, a club where avant-garde plays were put on and the most modern music played and the spirit of Victorian music-hall kept alive, all without solemnity or vulgarity. He was the leading English authority on the music-hall and on much else as well. His reading, and not only that connected with theatre, was both wide and deep, his knowledge of painting very considerable, and he knew

London as few have known it. If his ghost is not clearing its throat quietly in the wings, before stepping on to a ghostly stage, then it is surely to be found in the Reading Room of the British Museum, a muffler about its neck, making notes in his exquisite hand for a book that will never be written.

He gave me hours of his time in that and other museums, so that I learned how to visit them and enjoy them on my own. He and Fanny took me to places of which I had scarcely heard, such as Greenwich and Soanes' House and Hampton Court, where I would almost certainly not have gone alone. When he was acting he found me seats; when not, we frequently went to plays together, the Old Vic perhaps, the best plays seen from the cheapest seats. He did not like spending money, and afterwards we would have a very cheap meal, perhaps kippers and a pot of tea in the Blue Cockatoo by the river just off Oakley Street. And then we would talk, and I learned what the word 'aesthete' really means.

Thus when I got to Berlin, where I was in large measure on my own in a strange city, I had some idea of what I wanted to do and wished to see. I went to the theatre, in the cheapest seats, and to concerts too, but it was the museums and the galleries that I really learned to know.

In Germany the status of modern painting was if anything even more ambiguous than that of contemporary literature. The Nazis were opposed to the whole modern movement, but in 1935 they had not yet got around to banning it altogether. Goebbels' perambulating exhibition of Decadent Art, perhaps the finest collection of modern paintings which had then been assembled, still lay in the future. It was difficult if not impossible for modern artists, particularly Jewish artists, to exhibit, and most of those who could emigrate had already done so, principally to France where they gave the moribund Ecole de Paris an injection of new vigour that kept it alive until the war. The museums on the other hand, or at least the Berlin museums, had not yet been stripped and spoliated, and past directors of these museums, men who had themselves mostly emigrated, had amassed upon their walls the best collections of modern paintings to be seen, at that time, in the world. Not even the works of the Jewish artists had gone, unless these were specifically political in tone, such as the drawings of George Grosz. It was in Berlin that I first encountered Klee and Kandinsky and Lipschitz among others, not to mention the great, and the less great, German Expressionists.

The reason for this hesitancy on the part of the Nazis was not hard to see. As with their Soviet colleagues, contemporary art angered them, since it implied thought beyond their control. What they liked were vulgar pictures of brawny men and simpering maidens or enlarged picture postcards of national beauty-spots and heroic achievements. The Russians rapidly went the whole way and banned everything else altogether. As allegedly internationalist ideologues, the Communists needed to feel no respect for any achievement merely because it was Russian. Stalin was not even a Russian himself. But Hitler, of course, posed as a German nationalist above all else. And modern German art was at least as German as it was modern.

Some was what might be called German-sickly. Franz Marc, for instance, was a Cubist, which was a bad mark against him, and in his use of colours he was also not strictly representational. On the other hand many of his more famous pictures, such as his *Red Deer*, exuded a positively chocolate-box sentimentality, which was very much in his favour. And then he had been killed, at a young age, before Verdun, and thus was something of a German Rupert Brooke. (Their work is not altogether dissimilar.) It was hard for the German authorities to ban this popular war-hero as a decadent.

This was true in another way of the Expressionists, Corinth, Beckmann, Schmidt-Rotluff and the rest. They too were intensely German, though with them sentimentality had been turned inside out, as so frequently happens and not only in Germany, to become savagery, even cruelty, often tinged with a sort of sadistic mockery. If the German writers of the Weimar years had warned their compatriots against Nazism, the best German painters of that period foreshadowed the times to come in another fashion. Looking

149

inwards in order to find what they had to express, they had uncovered aspects of human nature which had hitherto been seldom acceptable on canvas. They, far more than Hitler's favourites or the caricaturists who hated him, were the real painters of Nazism. They seldom became Nazis, and indeed they usually emigrated, and as a group they certainly had no wish to help the Brownshirts to power. But that such artistic brutality was acceptable to the most educated German public in the 1920s is surely not unconnected with the fact that this same public was also and in large measure ready to accept its political equivalent. Nor is it without significance that those artists, and this type of painting, remained almost unknown outside Germany until they, and their successors such as Francis Bacon, began to enjoy great esteem and popularity, in England and elsewhere, in the 1950s.

It must not be imagined that I spent all my time in the art galleries before these often fine, if frightening, pictures. I visited all the other museums, too. (The hours thus spent were marred by one silly misfortune. In order to save me shoe-leather my mother had taken the advice of Geraldine's friend and had had my shoes toed and heeled with strips of iron. The clatter that I made upon the stone floors as I walked about the Pergamon, say, caused others to turn their heads, and me acute embarrassment. Going on tiptoe was no solution. This same person had recommended that my only suit, apart from my old blue school one, be purchased from a firm of multiple tailors who sold suits for £2 10 0. It was made of thin grey flannel, and fitted me excellently for a few days until I was caught in a shower without a raincoat. It immediately shrank, as rapidly and as drastically as Alice in Wonderland. Henceforth I could scarcely button the jacket, while the trousers were so tight as to be positively indecent and I moved in constant terror of the fly-buttons popping off, which they sometimes did.) But if I learned something of the great pictures and sculpture of the more distant past, it was the German Expressionists that affected me most.

The reasons for this were two-fold. Subjectively, I felt that I had 'discovered' these painters. Nobody I knew in

England had ever mentioned them to me, or had perhaps even heard of them. For my English friends, modern art existed in Paris, principally in the period before 1914, and had been chronicled and explained by Clive Bell and Roger Fry. With the exception of Surrealism, which was then little known in England, what was new since the First World War was essentially only a prolongation of what had been new before it. Picasso and Matisse, Derain and Chagall were considered outrageous by some, utterly up-to-date by others. That they and their school were, in general, far better painters than the Germans I did not deny then and certainly would maintain now. But painting is no more a competition in excellence than is poetry. The men of the Ecole de Paris painted for an older generation than mine, the pre- and post-First World War generation. I sensed, and I think correctly, that those Germans painted, as no one else did, for my own pre-Second World War generation, and therefore I was not only subjectively excited because I felt that I had discovered them for myself—as I might have found a merlin's nest with four eggs, three years earlier, in Devonshire—but also objectively thrilled because here was a sort of painting that addressed itself directly to me, without the assistance of intermediaries. It was this experience which made me now decide not to become a *New Verse* poet, as I had intended, but a painter.

For in Berlin I was slowly becoming aware of the reality behind the words: 'War is coming'. Not that any of my German friends spoke of a future war as anything other than a horrible impossibility. Still, the daemonic was in the air. I heard Hitler speak from a balcony, welcoming the Anglo-German Naval Treaty. His speech was filled with friendship for Britain, of course, but the hysteria of the crowd's applause frightened me: it frightened me all the more when I could not myself resist those massive emotions, and with a sort of disgust I heard myself cheering with the rest. I saw soldiers march down the Unter den Linden, in some memorial parade, for Tannenberg perhaps, and I knew that these were not at all the toy soldiers I had seen outside Buckingham Palace nor the type of march that I had witnessed when

George V and Queen Mary celebrated their Silver Jubilee. The goose-step sounds silly in English, but that crashing down of boots in unison, boots more solidly shod with iron than were my own, is meant to inspire martial fear, and it does. Göring's Air Ministry, which was then a-building, was the architectural equivalent, an insolent assertion of power in grey stone. Even the German workers in their blue dungarees and black peaked caps, with their beefy red faces and rough gestures, did not at all recall the English proletariat. I was supposed to be on their side, but they looked dangerous to me, dangerous and hostile.

And finally I was seeing something of Berlin life beyond the safe walls of the Schackwitz flat.

Gunther and Herbert had introduced me to a few of their friends. One of these was Jewish, but looked like a recruiting poster for the SS, tall, with reddish-blond hair and a profile that was two hundred per cent Teutonic. This was a joke, but not a good joke. Another was called Peter. He was a photographer, and also Jewish, and looked it, and that was no joke at all. However, he told me that he had a Hungarian passport, his life-line. We became friends. When I met him and his girl, we avoided the obvious cafés. Even in the ones we frequented, he preferred to sit with his back to the street, or to the room. She was a pretty girl and belonged to the quarter-world of the photographer's nude studies and the chorus line of the cheap revue, which is only one remove above the prostitution line. She in turn introduced me to a friend of hers who lived the same life as herself, and whom I shall call Mitzi.

Mitzi was a pretty girl, whom I thought a ravishing beauty. It would not be correct to say that she was my mistress, though it amused her to go to bed with me once or twice, for which I was immensely grateful. She taught me what to do—I was so innocent that on the first occasion I had only the very vaguest idea: it would have been awful had she laughed at me, but this she did not do—and she tried to teach me how to make love properly, though I fear that I was too young and altogether too ardent to profit as greatly from her instruction as I should. And we talked.

She told me about Peter's girl. Did I know that she was half-Jewish too? No, I had no idea. Well, she was. And she slept with this Nazi swine, a beastly man, a big-shot, quite old and perverted like most of them. He made Peter's girl do disgusting things. What sort of things? I asked. She looked at me for a long moment, then shook her head. No, she would not tell me. But Peter's girl was often hysterical after she had been with the Nazi swine. Then why, I asked, did she go with him? For Peter's sake, of course. If she refused, the Nazi would have Peter's work-permit revoked, and even have him expelled from Germany or worse. And for her own sake, too. Because of her being half-Jewish. It was re-insurance. Did I not understand? I was beginning to understand. Though I never met him, I knew that I had seen the prototype of that Nazi's face, and his expression when he looked at Peter's girl, painted and hanging on the walls of the elegant gallery in the Unter den Linden.

One night I was in Mitzi's bed-sitting-room on the Aschaffenburgerstrasse. Peter's girl had a room on the same floor. She knocked, and came in, and saw the little meal, black bread and sausage and beer, that Mitzi had prepared. She took a piece, distractedly, and said as she ate:

'I must go out tonight.'

Mitzi asked:

'Him?'

Peter's girl made a face and nodded. She soon left us, after taking another piece of bread and sausage.

Later Mitzi suddenly whispered:

'Listen!'

For a moment I could hear nothing. Then the sound of singing came rapidly closer. So they were in a truck. I had seen those truckloads of Brownshirts driving down the street, always singing. I knew that they were less frequent now than they had been before the murder of their boss, Ernst Röhm, in the previous summer, less frequent and on the whole less dangerous. But one never knew.

'Hold me,' said Mitzi, 'hold me tight!'

I put my arms around her thin body, and she gripped me so that her fingers dug into my flesh. As those hoarse voices grew nearer and louder, I wondered what earthly protection she could hope to get from me: I was proud that she should seek it and I wished that I could do more. Then the hoarse chorus was immediately beneath the window. As it faded away, her grip loosened. She shivered, though her room was warm despite the autumn winds in the streets.

'When are you going to Munich?' she asked, in tones of deliberate calm. The singing men were out of earshot.

'Next week,' I said. I was going to Munich to study painting. The arrangements had all been made, a room with a lady who 'took in' foreign students, an art school that was cheap and near-by. Munich was said to be the artistic capital of Germany. My mother had given her approval. She had sent me a bit extra, to cover the expenses of the move. I even knew which train I was catching.

'I shall miss you, Conny,' she said.

It was over twenty years before I saw Berlin again.

IO

I HAD LEARNED much in Berlin. Above all, it was there that I had first tasted something like adult freedom, nor is it quite as paradoxical as might first appear that I should have done this in the capital of Nazi Germany. For there I not only found a quite adequate freedom from physical restraint (which I could equally have enjoyed in London) but also from intellectual and moral pressures. Nobody in Berlin tried to turn me into a model North German, let alone into a Nazi, nobody tried to 'mould' my views and certainly not my character. My physical needs were cared for by Frau Schackwitz and her family and so, in some measure, were my intellectual and social ones too. For the rest I was free to follow, and develop, my own interests, to use my own five senses. As Dr Schackwitz knew, the climate of Berlin is bracing.

The climate of Munich is not. It turns to fog in the winter and to a depressing damp heat in the summer. It even catches from time to time the tail-end of the pernicious Mediterranean south wind which they call *scirocco* in Italy and *Föhn* in Austria and *mistral* in southern France, a wind that simultaneously stultifies the brain and exacerbates the nerves.

The intellectual climate in Munich, when I was there, was not at all refreshing. If Berlin was the national capital, Munich was the acknowledged capital city of the Nazi movement, *die Hauptstadt der Bewegung*, where the Party had its Brown House and Hitler his home. In Berlin Nazis in uniform were scarcely more in evidence than soldiers in London. In Munich they seemed to be everywhere, SS men rattling collecting boxes at street corners, SA men marching about and singing or seated in large clumps in beer-halls, banging their tankards upon oaken tables. This was their city, and they knew it, and they made sure that everybody else remembered it too.

I have never understood the apparent affection of the British for Munich and the Bavarians. True, the beer is very good, though the food is not. The rococo architecture, too, is exquisite, though in Munich this is scarcely in evidence: what there is of it is swamped by the heavy mock-Florentine of the huge nineteenth-century streets laid out by Ludwig I, a typically futile Wittelsbach megalomaniac, or lost in the drearily quaint and narrow, mediaeval lanes around the Cathedral and the Town Hall. The music, and its Bavarian setting were also most lovely and to hear Mozart's operas sung in the little Residenz Theater, all blue and silver, was indeed a delight. On the other hand the Bavarians' own taste was for coarser and for gamier fare, for Bizet and Puccini and above all for their own beloved Wagner.

But it is when the English talk about the charm of the Bavarian character that it seems to me time, as the Persians say, to put one's trust in God. Perhaps it is because the thick

and glutinous accent, punctuated by a recurrent '*Jo! Jo!*'
is almost incomprehensible even to other Germans that
the foreigners claim to be enchanted by a humour as pawky
as it is cruel. Perhaps they do not know that these remarkably ugly people—often beer-swollen into a waddling
deformity or twisting like gargoyles—not only provided the
backbone of the Nazi movement but along with the Austrians
were the keenest recruits to volunteer for its foulest organisations, to guard the concentration camps and exterminate
the Jews, the Poles, the Russians. Even in the First World
War the Bavarians had won a reputation for brutality:
in the civil wars and the uprisings that followed, more blood
was shed, and shed more deliberately, in Munich than elsewhere, so that its pavements were well prepared seed-beds
for Hitler's sowing: and in the Second World War they
really excelled themselves. In 1935 and 1936 the atmosphere
was heavy with Nazism. The most notorious concentration
camp of the period, Dachau, was only a few miles away and
everybody knew of its existence and, more or less, what went
on there; the jolly, beer-swilling Bavarians shrugged their
shoulders and said: '*Jo! Jo!*'

I spent most of the late autumn and early winter of 1935–
1936 in Munich, and was back there again for several
months in the summer and autumn of the latter year. As
will be seen from what I have already written, I did not enjoy
the place, the first visit less than the second. For this Munich
was not entirely to blame.

I had gone there in order to learn how to paint and in the
search for a greater measure of adult freedom than I could
enjoy in the Schackwitz household. I had read about the
artistic life, *la vie de Bohème* in garret and studio. I knew that
the 'artists' quarter' in Munich, called Schwabing, had
enjoyed a certain fame and even notoriety. I imagined a gay
and carefree existence among young people as interested in
the arts as was I, with many a Trilby thrown in, poverty a
lark, hard work a pleasure, funny clothes a defiance, and
love a perpetual delight, maybe with ballerinas, too. I was,
after all, only sixteen.

If what I was really looking for were more and better

Mitzis, such ingratitude was rapidly punished. In Munich there were no Mitzis at all, or at least none that came my way, no, not a single one. Nor were my attempts, and steady failure, to draw the fat and rather elderly nude model at the art school any compensation.

The art school, indeed, was a grave disappointment. It was presided over by a stout little turkey-cock of a man, a keen Nazi who sometimes appeared in his Brownshirt's uniform and boots. (Once when the elderly model failed to turn up, he made us draw from a bronze bust of Adolf Hitler.) I dreaded his rounds of his students. He would seize my india rubber, angrily erase most of my wobbly and inaccurate lines, grab my stick of charcoal from my hand, draw in a few rapid lines of his own, usually breaking my charcoal several times while so doing, and all the while shouting instructions at me in a thick and rapid Bavarian. Then he would stand, feet apart, arms akimbo and chin thrust forward like Mussolini, and bark out: '*Verstanden?*'

Though I had understood very little I would nod and miserably return to my ruined drawing. As the weeks went by it became more inescapably apparent to me not only that I could not draw here and now, but that I would never learn how to draw later on, presumably, anywhere else. It was a depressing realisation, but I struggled on for a couple of months before I finally abandoned my ambition to become the greatest painter of the twentieth century.

As for my fellow-students, they were far from what I had imagined. Thin and pallid young men, patently terrified of their teacher, they seemed most unlikely to live the *Künstlerleben*, even in the unattractively named district of Schwabing. They were all anxious to obtain a diploma, which would enable them to get jobs as commercial artists. To begin with I tried to engage them in conversation when we left the art school, and occasionally, after some hesitation, one or two of them would accept my suggestion that we drink a coffee or a beer together. Their conversation, however, was limited, principally to the subject of the wretched diploma, the absolute need of obtaining it and the immense difficulty in so doing. It was said to be easier to get one if one were a member of the Nazi Party, but joining the Party was itself a most difficult undertaking, involving physical examinations and the production of proofs of Aryan blood stretching back generations. Yet if they failed to obtain the diploma. . . .

As for the people with whom I lived, they were scarcely better company. The Countess alleged that she took foreign students into her family, but she had no family. In fact she ran a small boarding house, where she economised both on food and on heat. We only saw her at meals. Like Louis Philippe she made a point of carving meat in slices so thin as to be well-nigh transparent, all the while engaging upon a stream of platitudinous small talk ('No politics please!' she would say with a smile, waggling her finger) designed no doubt to make us forget our hunger.

The other boarders consisted of two American Rhodes Scholars and a rather pretty English girl. Here I hoped for better things, but was soon disappointed. The English girl took one look at me and never bothered to look again. As for the Rhodes Scholars, who are chosen, I believe, as much for moral worth as for intellectual ability and athletic prowess, when one of them was not escorting the English girl skating or dancing, the other was. And the one who remained at home then proved his moral worth by sticking his pipe between his teeth and really getting down to his studies. I was thus left strictly alone, and began to get very lonely. After a little while I moved out of this boarding house and into the students' hostel where I was lonelier still, but at least I could buy my own meals and thus get enough to eat. I was also spared the Countess's forefinger, and could read while eating.

I began by visiting the Munich museums, as I had those of Berlin, yet it was not the same. There was then very little modern painting to be seen in Munich, though I remember some French post-impressionists in the Deutsches Museum, and particularly one picture by Matisse, which I frequently went to see. (I do not know why they were there. It was really a technological museum and contained a coal mine, among other ponderous exhibits. Perhaps the pictures had been overlooked.) The collection of Old Masters in the Pinakothek was magnificent, but I fear I wearied of them. Perhaps I was becoming satiated with looking at paintings, or maybe it was the effect of the art school. The first halls that one passed through in the old Pinakothek were hung with vast canvases by Rubens, depicting huge fleshy nudes, godesses and whatnot, twisting their great red limbs in the sky. I began by disliking these and quite quickly developed a positive loathing for them. I walked through those halls with clenched teeth and my eyes on the ground. I still do not care for Rubens's lush, plain, fat ladies (or for Cézanne's either, come to that). Perhaps they reminded me gloomily of the model in the art school whom I could not draw.

I went to the opera a great deal, more than I have ever been able to do since. Students were then allowed to buy, for one mark, any seat unsold five minutes before the curtain rose. I queued up almost every night, and the unsold seats were usually the best in the house. The royal box, for instance, was almost always empty. It was thus that I met Adolf Hitler.

I and a dozen other students, all unknown faces to me, had taken our seats in the royal box when two gigantic SS men appeared and ordered us out, and fast. The Führer was coming. In the drawing-room behind the box we met him and his party coming in. The SS men ordered us to stand aside, but he stopped and shook us each by the hand, and spoke to us in turn. When he came to me he asked me my nationality. I told him. He congratulated me on my German and enquired what I was studying. I told him this too. He was delighted that a foreign boy should have come to Munich to study art. An artist's life, he said, is best. Then he moved on. His voice when talking to me had been gruff but not unmelodious. His blue eyes looked straight into mine, but I did not feel the hypnotic power of which others have written. Rather did he put me surprisingly at my ease, but in view of the circumstances this in itself may have been evidence of hypnosis. Then he apologised to us collectively for disturbing us, and said that there would be seats for us in the stalls. And after this display of charm and good humour he moved on, followed by his entourage, into his box. I saw him once again, a few weeks later, in private as it were, when he entered the Carlton tea-rooms and sat at a table near to mine. I hoped he might recognise me, but of course he did not.

I had one other encounter in Munich which I have recorded at greater length elsewhere but which is worth repeating here. It happened in a steamy little corner bar near the students' hostel. I had stopped in there for a glass of beer on my way to bed, perhaps after another visit to the opera.

There was an SS officer there, who had been drinking and who engaged me in conversation. He had, it seemed, recently returned from Russia. I asked him about that country, expecting the usual abuse that I read in the Nazi press. But not a bit of it: he had nothing but praise for the Soviet Union and for the Communist system. The Germans, he said, were political amateurs by comparison, efficient in other ways it is true, but politically incurable sentimentalists. He said that he regretted, really, that Germany had gone Nazi and not Communist in 1932.

I was flabbergasted. This seemed to me the height of treason and, coming from an SS officer, almost incredible. What about ideology, I asked, what about the Bolshevik peril? He gave a tolerant laugh. That was all child's play, all propaganda-nonsense. Ideology was a lot of hot air. Did I imagine that Russia was any more of a socialist state than Germany was a national socialist one? No, what counted, and all that counted, was power. If Germany had gone Communist in 1932, by now, thanks to superior German efficiency and technological skills, the Germans would be running the most powerful consortium of states in the world, and the globe would be theirs for the taking. *That* was what mattered, power and only power. And then he got up, paid for his drinks and mine, and left.

Who he was I do not know, nor why he talked to me in this fashion. As a foreign boy, I obviously could not hurt him and he may have felt an uncontrollable lust to express these ideas to someone. Or maybe such ideas were commonplace in certain SS circles. In any event this conversation was an eye-opener to me. It was a long time before I understood all its implications, but it gave me an inkling that power cannot be brushed aside, as the pacifists would do, and that it is not often to be strait-jacketed by moral principles, as the left-wing progressives like to believe. Furthermore, the whole neat spectrum of Left and Right on which I had relied as if it were a law of nature was henceforth open to question. I did not immediately abandon my belief that the Communists were our friends, and I have never ceased to believe that the Nazis were our enemies, but somehow, and from then on, I suspected more and more that the political realities were considerably more complicated than the version of them I had hitherto accepted devoutly from the pages of the *New Statesman and Nation*. That great movement of thought which calls itself liberalism was born of French eighteenth-century sceptism. To be sceptical about its credo in this century has been to arouse its intense hostility. I first began to doubt the infallibility of the intellectual Establishment and of its popes as the result of a conversation in a steamy Munich bar thirty years ago. Little has happened since that has not increased my scepticism. Yet when arguing with progressives one is dealing with faith and not with reason. For them it is not a revelation, it is mere *lèse-majesté*, to suggest that Pandit Nehru or Bertrand Russell or the Bishop of Woolwich have really got no clothes on at all.

The introduction here of these Grand Old Men of what 'the Left' like to call 'the Left' is not done solely that I may find a chance to be rude about them. Some years ago, in a novel, I constructed a composite caricature of the left-wing father-figure and this caused a great deal of ill-feeling. Because my progressivists' Pétain was a political ninny and as old as Bertrand Russell I was accused of having insulted that distinguished philosopher, and was looked at askance by several of his well-known disciples, when I certainly had no such intention. Indeed they are extremely touchy about their old men, far more so than conservative intellectuals appear to be about theirs. But then conservatives have seldom claimed absolute moral superiority for themselves or unique political wisdom for their chosen leaders.

Why the progressives' syndrome, in England at least and to a lesser extent in America, should include this lust for intellectual and moral authority I do not know, though I suspect that it is not unconnected with their customary rejection of God and of ethics, just as their professed anti-militarism finds expression in a most martial and unsuitable vocabulary. (They are for ever marching into the future and conquering unemployment and building defences against inflation and so on and so forth.) With religion gone, surro-gates, usually even more unsuitable than this staff officer's jargon, are found for God the Father, eagerly embraced and even worshipped. True, their pseudo-divinities seldom last for long. It does not take many years for even the most devout and dim-witted progressive to realise that the wise-cracks of a Bernard Shaw or the pleas of birth-control by a Marie Stopes are not quite in the same category as the Ser-mon on the Mount. On the other hand there are always new *gurus* available, eager to accept the mantle. Indeed one can see them queueing up for it, at quite an early age. I, and some of my friends, have started a book, not this sort but a bookmaker's book, and are prepared to offer odds whether Norman Mailer, John Osborne, Wayland Young, Brigid Brophy, Ken Tynan or any one of a dozen other starters will be 'the wisest man in the world' when the progressives, shoulder to shoulder, bayonets fixed and watches synchronised, march into space and the Third Millennium.

Whatever their reasons for having father-figures may be, I know that the mere existence of these usually very grey eminences has always repelled me. My limited knowledge of the Freudian discipline tells me that within its closed system of thought everybody suffers from, or perhaps enjoys, an Oedipus complex. If this be true, then I can only assume that in my case the absence of a father or even of an accept-able father-figure during my youth turned my anti-paternal-istic feelings elsewhere, first against the authority of my schoolmasters—which led me into the rebels' camp—and then against the intellectual authoritarianism that so often flourishes among rebels, missionaries and the like. Certainly I developed, quite quickly, a sixth sense for detecting those who were determined to order me, and by extension anybody else about. So far as I have any coherent attitude to politics, it is this: how people choose to exchange their goods and services seems to me a fit subject for debate and for recurrent decision on the part of the people; but a system that in the name of any abstraction, racial, religious, economic or social, murders its conquered enemies or really ruins them financially or locks them away in camps, for any reason whatsoever, ought to be destroyed as quickly and as painlessly as possible; and, finally, that in the comparatively happy society in which I have had the good fortune to live for the last half-century, the idolaters of abstractions are the enemy. Respect is not only no alternative to love, it can breed its very antithesis. Intellectual bullies, no matter what the causes they may claim to represent, can at any time become the half-forgotten trumpeters for bullies of an even nastier sort, and those who respect them may be succeeded by other men, obediently patrolling the concentration camp wire. Such an attitude as mine towards politics may be the result of an Oedipus complex that lacked a physical object, but it may also be defined as a hatred of tyranny and a love of freedom. Disrespect by no means rules out love or even admiration, both in public and in private: what it does rule out are attitudes that are usually best dispensed with in man's relationship with man and his pretensions.

Before leaving this subject of freedom, and returning to my own story of which it is also part, I would tell one anecdote. I heard it from Don Salvador de Madariaga, that great Spaniard and a great liberal in the true sense of the word.

After the American conquest of the Philippines, the troops and administration of the occupying power were rough with the Spanish inhabitants. At a Spanish school the younger children were asked by their teacher to write an essay: subject 'The Cow'. One little boy wrote:

'The cow is a large, square animal with four legs, one at each corner. It produces the milk we drink. But give me liberty or give me death.'

One of the very few masters at Wellington for whom I had felt friendship was George Browne, 'Bouncy Browne' as we called him with schoolboy wit because of his springy step. Indeed of all those six hundred and some boys and several score masters, he is the only one who has remained a friend. This may be explained not only in terms of his amiable, resilient and even bouncy character and our shared interests but also because of the fact that he did not teach me in class—he taught me a great deal out of class—and was thus never set in authority above me. He never really belonged to 'them'. Only a few years older than myself, he would give me coffee in his rooms out of green cups and discuss books and come for walks with me and generally treat me more or less as an equal. I appreciated this and was anxious to follow his guidance during a time when I was most loth to accept instruction or obey orders.

He had told me that it was my rebelliousness against authority which first aroused his interest and he certainly never tried to crush this. Indeed he himself was something of a rebel—he is an Australian—and soon gave up the profession of schoolmaster with the conformism that it usually entails. His nonconformity differed from my own. His dated from the 'twenties and inclined towards the flamboyant aestheticism of the period. In those distant days he had chosen green as his symbol, and he wore green shirts, green ties, green socks. His was not the green of *The Green Hat* but rather of *The Green Carnation*. However the faint scent of 'nineties decadence with which he doubtless wished to surround his personality in his Cambridge days was effectively blown away by the brisk and breezy trade winds of his Australian childhood.

When I went to Berlin he wrote to me, in dark green ink on pale green paper, long and interesting letters to which I looked forward and replied at length. Now he turned up in Munich, for Christmas, and gave me good meals in restaurants I could not myself afford and we went sight-seeing together. (South German rococo was then all the rage among the aesthetes, in some measure because of Sacheverell Sitwell's book, and I remember most vividly a trip to Nymphenburg early on Boxing Day morning. The snow lay deep. The paths to the Amalienburg and the other gazebos had been rolled smooth and there were no footprints. We had the place to ourselves, beneath a bright sun shining out of a cloudless blue sky.)

He found me in a somewhat disconsolate mood, and it was he who suggested that I go to Oxford. No doubt he sensed that I had been alone long enough and also that I needed some goal for which to aim now that I had realised I could not learn to paint. I was a bit young to live the life of a remittance man, or rather of a remittance boy. He assured me that my reading had told me the truth, that Oxford was not at all like school, and that I should enjoy the life. So I wrote to my mother, who agreed I go there, but with the proviso that I must win a scholarship: since she had to support my three sisters as well as myself, she could not afford to send me to Oxford as a commoner. Early in January I went to Jersey to discuss it with her.

I travelled by way of London, where my and George's plan met formidable opposition on the part of my sister Geraldine, now ensconced in damp domesticity beside the Thames. She herself had profited nothing from Oxford: since this could not conceivably be her fault, it must be that of the university: therefore it would be a great mistake for me, or indeed for anybody else, to go there. She advocated instead that I be trained as a chartered accountant. Why she should have chosen this rather grey profession, I do not know. Perhaps its very greyness appealed to her. (On this same principle the father of a friend of mine, when slicing the loaf of bread at mealtimes, invariably inquired of his son: 'Crust or crumb?' and gave him the portion he had not chosen.)

She might have got her way, too, had my mother not made a new friend in Jersey. This was Dr R. R. Marett, the anthropologist and Rector of Exeter College, Oxford. Old

Dr Marett liked unorthodox young people and he approved of my plan, perhaps because that, too, was unorthodox. He did more than merely approve. It was, he said, extremely difficult to win an Oxford scholarship without the benefit of the specialised tuition provided at English schools. He would help me overcome this barrier, which he disliked as he disliked standardisation in general. He would arrange that his secretary give me a little instruction, by post, in how to answer the sort of questions that I would face when I sat for my exams. He suggested that I put down Christ Church as my first choice of college, his own as my second. He said that if I worked very hard, a year's study might be enough. Modern languages was the obvious choice, and before I left Jersey in early February of 1936 it was agreed that I should sit for an open scholarship in December of that year.

I went first to Paris, where a lodging had been found for me by Bertram's French partner with a certain Monsieur Perseil. He was an *agrégé* of the University, and lived with his wife and daughter (who had a black moustache and gave singing lessons which drove me out of the flat) behind the Montparnasse cemetery. He gave me lessons and arranged that I attend lectures at the Sorbonne. When he was not otherwise engaged he listened to the French radio, noted the precise hour and minute of every mispronunciation and false liaison, and wrote a letter enumerating these, each evening, to the Minister responsible for French broadcasting. What with this and the singing lessons he was, not un-naturally, in a permanent foul temper.

The summer term I spent at Angers in the Ecole des Hautes Etudes, a clerical establishment connected with the Catholic university there. Most of the other inmates were studying for the priesthood and we were looked after by motherly old nuns, who gave us ample and delicious food and saw to it that our clothes were spotless and well pressed. There I wrote essays which were corrected by the Dean, a most charming and highly cultured elderly canon with a real love of the French language. I remember hearing him deplore that Voltaire's prose style had not been employed in a better cause. There was a fine library, containing almost all of French literature in leather bindings. Its main door opened on to a small garden filled, when first I saw it, with lilacs in blossom. At the University I refurbished my Latin, which I would need for the exam, and hearing it in French, as it were, realised for the first time that people had actually spoken that strange language. I also attended courses in French literature and history. By the time I returned to Munich in the late summer I was once again more or less bilingual in French. I had read an immense amount of French literature and had acquired a passion for Racine. I was also determined that one day I should write novels as good as those of Flaubert, or maybe Stendhal, or perhaps Balzac.

Munich was much better, now that I was fully occupied. The family with whom I lived were delightful people. The mother, widow of a musicologist, was a painter of talent who had lived in Paris. Frau Beer-Walbrunn came from Lübeck, where she had been a childhood friend of Thomas Mann's. Indeed she told me that she was the original of the girl in *Tonio Kröger*. She really loathed Nazism, as did her son and daughter. I agreed with them.

Here again I attended lectures at the University, and studied with a charming, white-bearded, velvet-jacketed old professor named Fritz Endell. Professor Endell knew more about archaic Greek bronze mirrors than anyone else in Munich and corresponded on the subject with Edmund Blunden. It may have been Dr Marett who sent me to him, for Professor Endell's brother was also an anthropologist whose life work, a study of the Australian aborigine, was about to be published. Indeed it appeared while I was there, and I well recall my Professor's dismay:

'Forty years my brother devotes to these people, and they are disgusting, their habits quite unspeakable. . . . Forty years! How could my poor brother have borne it?'

He advised me simply to learn as much as I possibly could about Goethe, and to go on reading the Romantic poets for pleasure. At first I was slightly repelled by the Olympian, but I realised soon enough that the sensual man was not at all the same as the blind marble bust. I became absorbed in his personality and therefore in his works. By the time I sat for my scholarship examination I knew much more about Goethe than do most English boys of seventeen.

The French papers I found easy. The German ones contained enough questions about Goethe, together with one good one about the Romantic poets and another concerning Thomas Mann. The German viva voce was again mostly Goethe, while the French one gave me an opportunity to talk at some length about Rimbaud, a great hero of mine in those days. Early in 1937 I heard to my delight that I had been awarded an open scholarship in Modern Languages to Exeter College, Oxford. For the first time in my life I felt the sweet, tired satisfaction of achievement. I fear I also hoped unworthily that this small personal triumph would cause at least a moment's annoyance to the authorities at Wellington College when they read my name, and not those of their candidates, in *The Times*. I was to go up to Oxford in the following October.

During that year when I was reading so intensively for my Oxford examination I had little time for anything else: little time but very considerable inclination. To use the jargon of the period I was, quite bluntly, sex-starved, and a very nasty form of starvation it is. During the thirty years that have since passed there have been periods of weeks or even of months when I have not made love to a woman. Sometimes the cause has been irresistible external circumstances, as once or twice during the war when there were simply no women to be had. Unpleasant though such enforced chastity was, at least I could look forward to its termination. At others it was voluntary, as when I was absent or even estranged from the woman I loved and did not wish to be unfaithful or feared lest she be therefore unfaithful to me through sympathetic magic. Sickness and certain types of nervous condition can also rule out sex, but usually the desire then goes first.

In 1936 none of these causes or palliatives existed. I was in love with no one, my health was excellent, my body approaching, if it had not already reached, the period of maximum sexual exuberance, and there were girls and women everywhere, in Paris, in Munich, even in Angers when I walked out through the heavy oaken front gate of the Ecole des Hautes Etudes. The trouble was that I knew none of them. Nor did my work, my reading, really serve to distract me. French, and to a lesser extent German, literature is, among other things, a great harem of delicious and desirable girls, not only desired but also usually obtained, seduced, tumbled and ravished. The bed is seldom far out of sight and is often squarely in the centre of the canvas. I read about love as seen and known by the greatest and most evocative poets and playwrights and novelists during three centuries when passion was almost always carnal and love's 'right, true end' was rarely in doubt. But their girls were even more untouchable than the beauties I saw in the Boulevard du Montparnasse, a smile upon their lips and their skirts blown by the March wind.

With Faust I lusted after Gretchen. I shared all of Frédéric's feverish impatience when Sophie Arnous kept him waiting, alone, in the little flat he had furnished so exquisitely for her seduction. My edition of *Candide* was illustrated: Cunégonde was plump, naked and eager upon her huge four-poster bed, and the caption read: '*Un jeune cordelier me séduit aisément.*' How I envied that *cordelier*! And as for reading *Les Liaisons Dangereuses* beneath the lilacs of Angers, well, there are limits. . . . When I hear of Anglican clergymen and English educationalists who maintain under oath that the reading of books cannot corrupt the innocent, I must assume that those progressive worthies are either very cold fish indeed or else have been remarkably selective in their choice of books. On the other hand such weird affirmation may be merely a contemporary variant of their long established fondness for hypocrisy. Tartuffe in his *chaste robe noire* could, and doubtless would, read through the whole spring list of the Olympia Press without the tremor of a visible muscle. Perhaps I could do as much myself, nowadays. but not in 1936.

Nor were my desires held in check by the fear which

comes of ignorance. As I have said earlier, women as such have never seemed particularly mysterious creatures to me. And thanks to Mitzi even the ultimate mystery had been partly revealed. I knew with a fair degree of precision what it was that I longed for. I also knew what I did not want. Masturbation, occasionally inevitable, seemed to me then, as it has done ever since, a most unsatisfactory business, producing depression, even disgust, and a gloomy sense of pointless hangover. It was no answer. Munich was not only the capital of the Nazi movement but also, in those days, of German buggery. My attitude towards homosexuality had suffered a metamorphosis since school days. At Wellington it had seemed yet another form of rebellion against authority. Here in Munich it became, for me, identified not only with my memories of that disagreeable school but also with the disagreeable realities around me. So this was not the answer either.

Whores might have provided the solution to my quandary, and I certainly eyed the flopsy-bunnies of Montparnasse and their less attractive sisters who lurked like alley-cats in some of the darker Munich lanes. However, two considerations held me back. One was the fear of venereal disease, a very real fear in those days before sulpha drugs and antibiotics. I had been told that if one caught syphilis one's nose fell off. A certain famous Hungarian Dadaist was to be seen almost every day, noseless, in the Café de Flore, as if to prove this. I had no wish to look like Tristan Tzara. And then there was the almost insuperable obstacle of money. The prettier and healthier-looking the girl, the more expensive she must be. Only a really ugly and rather elderly one would be cheap enough for me, and she would almost certainly be diseased as well. So this, too, was no solution.

I did make the experiment once. It was a hot summer's night in Angers. Inflamed by some eighteenth-century novel—Manon Lescaut was, I believe, to blame for this, as her charms had been to blame for so much else so long ago—I went out into the streets of the town to cool my blood. A girl leaning on her elbows in the embrasure of a ground-floor window spoke to me softly. I stopped. She asked me for a cigarette. With an unsteady hand I lit hers and my own. Would I not care to come inside? She looked, in the dim light, pretty and healthy and young, scarcely older than myself, and her voice was low, husky, sensual. She mentioned a sum of money. It was more than I had. Never mind, she said, I looked a nice boy, she would take that. I recall her body exactly. When first I saw Goya's *Naked Maja* some years later I knew that I had twice made love to that Duchess of Alba. But when I wished to make love yet again she told me that she must get back to work. What work? I asked in my innocence. Only a few moments ago we had been sharing a climax which was no more feigned on her part than it was on mine. Now she became cold, almost sardonic.

'*Mais voyons!*' she said sharply, and began to get dressed. Once more, I asked, once more, I begged. I had thought it was for the night. She became cross and ordered me out. I protested, though affectionately. Angrily she pulled on her dress. She began to swear at me, and I left, more or less satisfied physically but emotionally hurt and penniless as well. Years later when somebody told me, in tones of mockery, that there was not a single prostitute from Cairo to Hamburg to whom some British private soldier had not proposed marriage between 1940 and 1945, his remark did not strike me as odd or even as particularly comical. In my young days I almost always felt affection for the women to whom I had made love. In later years, with more knowledge and less impetuosity, the sequence of emotions has usually been reversed—with disastrous consequences when not. One way or another sex and love have almost always been intertwined in my life. (And when friendship is also present, then for me real happiness is possible.) I am aware that this is not true of all men, and particularly not of many complicated ones. I neither envy nor censure those who can dissociate their lusts from their emotions. I only know that I myself am almost as simple as those British private soldiers in their progress from Egypt to Germany.

Next day I had to tell the old Dean a lie. I had, I said, lost my money. His expression was entirely impassive as he dug out his purse from beneath his soutane and lent me a few francs for pocket money until my next monthly allowance should arrive. I assumed he had guessed. Anxiously I examined my body in the days to come for ominous symptoms concerning the exact nature of which I was much in doubt. My nose at least seemed safe. With perhaps more positive results I examined my emotions. Since then I have only very seldom bedded with a prostitute whom I have had to pay beforehand, and only once with a woman who extorted money afterwards. That, of course, is the really nasty sort of whore, as she is the most successful. They often die quite rich. And quite alone.

1936 was a year of political importance in Europe. In March the Germans re-occupied the Rhineland. War was drawing closer. In July it came, though at first in Spain alone, where the Civil War broke out. 1936 also saw the victory of the Popular Front in the French elections. The 'Popular Front' concept was accepted by most people with leftish views and the slogan 'No enemy on the Left!' was generally agreed. At the same time the great Soviet mock-trials made it apparent to the few who could see that Russia was administered by men and methods far closer to those of the Fascist states than to those which prevailed in the West. The exportation by the Communists of their methods to Republican Spain was soon to undermine the Front Populaire there and, by extension, elsewhere. Among the larger European democracies it was only in England that the Popular Front idea never assumed any political reality: and it was in England that the intellectuals contrived to believe in it, and to trust the Stalinists, long after their true intentions had been unmistakably revealed.

I remember the day the German troops marched into the Rhineland. I used to leave the Perseil household for an hour or two each morning, when the singing lessons reached their discordant crescendo, and would walk to the Café du Dôme where I read a book or a magazine after glancing through a left-wing newspaper, seated in the sun. I sometimes wrote there, too, for I had heard that such was the habit of some French writers. I liked to feel that I was surrounded by painters and writers, even if I neither knew nor recognised them, for I hoped that the atmosphere would somehow help me in my own attempts to express what I wished on paper.

On that sunny March morning the atmosphere was not artistic. Rumours flew: France was mobilising: an ultimatum had been sent to Hitler: within a matter of days we should be at war. I drank my coffee—a glass of white coffee, a *croissant* and a Balto cigarette were what I and my budget allowed me each morning—and listened and wondered. There were knots of people talking at the street corner and grabbing the latest editions from the hurrying newsboys. What would the English do? Somebody even asked this question of me, but before I could give a considered reply somebody else said that England would betray France—as usual.

The air was filled with perturbation rather than excitement. My own feelings were inevitably mixed. I disliked Hitler and the Nazis, and I thought the French ought to slap them down. On the other hand I had no wish to fight the Germans. I wished to go on with my reading, and maybe get to Oxford. War was coming but, I hoped, not just yet.

Within a couple of days all was back to normal. A German Communist refugees' magazine which I then read informed me that the last chance of stopping Hitler without a war had been lost. I wondered if this were true. I was beginning to feel sceptical about the Communists' pronouncements and to find distasteful the authoritarian tone in which these were delivered. On the walls of Paris a Communist electoral poster portrayed Hitler with a dagger between his teeth and blood dripping from his fangs: CONTRE ÇA VOTEZ COM-MUNISTE. I was sceptical about this, too. It seemed to me an extremely uncomfortable, and even improbable, way of toting a dagger. I gave up reading *l'Humanité* in favour of the Socialists' *Le Populaire* or even the Radicals' *l'Oeuvre*. The tone of the Communists' daily was reminiscent of the newspapers beyond the Rhine. I knew that the Communists had on occasion collaborated with the Nazis before Hitler came to power. I also knew that many thousands of German Communists had later joined the Nazi Party. I remembered what the SS officer had said to me in the Munich bar. And I did not see why I should be deprived of my education and perhaps of my life, just to please them.

I was visiting my mother in Jersey when the Spanish generals' *coup* began their civil war. Mimi was there too, and so was a Spaniard who had come to ask my mother for Mimi's hand in marriage. Francisco was a delightful man. From my reading I had expected Spaniards to be tall, gloomy, haughty and reserved, like Chimène's father in *Le Cid*. Francisco was a fat, small and extremely merry young man. He was also most generous and gave me a silk sash or cummerbund, which had belonged to young Belmonte, the bull-fighter, a close friend and hero of Francisco's. I have this relic still.

On the day the war started in his country Francisco's bright black eyes were sad. Immediately he announced that there would, alas, be no question of his proposing marriage at this time. My sister should consider herself in no way obligated to him, for he must return to Spain immediately, to fight. Later that day, while helping him with his bags, I asked a question which nobody else had thought to put to him. I enquired on which side he intended to fight. He straightened up from his packing and said:

'I have no interest in politics. But I have seven brothers. When I return home I shall learn which side they have chosen, and I shall join them. That is what happens in time of war.'

This was another lesson for me in the realities of politics. Mimi never heard from him again and perhaps he was killed very soon. I therefore do not know whether he died—if he died—fighting for Christianity and the ideals of Spanish chivalry or for Democracy and those liberal values in which I then believed and still believe. But I did learn that it is not absolutely necessary for an honourable and a kind man to accept the ideas which I have accepted. Seven brothers are in some circumstances a far more convincing argument than seven volumes published by the Left Book Club.

Later that year, after spending some months in Munich, I found myself once again in Paris. I there attended a huge meeting in favour of the Spanish Republic at the Vélodrome d'Hiver. Volunteers were being sought for the International Brigades. Although I was to sit for my Oxford exam within a few weeks, I decided that I should be better employed fighting in Spain. I therefore went backstage, as it were, after the meeting and joined a queue of other young men. I was turned down, on the grounds that I was too young, by the three men seated behind a table.

My memory no longer recalls what was my immediate reaction, but I do not believe that it was really one of disappointment. I was becoming wearied—disgusted would be too strong a word—with the strident propaganda of the French and British Left in the matter of Spain, though I agreed with their basic contentions. Their style, and particularly that of the British intellectuals and poets, was to me reminiscent of First World War propaganda. Though my opinions about many matters have changed since those days, I still have a feeling of contempt for people who, in soft safe places themselves, cheer others on to risk their lives, particularly when such voices are housed in the bodies of healthy young males. I felt that I would rather fight in Spain than talk about it, though I am myself the least military or bellicose of men.

When I was turned down my reaction, as I say, was not one of disappointment. It was closer, as the days passed, to relief. I had really no wish to fight in Spain. It was only a sense of what was fitting that had led me to volunteer. That done, a debt was discharged. This debt had been incurred by my acceptance and propagation of the standard ideas then current among people of my sort and my age. Although I did not reject them, I was beginning to be bored by them. I now think that my volunteering for Spain was also a desire to escape from the preoccupations of the 'thirties in England, for I sensed that they bore little relationship to the realities that existed upon the continent of Europe. Since I was not capable at that age, and against that massive pressure of left-wing conviction, of creating a new political philosophy, I was prepared to substitute action for talk. I wished to *think* about other things. And when I was refused the opportunity to act, I was still free to accept gratefully this chance of putting my boyhood politics into the lumber-room of my mind and thinking, as best I could, about what it was that I wished to write and how best I should do so.

Thus by the time I returned to London at the end of 1936 I had, in a way, walked straight through the categorical imperatives of the English left-wing intelligentsia of the day.

As for what I wished to write, during 1936 it was poems, pale imitations of Eliot, of Pound and of others. They are all lost, and literature is none the poorer. Only those inspired by Arthur Rimbaud might, perhaps, now have some slight interest. But I was becoming less interested in words than in the connection between words, less of a poet and more of a prose-writer. *Une Saison en Enfer* gave me the sort of artistic bridge that I needed. I began to write prose-poems, a mule of a form, though I am far from despising the mule. When in Oxford for my examination I met the under-graduate editor of a new magazine to be simultaneously published in Oxford and Cambridge. I showed him, Patrick Terry, two of these prose pieces and he accepted them for *Light and Dark*. This pleased me at least as much as passing my exam. They appeared in the spring of 1937. I had by then decided that I would be a writer until such time as I was killed in the coming war.

I I

GISELLE, AS I shall call her, and I became lovers in the very early spring of 1937. To describe her as my mistress would perhaps be technically correct—we lived together, on and off, for over two years—but would be misleading, implying a relationship far more formalised and even more secretive than was ours. In another sense, she was no more

176

my mistress than was I her master. We were both entirely
free agents and we came and went as we chose. We were, and
have remained, very good friends. If we were also in love, and
I imagine that we were, ours was an easy, frank and sensual
love, quite unconducive to guilt or even to introspection.
Indeed I do not recall discussing our love for one another
with her at all except perhaps in terms of irony—'love' was
not an O.K. word at that time and in our circle—just as we
only ever spoke of marriage with the utmost cynicism: what,
if anything, could be got out of it in material terms? I do
remember discussing possessiveness, which we both regarded
as immoral and bourgeois, and of those two adjectives
bourgeois was far and away the more damning. As for its
normal manifestation, jealousy, we agreed that this is a
shameful and destructive emotion—destructive was another
period word, less pejorative than bourgeois—but we feared
that neither of us could shed it completely. This was a good
subject for conversation, as was 'the equality of the sexes'.
I remember that, to begin with at least, I was rather more
in favour of such equality than was she.

'But men and women are not exactly alike,' she would
say with a puzzled frown.

'In essentials they are,' I would reply and with masculine
superiority I would then explain to her the principles of
egalitarianism.

'I would say they are more like cats and dogs,' would be
her conclusion, though we never quarrelled or fought.

She was a year or so older than myself and had been
knocking about the Soho pubs for about that length of time
when first I met her in London's Bohemia. She was small,
sturdy and slightly shaggy, like a strong, wild little pony off
the moors. She had thick, black, very curly hair, a full figure
and a most sunny disposition. Her eyes were very dark and
filled with laughter, even when she had little or nothing to
laugh about. She was brave and she was gay, and if she had
one very obvious fault it was that she talked too much. She
was in fact a proper chatterbox, completely outspoken and,
to use another fashionable word of the day, entirely unin-
hibited. In my first novel, *The Arabian Bird*, which I wrote

in 1946 (that is to say immediately after my story, as told in this volume of autobiography, ends) I gave some of her qualities to a character whom I called Katherine.

She used to say that she had no idea how her family had managed to produce her. She spoke of that family in terms of fascinated horror, as one might describe some weird collection of freaks glimpsed at the circus long ago in a thunderstorm. Their deformities, she told me, were both physical and mental. Her father was a lowland Scot, a race of men she despised utterly. For many years he had served his King and Country in the nethermost regions of the British Empire.

'For years and years,' she said, 'he made those poor black men dig drains, miles and miles of drains. But they didn't want any drains. And that embittered him.'

He was very small, almost a dwarf, 'about so high' she would say, holding her hand a couple of feet above the floor. Furthermore he seemed to have grown smaller with the years and she speculated whether perhaps those black men had put a curse upon him, like Tutankhamen. So bitter was he that he scarcely ever spoke and he hid himself inside a small cloud of smoke.

'Like a squid,' she explained. And his pipe tobacco gave off a peculiarly foul and repellent smell. 'Nobody knows where he gets it,' she said: 'it just arrives, in huge parcels, from London.'

She believed that he was hiding from her mother whom he also wished to repel by these noxious stinks. Her mother, she said, was enormously fat, a great wobbling jellyfish of a woman who was never fully dressed nor, she devoutly hoped, entirely undressed. She slip-slopped about their rather dirty house in dressing-gown and carpet slippers, her hair always in curlers. Her principal activity was a prolonged and unsuccessful attempt to make her husband eat something, anything, at any time of the day or night. This, however, he steadfastly refused to do, though she cooked half a dozen three-course meals a day with hot and cold snacks to fill the interstices, though the dining-room was never cleared of food, though she and her other daughters—Giselle had two sisters who lived at home—attempted to encourage him by themselves steadily eating their way through all the meals, all the snacks and ten-pound boxes of chocolates as well. According to Giselle, her mother would really have liked to nail her husband's feet to the floor, like a Strasbourg goose, and force her meals down his throat with the handle of a large wooden spoon.

He, in return, treated her with contempt, not answering from within his cloud when spoken to and occasionally ordering her to clean his boots *while actually wearing them*, though he never set foot out of doors. No more did Giselle's mother or sisters (who had names like Myrtle and Ireen) and these younger females were also swelling to strange proportions. The women of her family, she said, were quite white and soft, like things that live under stones. Her diminutive father, on the other hand, was nut-brown in colour, smoke-cured presumably. They lived in a bungalow, on the outskirts of a third-class seaside resort. The bungalow had a name like Dun Roamin, a lowlands Scots touch, and no drawing-room. They passed their entire lives in the dining-room, surrounded by uneaten meals. The walls were decorated with poker-work mottoes, some in incomprehensible lowland Scots spelling, others in English. One read: DON'T WORRY, IT MAY NEVER HAPPEN.

I used to listen, spellbound, to these tales of domestic horror, which I assumed to be creations of the purest fantasy. When, however, I eventually visited Dun Roamin I realised that Giselle had only exaggerated, and no more than was her custom. She was fond of exaggeration, and good at it.

Such was her background. She herself could not understand why she had been given so weird and pretentious a first name: certainly neither of her parents could ever have heard tell of the ballet. In her childhood she had hoped that she was illegitimate, that after one passionate night with a romantic stranger—a foreign nobleman of course, named Rodriguez or Vladimir—her real father had said to her mother:

'And if it is a daughter, name her Giselle!'

As she grew older, and more aware of her mother's

appearance, she had had reluctantly to abandon this explanation.

At school she had played the lead in the school plays. She had persuaded her father—who was, she assured me, immensely rich but almost incredibly mean—that he let her attend a dramatic school. He had insisted on a cheap, rather bad school, which was why she had so far failed to get a job. She had drifted into Soho and a life of modelling and moderate promiscuity. One of her major activities was the extortion of money from Dun Roamin, whose bourgeois inhabitants she regarded as merely fit for looting. On one occasion she had bought a lot of jewellery on her father's account with a large but dingy department store, and immediately pawned it.

'They'd have sent me to gaol for that,' she said, 'if they'd had the guts. But they hadn't.'

I met her in a pub called the Wheatsheaf, where I met so many of my future friends. It had taken me rather less than six weeks to find my way there, once I was living in London.

It had been decided that I must get a job. So, like many another would-be writer before and since, I went to see a well-known scholastic employment agency which purveyed schoolmasters, tutors and other educational hacks. It was one of the few places where an allegedly educated man or boy with no further qualifications whatsoever could hope to find modestly gainful employment.

I was sent for interview with a very High Church clergyman, the father of seven, in an icy country rectory. We did not take to one another. The agency then found me a job in London with a correspondence course.

This was a deliciously corrupt concern. It catered for ambitious labourers anxious to better themselves by passing examinations which would enable them to become minor civil servants in, say, the Customs and Excise Department or to obtain other clerical employment. For this second ambition, a strange language called Commercial Spanish was apparently essential. It all recalled the diploma which had played so large a part in the lives of the Munich art students.

The entire staff consisted of the owner of the course, a thoroughly dishonest-looking old man, his secretary and myself. The old man dealt with advertising and administration in general: I corrected all the papers: the secretary sat upon his knee and licked envelopes with a sharp tongue when not brewing very strong tea.

The old man explained my duties to me. The advertisements promised three FREE lessons, after which the subscriber must pay to complete the course. (There were a dozen or so courses in various subjects.) My instructions, when marking the original FREE papers, were to give good marks that also showed improvement but indicated the need for further lessons. I was told that the first three papers should be marked 30 per cent, 40 per cent and 45 per cent and that my instructor's corrections should be made with some care. Thereafter, that is to say once they had sent him the fee, which was for the whole course, payable in advance, it did not really matter what marks they got, but it was better that the apparent progress of the FREE period should not be maintained. Indeed, a decline was advisable, and their final papers should earn only about 20 per cent. Thus when they flunked their examination or failed to get the office job, they could not turn round and blame us. It was on the whole preferable that they should fail, since the old man could then send them a mellifluously worded letter of condolence: were they but to take the course again, he would say with paternal encouragement, they would surely pass next time. Some poor boobies took it over and over again, I believe. No doubt doing long division or translating small French sentences helped fill in the long winter evenings. Nowadays, I imagine, they do the football pools instead in order to make their fortunes and with identical results.

Since I had to correct all the papers in all the subjects, including Commercial Spanish and Journalism, I could only glance very briefly through the answers laboriously scrawled by horny hands more accustomed to the pick-axe than the pen. Indeed I reckoned that I could devote approximately fifteen seconds to any one paper, if the huge pile that awaited me each morning were to have disappeared by five o'clock. In the advertisement and circulars I was described as 'a large staff of skilled specialists, many with the M.A., the B.A. and other high academic distinctions'. I was paid, if I remember correctly, five pounds a week, and we worked in a snug little office behind St Giles' Circus. Since I also had my allowance from my mother I considered myself rich. I found the cynicism of the whole enterprise moderately invigorating. It appealed to my youthful nihilism, though I did feel an occasional pang of pity for those poor, deluded workmen.

After staying briefly with my sister Geraldine in her flat on Cheyne Walk I rented a furnished room in Oakley Street, Chelsea. Like so many houses in Oakley Street, this one consisted entirely of bed-sitting-rooms. It was run by a couple of happily married homosexuals who lived in the basement. The male member of the team pranced about in open-neck shirts, and made the most of his handsome, bronzed profile. The female wandered about the house with a feather duster or was to be found puttering about the King's Road, clutching a large basket and gloomily comparing the prices of vegetables in the shops. His husband, whose lips seemed ever about to part in a shout of Shelleyesque affirmation, clearly bedazzled his mate's hen-like wits.

My single bed-sitting-room was small and cheap, with a gas fire and ring on which I boiled a kettle to make my breakfast tea and simultaneously cooked an egg inside the kettle. I also kept a large box of Ryvita in my closet. The gas fire quickly warmed the little room, and there was a table at which I wrote or read when I spent the evenings there. To begin with I passed many of my evenings in this way. The gas was fed through a meter into which one put shillings. Ours was a gas-meter and pub society, but at first I did not know about the pubs.

The other residents were strangers to me. I looked at their names beside the row of bells outside the front door, and tried to match the names to the people I saw hurrying in dressing-gowns to the bathrooms. Before I left I was to become a close friend of a couple who had the big double room beneath mine, though I first met them in the Wheatsheaf and not upon the stairs. This was Michael Wharton and his wife, whom he called Pépi. (Like so many English girls of the period, she was really called Joan. He had renamed her Pépi, for he detected a resemblance to the barmaid of that name in Franz Kafka's novel, *The Castle*.)

Michael had no money at all. Pépi, who looked like one of Renoir's prettiest girls, made a little cash, modelling for the Chelsea painters. She did not, however, make enough to pay the rent. Michael was writing his novel, *Sheldrake*, a most witty and haunting surrealist fantasy which was not published until after some twenty years had passed. He was also, though a Yorkshireman, a keen Welsh nationalist. Thus the rent did not get paid. This worried the domestic hen in the basement. Michael offered, very generously I thought, to pawn his typewriter in order to pay it, but the hen became extremely flustered and said that on no account was the typewriter to be removed from the building before the rent had been settled. A state of deadlock was thus reached. Michael stayed at home, typing his novel: Pépi modelled for the beards: the rent was not paid. How the situation was at last resolved I do not know, for by then I had left England.

There were two main sorts of artist in London in those days. There were the bearded Chelsea academicians, who made money and painted badly. They ran to cloaks and shepherd's crooks and strange velvet tam-o'shanters reminiscent of Richard Wagner. And then there were the Soho artists, the moderns, who also painted badly—with a very few notable exceptions—and made no money. They were more or less clean-shaven and wore stained grey flannel trousers and tweed jackets over dark flannel shirts. They were inclined to be dirty and to bite their finger-nails. The Chelsea ones frequented a pub called the Six Bells in the King's Road. I began by admiring their curious charade— they tended to talk in very loud voices, addressing younger men as 'laddy'—before I learned better. The Soho ones were usually to be found in the Wheatsheaf or the Charlotte

Street pubs. The girls preferred to model for the Chelsea beards: the pay was better and the old men's advances more easily rebuffed.

I am not quite sure when or how I graduated from bar-billiards with former schoolmates in the Chelsea pubs to witty repartee with poets and painters and their girls in the Soho ones. I imagine it was Harold Scott who led me there, though he was never a drinking man himself. Certainly his great friend, Wilfrid Hanchant, was a regular figure in the Wheatsheaf, carefully preserving his reputation as a wit by puffing steadily at his pipe and saying nothing. (Occasionally he would clear his throat, and we would lean forward, awaiting the epigram that never came.) Or it may have been one of my new Oxford or Cambridge friends whom I had met through my contributions to *Light and Dark*. In any event I started by making an occasional outing to Soho from Chelsea. Quite soon I did not bother to go home but walked straight to the Wheatsheaf or the Fitzroy after finishing my day's work with the correspondence course. And I rapidly discovered that I was not as rich as I thought.

I have tried to describe the life of those pubs, and of the cheaper half of the Café Royal where we often went after they had closed, in my *Life of Dylan Thomas*, but as the Duke of Wellington remarked, one can no more describe a battle than a ball, and the Soho pubs had many of the qualities of both. It was a constant coming and going, a swinging of swing doors, a borrowing of half-crowns and attempts to attract the barman's attention, flirting and arguing, gossiping and kissing, discussing and liking and disliking, amidst clouds of cigarette smoke and empty beer glasses. Almost all the painters and writers who have since become famous must have passed through those pubs in the six or seven years immediately before the Second World War, and many, many more who have not. There is no purpose in listing names that are now well known, for their owners were not necessarily, in those days and in that pseudo-society, the best liked or the most spectacular. Dylan Thomas, for instance, was frequently there but was no more outstanding than half a dozen others who are now unknown. If he attracted attention it was not

184

because he was particularly outrageous or drunken, but because he was very amusing company and already a famous poet with two books published. But Michael Wharton was at least as amusing when he saw fit to speak, and Bernard Spencer, who stayed sober longer, was better company.

It was a great place for finding girls and I managed to go to bed with three or four before I met Giselle. (One was the traditional 'older woman' who taught me the only essential lesson about making love, namely that pleasure comes from the giving of pleasure.) It was all very exciting for me, but Soho was also skid row for some and therefore there was much unhappiness as well.

Giselle was in a bad way when I first met her. She had had a love affair with a well-known sculptor. The sculptor had been in love with his beautiful wife, who had left him because the sculptor had discovered that he was really homosexual. In an attempt to put this right, and no doubt to regain his wife's affection, he had had an affair with Giselle, who had fallen in love with him. It had all become too much for the poor sculptor, who had committed suicide. By then Giselle was pregnant, and on hearing of his death had miscarried. An acquaintance had persuaded her that she take drugs, principally veronal, to ease her pain, though of this I was unaware when first I met her. All this had happened some weeks before I made her acquaintance, though I had seen her about and knew her by sight. At that time she had no home and dossed down where she could, frequently in John Pemberton's studio where she shared a double bed with John and his pretty wife Barbara.

John Pemberton was painting her, a large nude which I later acquired and, later still, lost. The pose was one that had been used, more or less, by Modigliani. Her head was in the lower left-hand corner of the canvas, her thighs in the upper right, and he painted in her pubic hair, bang in the centre of the picture, which was regarded as very bold in those days. It was probably through John Pemberton that I met her. Later that evening, in the corner of the Wheatsheaf, she began to cry. She had, she told me, no place to go, no money, nothing save a little cardboard attaché case that she carried with her. She had decided to commit suicide by jumping into the Thames.

I took her back to my room in Chelsea—I had never done this with a girl before—and she asked if she might have a bath. She was very grimy indeed and the tub was filthy. We then sat in front of my gas fire, she in my dressing-gown, and ate Ryvita and Gentleman's Relish, and drank tea, and gradually she cheered up. We made love and slept soundly in my narrow bed. Next morning she was not at all suicidal, and made me my simple breakfast before I went off to work. I met her that evening at the Wheatsheaf, where she was waiting for me. Her clothes consisted of an old plum-coloured woollen coat and a borrowed black dress far too tight for her. Her shoes were hopelessly down at heel. We slept at Oakley Street again. The next morning was a Saturday. I had drawn my week's pay and we bought a few cheap clothes before meeting Michael and Pépi in the Six Bells. By the time we got to Soho that evening, it was a fact accepted by us and our friends that she was now my girl. So easily were arrangements ratified in Soho in those days. I was very proud to have a girl of my own. She held my arm tightly when we walked about the streets. I liked this too.

When she told me about her doping, I was frightened. I had long known about my father's downfall, for in 1933 or 1934 he had been sent to prison and my housemaster at Wellington had been instructed to inform me. He had done this in such a way as to make me feel not only that my father was thoroughly disgraced but also that some of that disgrace had rubbed off on to me. I had thus developed a fear and hatred of drugs which I have never altogether shaken off. To find that my girl was taking them chilled me. I told her this, and I told her why. She immediately promised to give them up, and together we made a parcel of pills, syringe and the rest, which we threw over the Albert Bridge into the Thames.

In return she exacted a promise from me:

'If ever you catch me doping again you must beat me, hit me, really hurt me badly. Promise?'

Doubtfully I agreed.

My homosexual landlords did not at all approve of Giselle sharing my room.

'It is most improper,' said the female one. 'You are paying for a single room. It is not proper that two people should live in a room intended only for one.'

I asked then if they had a double room to let, but they had none. So we moved a few doors up the street, to another and larger room.

One evening when I came back from the correspondence course, I found her on the bed. At first I thought she was asleep. Then I noticed that she had broken open the gas-meter and emptied it of shillings. This frightened me. I examined her more closely and saw that she was clutching a bottle of pills in her clenched fist. I shook her. She half came to, her eyes glazed and her speech blurred. I remembered my promise and I began to slap her face, harder and harder, until she had come to and was begging me to stop. When at last she was really crying with pain I took the pills from her and threw them out of the window. For a long time she went on sobbing, her head in the pillows, while I sat on the edge of the bed and stroked her rough curly hair, and felt utterly miserable. She never took drugs again. The new landlady was very good about the gas-meter. When I told her that it was 'all an accident' she replied enigmatically that she knew how these things do happen.

If we did not dope, at least we could drink. How much Giselle and I and our friends drank in those days, it would be hard to say. Certainly we posed as hard drinkers, for that, too, was a symbol of rebellion against the bourgeois values. On the other hand, like most people in most places and at most times, our drinking was limited by our finances if by nothing else, and we had very little money. Thus we drank beer and only occasionally spirits. At this period of my life, that is to say before I went to Oxford, I have no memory of ever owning a whole bottle of whisky or of gin. We did not drink 'at home', but in public, and if we went to one another's rooms or flats after the pubs had closed, we took beer in bottles, if we could afford it. Should there be some millionaire in the party who could actually buy a bottle of spirits, this was regarded as a great treat and the millionaire was insulted or fawned upon according to taste and temperament.

There were potential alcoholics in those long-ago pubs, as there are in every social group, and some have sadly gone that way; but most of us, whatever we may have said and thought, drank for the company rather than for the alcohol. This was revealed by an expression of the period: 'having one's entrance fee'. The entrance fee was the price of the original half-pint of bitter, fourpence in those days, which enabled one to join a group of friends and acquaintances with a glass in one's hand. Thenceforth, if one were penniless, one took what was offered as the more affluent members of the group bought rounds in turn. By well-timed retreats to the lavatory or sudden immersion in profoundly interesting conversation it was possible to avoid one's own round. This was acceptable behaviour, provided that one was genuinely broke and not merely mean, and also provided that one did not arrive entirely empty-handed and thus patently expecting support throughout the whole evening. Indeed young men would on occasion hang about outside the pub until a friend turned up from whom it was possible to borrow the entrance fee. We had our code, like anybody else. As for the girls, they were not expected to buy drinks, but if they chose to do so their contribution of a round was quite acceptable. Some girls apparently could not drink beer and asked for more expensive drinks, gin and lime being a favourite. Unless they were extremely pretty or amusing they were not very popular, and I imagine that they rapidly moved on, to richer, older men and lusher pastures.

Etiquette so far as cigarettes were concerned was less rigid. If one took a packet from one's pocket it was bad form not to offer it around, and failure to do so rapidly won an unenviable reputation for being tight-fisted. On the other hand, the entire contents of a packet of ten Players or Woodbines could easily disappear before their owner had a chance of a smoke himself, and he might not then have the price of another. If, however, there were only one cigarette in the proffered packet, the question was always asked:

'Is that your last?'

The cigarette was then refused. One painter was detected exploiting this convention. It was possible in those days to buy cigarettes in packets of five. He used to fill his pockets with those, a single cigarette in each. He could thus not only smoke those of others but could offer his own, confident that his would be refused. This trick when discovered caused unfavourable comment, but he was not dropped.

Indeed nobody was ever dropped. There was no membership of the Soho pubs, no blackballing and no expulsion, except occasionally by the management. Men might quarrel or even fight one evening, but the next day neither thought he had the right to order the other out. If he disliked his enemy so much that he did not wish to see him, then it was up to him to stay away, or he could ostentatiously cut his enemy and take up a position at the far end of the bar. Usually these enmities, even when based on really serious causes such as a girl or an artistic allegiance, were of brief duration. Only on the part of the Communists did political odium lead to lasting feuds. They were at this time riding the highest of moral horses and everybody else was expected to regard those of their number who were in Spain as heroes while alive and martyrs when dead. The rest of us more or less accepted this view of current events, and did not argue with them. Those who denied their hagiology were slandered, insulted and even persecuted by the Communists, so far as this lay within their power. It was not only tedious and potentially dangerous to argue with Stalinists, it was also considered rather bad form, like arguing about the existence of God with a Roman Catholic priest. The Communists were said to be 'dedicated', whatever this may have meant; most of us, who were not, were quite content to leave it at that, though some claimed to envy them their 'dedication' as certain agnostics will wring their hands and lament their inability to believe in God. I was not of their number. At about this time a well-known poet published a poem in which he stated that when he saw a Communist he felt ashamed: the reason for his shame was that he himself was not a Party member. A well-known critic, who was, felt

189

ashamed for another reason: some of his relations were aristocrats. I refrain from comment now, though I did not then.

Once Giselle had got her health back, we resolved to go to France together. There was little to keep us in England. She had agreed to play the lead in a play that would run for one week at the Barn Theatre, Shere. This, however, was not until late July and till then she had nothing to do nor any prospect of work. (This statement was much more banal then than it would be today: there were then some two million registered unemployed in Britain, and few of our friends had regular jobs.) As for me, the correspondence course was a dead end. I would do better talking and reading French. France in those days was much cheaper than England and my sister Fanny, who was at Cassis, on the Mediterranean between Marseilles and Toulon, wrote that there were little cottages to be rented for almost nothing. My mother, who was moving into a very small cul-de-sac house in Cheyne Row, approved of this plan. She had met Giselle, and whatever doubts she may have felt about the advisability of my setting up house with her, she kept these to herself.

The problem was money, a problem with which I was to grow only too familiar in the years to come. I had my allowance, and my mother was prepared to pay my fare and expenses to Cassis, but beyond that she was not willing to go. Dun Roamin seemed the only solution.

Giselle wrote to her father. She said that an English couple by the name of Mr and Mrs Robert Dillon, reliable, middle-aged people, had offered to take her for a holiday to Cassis, but that she had debts in London and could not afford the fare. Almost by return of post a fairly substantial cheque arrived. No doubt her miniscule father was only too glad to get his daughter out of London before she visited the dingy department store again. Furthermore, a letter was enclosed for the mythical Mr Dillon. (Giselle had drawn rather over-elaborate portraits of this couple, he a grey-haired writer fond of hiking, she a charmingly vague lady, an amateur painter, keen on gardening, and an excellent cook.) Giselle's father was immensely grateful to them for giving his daughter, who he understood had not been in good health, a holiday in the country. On the other hand he did not see why Mr and Mrs Dillon should be out of pocket as a result. Would they permit a contribution on his part towards household expenses? He would prefer to send the cheques—would £20 a month be acceptable?—direct to Mr Dillon, and he was 'Yrs sinc'.

Thus the money problem was solved. For some months I, or Robert Dillon, wrote him regular letters, my first attempts at realistic fiction. It was an awkward moment when Giselle's mother joined in and wrote to Mrs Dillon. I attempted to answer left-handed, but we decided that the result looked too strange even for Dun Roamin. So Mrs Dillon broke her right arm, and Mr Dillon answered for her, a long, chatty letter about the beauties of the Mediterranean seascape, zinnias and the difficulty of getting well-hung meat in Cassis. In general I am against the telling of lies, but there are certain falsehoods which only serve to increase the general sum of human happiness. In Dun Roamin they were reassured, in Cassis we were as happy as mice in a cheese, and the sun shone.

We spent a few days in Paris, where Giselle had never been before. I realised that it was thus my beautiful city, my Paris-in-the-Spring, that I was showing to my girl. We bought her some summer clothes from the Galeries Lafayette and in the evenings I knew which cafés we should visit. The Dôme and the Rotonde, the Coupole and the Flore were not what they had been to me a year ago, when I sat there alone in the morning with my glass of white coffee. The coming and going between literary and artistic London and what was then still the acknowledged capital of our world was very great. We ran into friends everywhere and made more, English and French. I could speak French very fluently and I thought I knew my way about contemporary French literature, painting and the Parisian theatre. The English intellectuals of the period had an inferiority complex so far as the French were concerned. The fact that I could chatter away about Céline and Montherlant and Kandinsky and

Arp in French to Frenchmen won me a measure of respect which I thoroughly enjoyed.

Our half-a-house on the edge of the pinewoods above Cassis was minute. The hall was also the kitchen, with bottled gas. There was a small room where I worked, and a bedroom containing a huge double bed and a muslin-swathed cradle, which made us laugh. We swam, and drank at the little café down by the port. I read and wrote and wore a pair of brick-coloured fisherman's trousers. But above all we made love, incessantly it seemed, when the sun shone, when the nightingales sang, even on the rare occasions when it was raining. This gave us a very healthy appetite, and Giselle turned out to be a good, adventurous cook. As a result of past misfortunes she had grown quite thin, but now she began to put on weight.

(The English and even more so the Americans of today seem to have an insatiable appetite for tips on sex. They must suspect that they are missing something, and long to be told what it is and how to get it. Perhaps many of them are, and maybe books about how the Indians do it, or what the gamekeeper did to Lady Chatterley, or even simple manuals of the *Sadism is Fun* variety do enrich many a bedroom. I have never liked self-appointed experts on this subject, regardless of their sex, whether in print or in bed. What I said earlier about giving pleasure and the giving of pleasure is true for both sexes, but it must be done for the sake of pleasure and not to prove expertise. Some women are so anxious to show that they know all the tricks, that bedding with them is more like taking part in a display of Swedish drill than making love. Such conscientious and gymnastic devotion to sexual duty can produce amazement, boredom or the giggles, thus leading to impotence as quickly, if not more quickly, than the ladies-don't-move business of the past. Wanting to do what the other person wants, and doing it with lust and if possible with love, is the only hope. Tip over.)

We cooked fresh sardines over olive twigs behind the little house. Halfway down the hill there was a grocer's shop, cool and dark as a cave, where we bought garlicky sausage and slabs of Parmesan cheese and good, cheap, nameless wine in large bottles: sometimes we would have a meal, sea-bass or a *bon bifteck de cheval* at the little café, and on Saturday nights we danced there, on the cobbles, to the music of an accordion, with the sailors and their girls. The occasional English or American tourist who passed through we eyed with a mixture of curiosity and disdain. There were few of these, for we were out-of-season residents. Cassis, in those days, was a sleepy little place. That Arcady and its like would seem to have been utterly erased from the face of the earth, though perhaps those who are this summer celebrating their eighteenth birthday, as we then celebrated mine, will have found other, different Arcadies of their own.

I had been given a lot of French and German books I was supposed to know before going up to Oxford, and those French ones I had not already read I had brought with me. The German ones I postponed. I had also some English books, different both in style and content from those I had taken to Berlin two years before. I remember Fr Rolfe's *Hadrian the Seventh,* and as many novels by Ronald Firbank as I had been able to find, and Edward Sackville-West's superb *Sun in Capricorn,* and *Ulysses,* and a couple of Kafkas and Yeats' *A Vision,* and books by Aldous Huxley, Evelyn Waugh, Ernest Hemingway, as well as the *Golden Treasury* from which we read aloud to one another. When the novels ran out I bought new French ones from the little book-and-paper shop on the hill at the far side of the harbour, and cut their pages with the blunt edge of a kitchen knife. I could afford these, for we had had a financial bonus: the new French government had devalued the franc and our cheques from England jumped twenty-five per cent in value. We seldom bothered with newspapers, and I assume that it was a new French government. It usually was, in those days.

It can be seen that my reading in English was erratic. I have never studied English literature as I studied that of France and, to a lesser extent, of Germany. Since leaving school I have only ever read English for pleasure. There are thus great areas of English writing, such as the eighteenth-century novelists and the nineteenth-century dramatists and the twentieth-century philosophers, which are almost un-known territory to me. I cannot solve the clues in *The Times* crossword which require a close acquaintance with *Martin Chuzzlewit* or the poems of Matthew Arnold. I shall never again attempt to read Jane Austen or George Meredith, and *Vanity Fair* was enough Thackeray for me. Only English poetry can I claim to know fairly well. But I write prose, and so far as that goes, while I have been influenced by some English and American writers a generation or so older than myself, the tradition which has always meant most to me, ever since I was steeped in it during those early years, is that of France.

Giselle learned her part for the play at Shere. If I remem-ber correctly she played Clytemnestra, but it was difficult to be quite sure since the play was less of a translation than an adaptation. The author or adaptor was determined to be up to date at all costs, and his text was peppered with Freudian phrases. (He had been most ingenious in his search for alternative ways of referring to the Oedipus com-plex, a metaphor too close to the home-life of his characters for comfort.) He had also done his best to strike a note of social significance, and Orestes and Pylades were definitely left-wing in their outlook. Finally, in distant Belfast where lay his home, he had heard tell of Surrealism. In an attempt to instil a measure of this modish convention into his work he had introduced non-sequiturs and near-gibberish that made it difficult for Giselle to learn her lines. As for his style, which was neither prose nor verse, it may best be described as 'free prose'. I am surprised that the play has not been revived. With only a little more emphasis on the cruelty of the plot it should be a West End sell-out nowadays. Perhaps the name of Euripides frightens off the commercial managements who do so well from such productions.

There was only one small cloud on our sky-blue horizon when we left Cassis for Shere. Giselle had not been having her periods. However, she had consulted the local doctor, who had told her that she had no need to worry. She was not pregnant, and the irregularity was doubtless due to past events. If her cycle did not become normal within a month or two, he advised her to see a doctor in England. Since she had always been most careful about birth-control and was feeling extremely well we did not worry. The muslin-swathed cradle, we decided as we packed up for England, had not been intended for us.

The System at Shere was simple. The theatre, as its name implied, was a converted barn that held an audience of about two hundred. Behind the stage there was a single large dressing-room. A very small semi-permanent staff of three or four people ran the place, though there was little enough 'running' to be done apart from the cooking of meals. In one old farm building the men slept on bunks, in another the girls. The actors and actresses were neither quite professional nor entirely amateur, being mostly in the same halfway house as Giselle. They paid a very small sum for board and lodging and were expected to help with the washing-up, the painting of flats and so on. Nor was there any charge to the public for admission. Seats were free, but the plate was passed round, as in church, during the interval. This was called 'the silver collection', which meant that members of the audience were not supposed to contribute less than a silver threepenny bit. Some gave much more— Charles Laughton, who lived near by, once dropped a neatly folded five-pound note into the plate I was carrying— others gave nothing at all. The money thus collected was used to pay for paint, the general upkeep of the barn and such items of costume as the actors could neither supply nor the actresses make themselves. Plays were put on every other week for one week only. Thus each cast had two weeks in which to rehearse. Some of the actors and actresses stayed there all summer, but most came just for their three weeks. They took their work seriously, but little else. I was allowed as a general handyman—running the car-park and so on— and I also played walking-on parts which caused me agonies of stage-fright.

There was a swimming-pool near by and a couple of pleasant pubs in the village where we drank shandy and ate crisps and played shove-ha'penny. Giselle and I had a small tent with an inflatable mattress and a black pekingese called

Buzz. I had given him to my mother some years earlier as a birthday present when first we had moved into Sandy Park House. Now she had asked me to look after him while she went to America for some months.

He was an unpredictable animal with a very protruding lower jaw: this gave his muzzle the look of a bulldog's. His teeth did not in fact meet, which meant that he could only eat very finely minced food, not easily obtained at Shere. Even so he was inclined to constipation and had to be dosed against it regularly, a procedure which he hated. Although still quite a young dog, he behaved like a very old one, even pretending that he was going blind, though he could see what he wanted to see quickly enough. My mother believed that he had a weak chest and bought him a scarlet turtle-neck sweater with a raincoat to match which he wore in the wintertime. Only when so dressed would he hold his magnificent tail on high. Usually he let it trail disconsolately behind him. He was also a homosexual and led a frustrating sex-life, being for ever rudely or even painfully rebuffed by male terriers and corgis. Buzz was understandably enough in a bad temper most of the time: he attempted to work this off by biting people. Owing to his malformed jaw, however, being bitten by Buzz did not hurt. This must have added to his frustrations. Although I think he liked me, and I know that I was fond of him, he bit me regularly, and always when I gave him his castor oil or whatever it was. Giselle would hold him, but as soon as he saw the bottle and spoon he would give a high-pitched snarl, wriggle out of her clutches, and attempt to sink his ill-matched fangs in my forearm or ankle.

Years later I was shown a letter from some forgotten actress to a friend, written at Shere during that summer. In it I read:

'There is a boy here I cannot understand. He has a mistress, says he is an American, wears red trousers, and owns a blind pekingese.'

How it all came back to me, the paint and the grease-paint, the morning mountain of bacon-and-eggs, the Canadian swimming-pool attendant as frustrated as Buzz in his attempts to make the young actresses, the taste of ginger-beer shandy, the moment of silence before the curtains parted for the first night, and Giselle's excitement next morning when she saw her name in *The Times* and read that her performance had been 'capable', the party on the stage after the last night with an incredibly potent punch which totally befuddled the bearded Belfast dramaturge, and the faint hiss of our air mattress as it slowly deflated throughout the hot August nights. I promised to translate Racine's *Britannicus* for production next year. Harold Scott agreed to produce it, and Giselle to play Agrippina. Then we returned to London.

A series of events now took place which I should like to pass over as briefly as possible. Indeed I would not mention it at all were I not convinced that omission would here be an unwarrantable falsification. As the reader may have guessed, when Giselle went to see a doctor in London he informed her that she was four or five months pregnant. Furthermore, since she had not been cared for after her miscarriage early in the year, her physical condition was far from satisfactory.

A time of nightmare followed. We agreed she must have an abortion, but how, and how to pay for it? With my mother in America, Geraldine was the obvious person to help and she also had control of the family finances. I went to see her and received a moral lecture for my pains, nor was any money forthcoming. Mimi was more helpful and made enquiries among her friends. It seemed that it was best to go to Paris, and she found me the name and address of a doctor there who had performed this illegal operation for a woman she knew. She even offered to come with us, but she was much involved with the man she was soon to marry, I believed I could manage on my own, and her presence, welcome though it would have been, must only add to the expense.

George Browne lent or gave me the money, and we set off, frightened and unhappy, for Paris. The doctor was suave, extremely expensive and quite definite. He was not prepared to perform the operation. In the first place it was too late: in the second it was too dangerous in view of Giselle's condition. He gave us each a brandy and said, with a light laugh, that I, as a man of the world, would understand that he could not risk Giselle's death at his hands. He advised us to have the baby, and he recommended that she be looked after by Norman Haire when we returned to London. He wished us the best of luck, was sure that we would love the baby, and said that I owed him so-and-so many francs. He even patted her shoulder in the hallway of his luxurious consulting-rooms.

A friend in the Dôme knew of an abortionist. We took a taxi for miles and miles and more miles, out to Charenton or Villejuive or some other part of the city known to me only from the Métro maps. We were shown into a small, stuffy, overfurnished drawing-room. Somewhere I could hear somebody groaning. A central table amidst plush-covered furniture bore a potted plant and other bric-à-brac upon dusty lace. I noticed a dirty tea-spoon. The abortionist appeared, a shrivelled old woman in carpet slippers, wearing pebble glasses that rendered her eyes almost invisible. She was drying her hands with a filthy cloth. Yes, she would perform the operation, immediately, for so-and-so many francs, payable in advance. I said we would have to come back with the money, though I had it in my pocket, and Giselle cried all the long way back in the Métro. Next day we returned to London.

I had heard of Norman Haire, for he was not only a very famous gynaecologist but also wrote books. These were liberal-progressive in intent. He advocated birth-control and, in certain circumstances, abortion. I hoped that he would solve our gigantic problem, and perhaps even do so for very little money, since the extreme luxury of his offices made it plain that he himself had more than enough.

As with other famous progressives in other professions with whom I have subsequently had occasion to deal, I soon discovered that his philanthropy was of a general, not an individual, nature, and that he certainly did not intend to allow his left-wing principles to affect his right-wing bank balance. He told me his fee, up to and inclusive of the baby's birth. When I spoke of abortion, hypocrisy was snapped down as a knight in armour might snap shut his visor. Did I not know it was illegal in England? It was, he led me to believe, unethical of me even to have mentioned such a word in the pile-carpeted splendours of his millionaire's consulting-rooms.

We agreed that he should look after Giselle. He scribbled a prescription for some medicine that she was to take, recommended that she do the exercises as given in one of his own books on pre-natal care, and said she was to come back and see him in, I think, a month's time.

We trailed back to the single furnished room, with its gas-meter and a paybox telephone at the bottom of the stairs, which we had rented in Walpole Street, Chelsea. There I wrote to my mother in America and told her what had happened. We had already decided that there was no purpose in writing to Dun Roamin. The best that could be hoped for from them would be that they insist she go back there. She wished to stay with me.

My mother sent me a cable. She would be back in plenty of time to look after Giselle in her last months. Meanwhile she had instructed her bank to let me have what money I needed. I was to purchase anything we required on her account with Harrods. And she sent us both her very dearest love. And so, suddenly, everything was all right again. I have had many opportunities to feel grateful to my mother for her love and understanding, but never more than on that morning when I received her cable from America, early in September of 1937.

During the weeks that followed we lived very quietly in our Walpole Street room, where I did my reading for Oxford while Giselle knitted and made little clothes for our baby. We took Buzz for his unsatisfactory walks and she hoped that his pre-natal influence would not make our baby whopper-jawed. She did not drink, took her exercises seriously, and went once to Norman Haire, who told her that all was going better than he had expected. My mother wrote that she would be arriving the day after my first term at the University began. She would rent rooms or a flat in Oxford for Giselle and herself. To us all seemed perfect, for we did not think much or seriously beyond our baby's birth. Marriage meant little to Giselle, even in those circumstances, and in any event Oxford undergraduates were not allowed to marry. That marvellous peace which envelops some women like a nimbus when they are pregnant was about her. We spent happy hours choosing our baby's name, and since both possibilities began with S she stitched SFG on to the little garments she was making. Because, as she said, and I knew, the child she was carrying was a little FitzGibbon, regardless of whatever the birth certificate might say.

And then she miscarried. I remember the awfulness of her pain, all night, in the Walpole Street room. I remember my attempts to get hold of Norman Haire and of the constant promises—presumably from servants who had orders not to wake him—that he would arrive immediately. I remember Giselle trying, when her pain was not too awful, to calm and console me, to tell me that all would be well, and then I would watch her become lost in pain and know that she was dying. I remember having no more pennies for the box telephone at five in the morning, and running to Sloane Square, and waking the reluctant porter at the hotel there in order that I might once again try to speak to Norman Haire, and getting the same answer, and running back to Walpole Street, terrified lest she be dead before I got there. I remember the sweat on her face.

He arrived at nine in the morning, freshly shaven and smelling of eau-de-cologne. He insisted that she go to the nursing home by taxi, since she might soil his Rolls Royce, and that I come with him. The baby was born at noon, and lived a few hours. This was just one week before the beginning of the Oxford term. I never saw her alive or dead. A nurse told me that she was a beautifully formed child, a seven-months baby.

Of the next twenty-four hours I recall little. Giselle was in an oxygen tent, I think, invisible at least to me. I took the little things she had made for the baby and gave them to a strange woman pushing a pram in the street. I can remember her face, but nothing else. Mimi insisted that I eat a meal: she was getting married next week, the day term began.

And then I was always in the nursing home, in a room I filled with Harrods' autumnal flowers, huge bowls of great bronze chrysanthemums which have preserved, for me, an especial and extra sadness of their own.

Giselle rapidly got better. She never cried when I was with her, though she told me later that she cried a lot when she was alone. Quite soon friends were allowed to visit her. John Pemberton gave me the picture he had painted of her, and only asked that I pay for its frame. My mother had cabled that she would look after Giselle. She was on board, on her way to Southampton. So I packed up Giselle's few clothes in one suitcase, and my own in another. Giselle was most anxious that I should not arrive late for my first term. She would be all right, she said, with my mother, who had said in her cable that she would bring Giselle to Oxford for her convalescence.

On that day, in the morning of the day term began, Mimi married Claud Mounsey. There was to be a wedding party that afternoon and evening.

'Go to the party,' Giselle said, smiling at me from her pillows between the chrysanthemums. 'Go to Mimi's wedding party, and get absolutely sozzled, and catch the last train. Promise?'

I promised, and I did. I arrived at my Oxford college, shortly before midnight, having finished my journey in that state of decreasing intoxication which produces a metallic taste in the mouth, careful, wooden gestures, and a feigned self-assurance. Of the two suitcases with which I had set off, I had mislaid one. I had not lost the large, unwrapped nude of Giselle, which I carried as best I could.

Next day the other suitcase turned up. Thus did I begin my career as a scholar of Exeter College, Oxford.

12

WHEN I HAD been at Oxford two or three days I was asked
if I would edit the *Cherwell*, then the principal undergraduate
magazine with any literary pretensions. I was flattered, but
declined, though I wrote for it fairly regularly from then on.
I did not see how I could edit a magazine for a university
of which I knew nothing, and I did not wish to make a fool
of myself. A little later I was asked if I would care to be
president of the English Society, but this too I declined and
contented myself with reading them a rather foolish paper
about Ronald Firbank. I had no wish to be conspicuous.

Oxford, like all other large organisations into which I
have wandered or been pitchforked, began by inspiring me
with a considerable measure of trepidation. In some ways I
have always been a timid person, and never more so than
when confronted with incomprehensible loyalties, conventions and *esprit de corps*. Although I did not at this time put
this into so many words, I desired to understand the place
before venturing forth into it. So for my first term I lived
very quietly, made few new friends, and felt my way.

This was all the easier since Giselle and my mother were
living in lodgings on the Iffley Road. I spent as much time
there as was allowed by college regulations. Giselle quite
quickly regained her strength and my mother—who must
surely have been very bored in Oxford—was marvellously
tactful and self-effacing. I brought my books but not my
friends to their lodgings.

Furthermore I had to take a very simple examination in
my first term, which was regarded as a walk-over for anyone
who had won a scholarship, but I failed in the German part.
For nearly a year I had spoken no German and had read
very little. What I had learned so quickly I was forgetting
with equal speed. I felt humiliated at flunking this simple
examination, which I would have to take again in the
spring, and I settled down to refurbishing my German. This
I found distasteful, like eating cold shepherd's pie, and it was
then that I began to develop a dislike for the German

language which I have never got over. (Someone once remarked that the trouble with German literature is this: there is too much ink in each letter, too many letters in each word, too many words in each sentence, too many sentences in each paragraph, too many paragraphs in each chapter, too many chapters in each book, and too many books. Certainly those huge composite words, like enormous molecules, and that cumbersome syntax which hides the operative verb, often at the very end of the sentence it is supposed to control, have bedevilled German thought. Only a real master can express himself clearly and elegantly in a language which, by its very structure, leads the mind into mists and quagmires of abstract thought. The Nazis were at this time busily exploiting the woolliness of the German language, which they further corrupted: they succeeded, easily enough, in persuading most of their compatriots that almost meaningless abstractions were the reality, while realism was a dirty Jewish-Bolshevist-pluto-cratic trick, played upon simple, honest-minded Teutons by sly and vicious Frenchmen.)

By the time the Christmas vacation came, Giselle had recovered her health. We visited Dun Roamin, which turned out to be much as she had described it, and then went to Paris where I became connected with a small literary magazine called *La Nouvelle Saison*. I translated poems by Dylan Thomas into French for that periodical, a rash under-taking and the first time that his poems had appeared in a foreign language. When I returned to Oxford she stayed in London, looking for work which from time to time she found, and visiting me in Oxford for the day on Sundays whenever she could.

It was now that I began to know Oxford, and I was on the whole disappointed with what I found. I had been led to believe that the atmosphere would be utterly different from that of a public school. Had I come there straight from such a school I might well have agreed. As it was I thought that the resemblances exceeded the differences, and the regulations about hours and meals, visiting pubs and having women in one's rooms struck me as childish and irksome.

Fortunately Exeter had a minimum of 'college spirit'. Once I had made it clear that I had no wish to row, play football or cricket, or join any of the college societies, I was left in peace. No gangs of hearties smashed up my rooms because I had prints by Toulouse-Lautrec and George Grosz upon my walls and played Vivaldi as well as Duke Ellington on my gramophone. On the other hand I found the conversation of my neighbours when I dined in Hall very dull indeed and remarkably similar to what I had heard from the older boys at Wellington, three years before.

This was hardly surprising, for those of my Oxford contemporaries who had attended public schools had in almost all cases only left them a term or two ago, and even if they had briefly visited Grenoble or Montpellier this provided but a flimsy bridge between their world and mine. Apart from Denys Sutton, the art critic, and John Gardner, the composer who was then Organ Scholar, I made no friends among the undergraduates of Exeter.

I was unlucky in the dons who taught me. These were pleasant, conscientious and painstaking men, but they seemed more like glorified, and not even very glorified, schoolmasters than men who could open vistas of culture and wisdom to an eager mind. I gather that in this respect there has been a remarkable and rapid deterioration over the past thirty years, but even then most of the younger dons attached great importance to the passing of examinations, the gaining of a good degree, in a word 'the diploma'. I was surprised to find that my teachers, though knowing a great deal about French philology and obscure nineteenth-century German critics, had apparently never heard of Existentialism or Karl Barth. Being still very young, I thought the worse of them for this.

And I found the syllabus, on the whole, uninspiring. The study of philology I quite enjoyed, much as I had enjoyed mathematics at school: it was neat, and there was usually a correct solution to each problem. I enjoyed, too, learning mediaeval French and derived real and particular pleasure from reading and understanding the *Chanson de Roland*, that great, wild epic like its own lovely, half-inhabited Spanish landscape. But my teachers, apparently, did not regard it as a work of art. This wretched 'diploma concept', as the Germans would put it, kept getting in their way. This was true both of the tutorials and of the lectures I attended.

Thus I was unlucky in what was most immediately available, but I could still look beyond my college and the Modern Language school.

Here the choice was apparently greater and indeed I did make a number of friends, most of whom are still my friends today. However I believe that I might have made just as many, if not more, in other circumstances. For supra-collegiate Oxford was to a very considerable extent stratified and subdivided into clubs and cliques and I have always been most reluctant, perhaps unable, to mould my manners to fit the one or my opinions to suit the other.

If one ruled out the diploma-seekers and the athletes, as I did, this left only a few hundred undergraduates. First of all there were the rich, Old Etonians, members of the Bullingdon and what-not, with private jokes from which I felt excluded, expensive tastes for motor cars which I could not hope to emulate, and frequently an interest in blood-sports, horses and racing which I did not share. They did not wish for my society, nor I for theirs. The glassy look that comes into a rich Englishman's eye when meeting a poorer contemporary is never more pronounced than when he is at Oxford.

Then there were the politicians. I myself had no wish to enter politics, and therefore did not join the Union or indeed attend a single debate there. (Twenty-five years later I was a guest speaker at the Oxford Union and I learned how right my instinct had been. The procedure was more abysmally fatuous even than I had been led to believe, the jokes more numerous and less funny, the standard of argument more puerile. Never again!) The political clubs were perhaps more interesting, though by now I had lost my sympathy with the Communists. The Labour Club, where I should have felt at home, had become a very dingy affair since the Communists had stolen their fireworks. Later I joined the Carlton Club, which was Conservative, but for social and gastronomic rather than political reasons. Indeed my interest in politics had evaporated almost completely before I went to Oxford, nor did I find any cause for its revival among the rather jejune polemics of the undergraduates.

The literary and artistic societies and groups should have been my natural milieu. However in the years just before the war there was considerable sterility in this side of Oxford life. The 'Oxford aesthetes' had been long forgotten. Auden, Spender and MacNeice had left no heritage behind them. There was a fashion for 'proletarian literature', a phrase I have never understood, and this I did not share. Some of my contemporaries certainly aspired to be writers, and most of these I both knew and liked. They never made it, for they lacked talent and the application that talent implies, and their names are not now known. I could not have foreseen this then, but it may explain why they did not become my real friends. I do not care for amateur writers in general.

Thus out of the thousands of undergraduates there were left only a few dozen from among whom I could choose my friends. These were, essentially, eccentrics or even misfits like myself. Some, like Anthony, were eccentrics first and foremost and only incidentally wits or scholars, in his case with a profound understanding of French symbolist poetry. Others, like David, were in essence charming, normal young men with a certain ostentation of temperament which led them to grow beards (when nobody else did) or play the flute, at dawn, on the top of towers. Some, like John, did not perhaps realise that they were eccentrics at all and believed that everyone else observed the world and its values with their own lazy, tolerant cynicism. Others, like Robert, were so busy in pursuit of their own egos, like a dog engaged upon an ever-accelerating pursuit of its own tail, that they scarcely noticed the world at all.

It was among people such as these that I found my friends. And there was one quality, and I think one only, that we had in common. We none of us conformed to, or particularly cared for, the standard picture of the English undergraduate of the day, the member of the future governing élite receiving the final pats upon the potter's wheel before being sent forth, honourable, C. of E., upstanding and well-educated, to take his place running his estates or in the forefront of the liberal professions, the civil service or in parliament. Clever we might be, but we were also, and almost without exception, foreigners or Catholics (both born and converts), flamboyantly Jewish or excessively Irish, homosexuals or quite unabashed lovers of women. And we all drank. If an Oxford education brought me no further profit, and I do not believe it brought much, going there was worth while if only to meet those young men who became, and have almost always remained, my friends. As for my sole friend among the dons, old Professor Dawkins was the most eccentric of the lot. He, alas, is dead.

We, or at least I, drank foolishly at Oxford. For this the university regulations were in part to blame. Undergraduates were not then allowed to visit pubs and the principal activity of the proctors and their bulldogs seemed to be the policing of them. No doubt the origins of this regulation lay in the remote past, like much that is pleasant and also much that is tedious about the University, and probably dated from the 'Town and Gown riots' of long ago. Or maybe it was modern-snobbish in origin, a desire to segregate the undergraduates from the workers. Whatever the reason, this ban on pubs meant that we could not drink beer in easy neutral surroundings. That we wished to do so is proved by the fact that we would drive, or even bicycle, miles out into the countryside in order to get away from the proctors.

We could drink beer in our college butteries, but this had numerous disadvantages, though the beer was cheap and good. I certainly had no wish to drink beneath the eye, as it were, of the college authorities nor to be then surrounded by the same young men with whom I attended lectures and often ate my meals. Such propinquity is in any event cramping to conversation.

Thus we drank mostly in our rooms or those of our friends. This meant that our customary drink was not beer but spirits or reinforced wines. Amongst the more sedate, sherry was the usual tipple, and the sherry party a recognised social function. But we did not wish to be thought sedate and therefore we drank spirits, often shaken up together to form noxious and highly intoxicating cocktails. And in my case, at least, to drink in this fashion was not only bad for me but was far beyond what I could afford, since I had only my slender allowance on which to live, though the college and university fees were taken care of by my scholarship.

Here, however, another ye olde Oxford custom came to my help or contributed to my downfall: This was the enormous facilities for credit available in the town. Particularly if one looked and sounded rich—and this, for reasons I do not understand, has always been the case with me, even when penniless—the wine merchants, for quite a long time, had no hesitation in sending round a dozen of this or a crate of that against a scribbled signature.

None of this applied during my first term, when Giselle and I drank bottled beer in the Iffley Road and ate our way through huge tins of small, cheese-flavoured biscuits while playing backgammon with my mother or reading. But once I was on my own I picked up the habit quickly enough, though I had only the haziest ideas as to how the bills would ever be paid. Never mind, war was coming, *edite, bibite, post mortem nulla voluptas.*

Before going up to Oxford I had been reasonably careful about money. In Germany and France I had usually managed to live within my income. In Soho I had learned a rather more elastic attitude towards personal economy and had readily accepted the view that strict financial probity is a bourgeois, and therefore contemptible, convention. At Oxford I found this view confirmed, not from a Marxist but from an allegedly aristocratic standpoint. Tradesmen, bank managers and such existed for our sake, and if we could exploit or even cheat them this merely served them right. (Thus one friend of mine, who was much richer than I and who later became a Conservative Cabinet Minister, evolved an ingenious technique for raising money from the banks. He had discovered that one could open a bank account by depositing two pounds, and that all bank managers would honour cheques that did not overdraw an account by more than five. Thus with an initial two pounds of capital one could, after a busy morning in and out of new banks, emerge with fifty. If the horse then won the 3.30, all was well. If not, there was always tomorrow. One frequently hears complaints that the Conservatives ape the ideas of Labour. Here perhaps is a case of the process in reverse.)

Early in 1938 I found myself launched into the world of tradesmen's accounts and bankers' overdrafts, and for some time all went well. Nor did I merely splurge the money I had not got on wines and spirits. The tailors and bootmakers and haberdashers were at least as accommodating as the vintners, if not more so. I had shoes made for me, including a pair in grey suède, very original and natty. I had suits tailored, a double-breasted black one with a tiny red pin-stripe, a green flannel one with a much broader yellow chalk-stripe, a heavy white linen affair. I bought pyjamas of black crêpe-de-chine, with my initials in silver on the pocket, and then a dressing-gown to match, black satin with silver revers. Dressed in all this weird finery, I thought myself a second Brummell as I guzzled Canadian Club mixed with crème-de-menthe and white curaçao.

And then there were ties. Really expensive, truly flashy ties came in pairs. That is to say the piece of silk was used to make two and only two identical ties. I recall one pattern that took my fancy, and in order that no one else might wear it, I bought them both. I gave one to my college servant, or scout, with instructions that he was only to wear it during the vacations. This coarse and repulsive gesture struck me at the time as the height of aristocratic refinement.

This sort of behaviour got much worse during my second year, until at last Dr Marett summoned me to his Rector's Lodge.

'I am told,' he said, 'that you have bills in the town which you are unable to meet.'

I admitted this, and when he asked me the amount I told him this, too. He said:

'It is quite preposterous, preposterous and immoral, that the Oxford tradesmen should allow a man of your age so much credit. They know that, being a minor, you are not in fact responsible for your debts, but they rely on the parents of undergraduates to pay them. They know that approximately a quarter of such debts will never be honoured, and they charge accordingly. My advice to you is to be one of the clever twenty-five per cent who let their bills be paid for them by the stupid seventy-five. Don't meet them.'

I was utterly taken aback by this. He went on:

'I have been examining your style of dress and have noted a certain ingenuity of taste. I have long felt that our university garb is far too drab. Our statutes lay down that the gown you wear must be subfusc. This has always been interpreted as black, but of course subfusc merely means "of a dark hue". I believe that if you were to wear, say, a bottle-green gown you could probably get away with it. Why do you not get your tailor to make you one?—though, if you don't mind, not on credit any more.'

The old scholar refilled my sherry glass and said:

'I am told that you drink too much, don't work, and ought to be sent down.'

He glanced at me from beneath his bushy white eyebrows. This was March of 1939, and the Germans had just occupied Prague. Half to himself, he continued:

'On the other hand Univ made thorough fools of themselves, sending down Shelley as they did. They've been a laughing stock ever since, in certain circles. Not that I think you're a second Shelley. But one never knows. Are you prepared to devote a little more time to your studies?'

I said that I had done quite a lot of work, I thought. He replied:

'I know a little about what work you have been doing. You have edited your magazine and, if I may say so, a very good magazine it is too. It has been published on credit obtained from the printers.' (He was quite right. I shall have a little more to say about *Yellowjacket* in a moment.) 'You have done a certain amount of research, and I understand original research at that, into the dating of the *Chanson de Roland*. I believe you are arranging to have the reference to it, in the mediaeval catalogue of the destroyed library at

Peterborough Cathedral, dated by a hand-writing expert, no doubt also on credit. And I am told that you know more than is perhaps good for you—certainly more than is necessary for an undergraduate—about the morals of certain great ladies who patronised the Encyclopédistes during the reign of Louis XV. But my dear Constantine, none of that is going to help you obtain a first, even if you manage to get a degree at all. Your German tutor tells me that you seldom attend lectures, that your knowledge of Middle High German is nil, and that while he shares your admiration for Hoelderlin, to know the precise nature of that poet's madness is unlikely to help you through your finals.'

I said that I found it difficult to concentrate on Middle High German when war against the descendants of those who spoke that odious tongue was obviously coming in the autumn. Perhaps, I said, it would be better if I went down? Dr Marett replied:

'Precisely. You think you are likely to be killed within a comparatively short period of time. Were I your age, and shared your belief, I too should be reluctant to waste my months with the drearier parts of an academic education. I suggest that you go down, and then if there is no war, or if you should somehow survive it, and if this college is still standing and I its Rector, we can discuss the possible resumption of your career as a scholar here, should that then be your wish. Meanwhile I can only say how much I regret that I shall not see you walking across the quadrangle in a bottle-green gown, when the Summer Term begins. Another sherry, or would you prefer something a little stronger?'

So I left Oxford in the spring of 1939. Whenever I revisited it, and for so long as he was alive, I always dined with Dr Marett.

I wasted my time at Oxford and did not even enjoy this very much. One cause of this sad waste was my almost total lack of ambition, or rather of ambition in any form that Oxford could help to fulfil. 'The diploma' meant nothing to me because I sensed, even if I did not then know, that a double-first will not help one to write any better. I did not despise the acquisition of academic honours, but neither did I see any purpose in them so far as I myself was concerned. Since war was coming, there seemed little point in laying the elaborate groundwork for a professionsl career even had I desired to pursue one. Less logically, there seemed little more point in preparing for the war. Others among my friends did so, joining the Oxford Air Squadron or the Naval Reserve and this, I believe, eased their passage from civilian into military life when the war finally began. I was far more fatalistic. The whole idea of the coming war filled me with such gloom and horror that I was not going to meet it half-way. If 'they' wanted their war, that was their concern. Once 'they' had got it, I would then decide on a suitable and appropriate course of action. Or so I thought, on the rare occasions when I considered the future at all. It was easier, and in some ways better, to have a drink instead.

The vacations were the part of my brief Oxford career that I really liked most. For the Easter one, in 1938, Giselle and I had my mother's little house in Uppper Cheyne Row. (My mother was in America.) We kept a barrel of Scotch ale in the little backyard and gave a lot of parties, testing my new Oxford friends against our London ones. Buzz enjoyed parties. People gave him titbits: if they forgot him, he could always nip their ankles.

In the summer we went to Shere again, for the production of my Racine translation. Harold Scott, who was the producer, had discovered from his researches in the reading-room of the British Museum that it was two hundred years since last Racine had been played in English and that nobody had attempted to translate him since Colley Cibber. This filled me with pride. The play went very well. Only one slight error of judgment marred the first night. Several of my Oxford friends had turned up for the occasion and were given jobs to do. Anthony was put in charge of the gramophone, on which a few bars of Gluck were to be played, by way of an overture, as the curtains parted to reveal a formal, austere stage. Unfortunately he sat on the record during the dress rehearsal, and on the afternoon of the first night was dispatched to Guildford to buy another one. He decided to improve on the producer's choice and to our surprise the curtains parted that evening to the hoarse and frenetic voice of Jean Cocteau intoning *La Toison d'Or* against a syncopated background. Nevertheless my *Britannicus* got good notices and I was pleased and proud. Indeed I was inclined to think of myself as something of a boy wonder, what with Colley Cibber and all, and me only just nineteen. Any elation of that sort, however, was soon dowsed by the arrival of the cast for the next play. They were headed by Peter Ustinov, who had done more than just translate it. He had written it, was going to produce it, play the lead, design the sets and, for all I knew, chant some equivalent of *La Toison d'Or* that he had himself composed as the curtain rose. And he was a year younger than myself.

After that I was supposed to go to Germany on my own, but I spent most of my money in Paris, fell sick and came back to England and Giselle. We rented a very small and primitive cottage in Hertfordshire. It had two rooms, a lean-to containing a gas cooker, an earth closet at the end of a minute and ill-kempt garden, belonged to a Hampstead lady, and cost five shillings a week. I played tennis with the son of the gardener at the big house, or read French eighteenth-century memoirs, while Giselle commuted to London in her search for work. I also devoted considerable ingenuity to outwitting the gas company. I had brought back a pocketful of French change, and I found that one-franc pieces worked as shillings in the meter. When I ran out of these I discovered that the old-fashioned twenty-five-centimes bits, the sort with a hole in the middle, were also viable if the meter were given a sharp tap. These, too, at last ran out. A few hundred yards away there was a single-line railway along which a very small train trundled to and from Buntingford once or twice a day. To my delight I discovered that a sixpence which had been run over by this train became the size of a shilling and was acceptable as such to the gas meter. I was trying to cut down further on overheads, by making similar experiments with farthings, when the man came to empty the meter. I naturally blamed the strange miscellany of foreign and battered coins on the Hampstead lady, but he made me pay up.

This was the time of the Munich crisis. There was no radio in our little village, so we often left our pub, where we usually passed the evening drinking Benskins and playing darts, and walked across the fields in the dark to hear the news, which got steadily worse, in a neighbouring village where I occasionally played on the cricket team, or to listen to Hitler's doom-laden voice in that pub's kitchen. Then we would make our way back, stumbling and depressed.

We discussed what we should do. I considered going to America, but did not wish to leave Giselle behind. Perhaps we should get married? It was all too complicated and worrying.

At the very height of the crisis the Hampstead lady arrived on a visit, in a very bad temper. She had joined one of the voluntary services and wore an arm-band. I thought she had come down to escape the bombs, but this misapprehension was soon corrected. She was a dynamo of patriotic zeal and wished to know when I was leaving the cottage as she planned to 'fill it with evacuees'. I remarked that it could only hold two, at the most, and that I should be leaving in about three weeks' time. My attitude infuriated her. She rounded on me. Everybody in London, she told me, was being perfectly splendid, digging trenches in the parks, drilling, and wearing gas-masks. And what was I doing? Sitting about in inns, she said, drinking ale, she added, and running up bills with the grocer, she concluded. Then she hitched up her belt and stamped back to London.

She seemed to me a perfect, and perfectly frightful, harbinger of what the coming war would mean. Even in remote country hamlets there would be no escape from 'them'. Still, I saw her point: perhaps I should do something to protect us from German bombs. So I borrowed a spade from the gardener's son and dug a very large, deep hole in her garden. Somewhat to my surprise the Hampstead lady was not a bit pleased by this patriotic gesture on my part, and told me to fill it in again. True, the emergency was now over and Chamberlain had given us peace in our time. Unlike the

Hampstead lady, I did not believe him and I foresaw a future in which our entire lives would be dominated for ever by people such as she.

That Christmas I went to Paris on my own. Giselle and I were drifting apart. She came to see me far less often now in Oxford, and I believed that she was involved with someone else in London. I did not, and could not, reproach her with this. I myself was becoming ever more attracted by a most beautiful member of Somerville College. Margaret Aye Moung was half Burmese and half Irish, an exquisite combination of looks. She had all the qualities which Giselle lacked, was quiet, extremely elegant and, to my mounting annoyance, chaste. I set about courting her as best I could, though I had very little idea of how this is done. There could be no question of plying her with drink. She had, however, a remarkably large appetite for so small and apparently fragile a creature, and I spent a lot more money than I could afford giving her large meals at the George, which was then Oxford's best and most expensive reastaurant. I had hoped up to the last minute that I might persuade her to come with me to Paris for the Christmas vacation, but she preferred to go skiing with a party of friends at Megève.

In Paris I arranged to translate Jean Cocteau's play *Les Parents Terribles*, which was then running. I did this, and its completion made me late for the beginning of what was to be my last Oxford term. Unfortunately I had no contract and when the play was eventually produced in English several years later, it was in another translation. That multilateral genius was most kind to me—we met almost every evening in the theatre bar between the intervals, to discuss my day's work—and I wish very much that it had been my translation of his brilliant play that was produced.

My last term at Oxford was principally devoted to my pursuit of Margaret and to the production of my magazine, *Yellowjacket*, of which she, needless to say, was secretary. My co-editor was John Orbach, who was supposed to look after everything that was not strictly editorial. Since he was at least as attracted to Margaret as was I, we spent a disproportionate amount of our editorial time watching one another. He put up a little money, as did I on the strength of a new overdraft guaranteed by Denys Sutton, who thus became art editor and wrote an article about William Coldstream. John Gardner was music editor: he wrote an article about Kurt Weill. The contributors included our friends (there were two stories by Dylan Thomas in the first issue) as well as Jean Cocteau, Henry de Montherlant, John Betjeman, T. F. Powys and other well-known writers whom I admired and to whom I wrote. It was a good little magazine and two issues were in fact published before our credit with Messrs Slatter and Rose, the printers, was exhausted. By then I had gone down.

At first I had a room in Bramerton Street, Chelsea. Margaret was in Oxford and Giselle with a provincial repertory company, but there were lots of other girls, and lots of parties. I was trying in a desultory fashion to edit the third number of *Yellowjacket* but becoming increasingly sceptical about the prospects of raising the money that Slatter and Rose required. I was also writing a novel, and showed part of it to James Ludovici, who was then connected with a now defunct publishing house. He agreed to publish it, but no contract was signed or advance paid. (It was never finished. A German bomb destroyed the uncompleted manuscript a little over a year later. But the plot, the rather over-ingenious plot of mirror figures which makes the heroes and the villains different aspects of the same characters, remained in my mind and at last became my second novel, *The Iron Hoop*.)

Then Margaret went to Corsica, with John, for their summer vacation. Several of the girls I knew in London had also left for the country, usually to stay with their parents in remote counties such as Suffolk or Monmouth. I became engaged to several of them. This is not quite as unscrupulous or dishonest as it sounds, for neither I nor the girls had any intention of getting married. At least they did not intend to marry me. On the other hand, if a girl told her parents that she was engaged, then I would be asked to stay and parental vigilance relaxed. By now everybody knew that war was coming.

So I hitch-hiked about the country, staying with my girl-friends and, I fear, not always delighting their parents. I ended up in Westmorland, where Michael Wharton and his wife had a cottage. They had a baby, my godson, Nicholas. There were no girls here, so we went to the pub and drank damnation to the Germans and the Russians and the Hampstead lady and her like and the rest of our enemies. On the day war broke out I wrote to the Air Ministry and volunteered as a pilot. That evening in the New Inn, Hoff, the landlady—a big, strong, red-faced woman with the nose of a Roman emperor—asked me what I was planning to do in the war. I told her. She gave a throaty chuckle, then said:

'And I shall pour a pint of bitter on your grave.'

Michael announced that he intended to stay in bed, preferably with his head under the bedclothes, until he was called up. His was the more sensible, and the more logical, attitude. He ended the war as a colonel in the Royal Artillery, which proves it.

Part Four

Part Four

13

THE LONGEST NATURAL period of time perceptible to man's senses is the solar year. With the renewal of the seasons, of each season, the cycle has come full circle. To encompass longer periods of time we are, in theory, reduced to the impersonality of numbers and such vague and fanciful terms as decades or centuries. 'A 'twenties figure,' we say, 'married to a woman who might have stepped straight out of the eighteenth century.' And we imagine that we have made a meaningful statement.

There are, however, other ways of defining temporal periods. 'During the Ice Age the sabre-toothed tiger purred in what is now Ongar,' refers to a natural megacycle, while: 'It was in the Depression that most people stopped eating off gold plate,' refers to a briefer and man-made period. Such periods are usually of catastrophic content and the most popular variant is war. The rest of this book covers the period of the Second World War. It is not, however, about the war, which rumbles away in its beastly fashion, usually in the background, and only on rare occasions is it shrill and screeching in the centre of my story.

For we also and fortunately have our private or at least our personal means for the subdivision of our past lives. 'That was in the days before I rose to Assistant Canteen Manager,' one might say, or: 'My whole life took a turn for the better once I had joined the Wentworth Golf Club.' Events of such significance need not, indeed usually do not, correspond in any way either to the mathematical or the politico-economic schematic. For most of us, and certainly for me, the importance of where my home was, as a definition of period, is exceeded only, but exceeded greatly, by the succession of emotional states through which I have passed. I can and do think of my Italian period, of the Hertfordshire years, of my life in Bermuda, of the time when I owned Waterston. These, however, are all post-war, for during the war I had no home. During this post-war period I can also, and rather roughly, break up my past according to my books or rather according to the intellectual interests which led me to write these books: Ireland, resistance to tyranny, Germany, contemporary politics, our society and its artists, the formation of my own character and attitudes. These interests, however, tend to melt the one into the other and even to survive in a torpid or a deep-freeze state. They are thus scarcely suitable compartments in which to store the years that are gone. Furthermore, during the war years I was not writing books. Therefore my tendency to measure the past in terms of my emotions is accentuated when I attempt to reconstruct what happened to me between 1939 and 1946. My war becomes, in retrospect and essence, my relations with three women, with Margaret whom I married in 1939, with a girl whom I shall call Charlotte, and with Theo, whom I married in 1944. It is their presence or absence, their warmth or coldness, their smiles and their voices that provide the background to those years, not machine-guns nor aeroplane engines nor staff conferences.

It is the reality of our private emotions that we must protect against 'them', and never more so than in time of war. 'They' would, of course, prefer us to have no personal lives, and therefore no personality at all, since all personality and hence all power would then belong to 'them'. In peacetime 'they' set about our destruction by corrupting our minds (newspapers, television and so on), destroying our moral and religious beliefs (pornographers, South Bank bishops, behaviourists and the rest of it), reducing our freedom of choice ('social' taxation, Freudianism, the egalitarian fetish, and much more in the same dreary catalogue), but in time of war 'they' can really roll up their sleeves and get on with the job. They can pay us what they like, tell us what to wear, make us do their wish instead of our own, lock us up in prison if they dislike our views, and eventually send us off to be killed while giving one another state banquets and state funerals. Our best, perhaps at last our only, defence is to dismiss all their claptrap about loyalties, countries, ideologies and above all about humanity and to love one another. The best way to start *that* is by loving one other person, preferably of the opposite sex.

Not that I had any doubts, then or later, of the absolute necessity that Germany be defeated and Hitlerism destroyed. Luckily we are not asked to volunteer for wars that are over and done with, but were this feasible I should once again, reluctantly, write to some Ministry or other and offer my services. (The only other past war about which I have similar feelings is the War between the States, and then only in its later stages. Once Abraham Lincoln had stopped playing politics and had come out in favour of Abolition, his became another just war. Just so, in the later stages of the Second World War, did our 'alliance' with Russia and our leaders' fulsome praise of Stalinist tyranny jeopardise, though it did not destroy, the justice of our cause.) But if I volunteered it was with reluctance and without enthusiasm. It was as if I were making an enormous appointment with a monstrous and totally unreliable dentist. And I remember remarking to my mother, early in September of 1939, that regardless of the war's outcome, what Hitler represented would win and what we represented would lose. If it did not turn out quite as badly as that, this was in some measure due to the fact that we were not yet aware of quite how evil were the forces which Hitler represented. Liberal democracy, on the other hand, is almost everywhere moribund where not actually dead, while variants of national socialism go from strength to strength where they are not actually triumphant.

This not very brilliant epigram of mine was uttered when first I visited my mother's new home, Church House, Hurley. She had given up her little house in Chelsea. Geraldine and her future husband were homeless. Fanny, who had had a nervous breakdown, was in a Swiss clinic from which she would have to be brought home. Mimi's husband, like myself, would soon be joining the Forces. And my mother therefore decided that she must once again create a home, or at least a base, for us all. It was not easy to find a place in the country at that time both large enough and cheap enough. Many people with more money than she were anxious to escape from the cities where massive destruction was expected immediately war broke out. She was fortunate to find Church House into which she moved almost on the day that the Germans invaded Poland. She remained there until precisely the day that war ended.

Church House was a rather gloomy, rambling, low-ceilinged house, cold and damp in winter, dark and almost gardenless in summer. As its name implies, it was ecclesiastical property and a mouldy odour of ungracious charity, unwashed vestments and large, unhappy Victorian families at their chilly morning prayers hung about its dark corners and the bend in the narrow, twisting stair. It was also said to be haunted, or at least Theo said so, and she claims to possess psychic powers. Her poodle, she said, used to growl at the ghosts. But the gloom with which I associate Church House may have been due to the war rather than to emanations from the spirit world. It is a place that I associate with boredom and, usually, unhappiness.

Hurley is a long, thin, straggling village, a single street running for about half a mile from the main road to the River Thames. In those days it had no shop but it boasted three pubs. One of these was a proper pub, for members of the working class, the others small hotels or roadhouses, and of these the one that we frequented, for it was only a few yards from Church House, was the Old Bell. Its well-stocked American bar, panelled, hung with sporting prints and brass or copper objects, always warm in winter with its fine log fire, became at times almost an annexe of Church House.

The Old Bell also had a restaurant which was expensive and good. Its owner in those days was an Italian naturalised British and his brother ran the catering department of one of London's largest department stores. They were thus in a position to acquire those delicacies which became increasingly hard to find as the war went on. They were both extremely patriotic men and I do not believe that they patronised the black market. In any event with their background, and with many envious eyes watching them, it would have been most foolish to do so. They simply knew where good, unrationed food and drink could be obtained and this they purveyed, at a price, to their customers. The dishes were excellently cooked, the wines served at the correct temperatures, the Soho-Mediterranean waiters polite and pleasant. I never visited the three or four bedrooms upstairs, but I imagine that the pile carpeting was very thick, the bathwater very hot.

There was a pleasantly *louche* touch to the Old Bell. The whole Thames Valley, once that river has left Oxford and before it enters the outskirts of London, is vaguely redolent of extra-marital sex. There used to be, for all I know there may still be, a dozen establishments in that region, not unlike the Old Bell, where half the couples are registered as Mr and Mrs Smith with no further questions asked and where the tactful discretion of the staff matches the grateful tips of the patrons. The tables in the dining-room were far enough apart for a man and a woman, talking in soft voices over a bottle of Moselle, to be confident that their conversation could not be overheard. One would meet them occasionally in the little hall, setting out for a walk perhaps, well dressed, their expressions happily vague. And their expensive cars, becoming rarer as the war went on, were tactfully tucked away in garages, their number plates invisible. I myself have always been rather bad at adultery. I fall in love when violent emotions are not wanted: I get found out: I suffer guilt: all ends in tears or even in divorce. This may be why I feel such admiration for those who can, in appearance at least, tread that slippery, treacherous path with grace and apparent happiness. Perhaps Dr Marett had been right: perhaps I did know more about certain aspects of French eighteenth-century life than was good for me.

The local residents who visited the Bell (the most respectable locals stayed at home) were *louche* in quite a different way and were far less elegant than the adulterers. The Thames Valley is also the stockbroker belt, was then the home of the now defunct British film industry and housed a scattered population of racing motorists, stunt pilots, company promoters, confidence men, *entrepreneurs* of dubious enterprises and other get-rich-quick Wallingfords. Their women tended to shrill voices, wrong or too much jewellery, and expressions which, in repose, fell easily into lines of dissatisfaction. They all seemed to live in an atmosphere of false bonhomie ('No, no, old boy, my round. I insist. Luigi! The same all round, doubles!'). Their jokes were dirtier than they were funny, and a certain boastfulness about their achievements in the black market struck, in my ears at least, an increasingly gloomy note. I much preferred the anonymous adulterers.

Not that I had any wish to commit adultery myself during that first winter of the war, most of which I spent in Hurley. On the contrary, I was set on marriage, and on marriage to Margaret before I should be called up and rubbed out. (The Royal Air Force did not want me. The Fleet Air Arm said they did. The Fleet Air Arm then flew obsolete planes, usually from obsolete carriers. Even without German assistance, life expectancy in the Fleet Air Arm was remarkably brief.) I had been accepted for pilot training by Miss Wright's Royal Navy: John Orbach was in hospital with hepatitis: and I took advantage of these facts to persuade Margaret that we get married at once. She agreed, though it must be a secret marriage since she intended to complete her Oxford career. Before John had recovered enough to intervene we were married, in late October, at the Chelsea Registrar's Office, the only witness being our taxi-driver who bore the curious name of Mr Pamplemousse. By then I had heard that the officers of the Fleet Air Arm, having discovered that I was an American citizen, were no longer interested in me. My relief was considerable, and I looked forward to a long and happy married life as I drove off, still behind Mr Pamplemousse and with my beautiful wife beside me, to the Café Royal, where my mother was to give us lunch or perhaps a wedding breakfast.

There is said to be a rustic game or pastime known as 'grinning through a horse-collar'. I have never had the good fortune to see this, but I imagine that my own expression must have been one of similar, fatuous self-satisfaction when I sat down to lunch, with my bride, my prize, in the Café Royal. Who precisely was of the party I no longer recall, but I do know that my father was present.

My father, now divorced from his second wife, had in some measure re-entered our lives. Later, when he had had a stroke, had finally been cured of his drug addiction and was a semi-invalid, my mother was to give him a home for several years in Church House, Hurley. My feelings for him were scarcely filial—how could they be?—but I liked him and found him, on the whole, good company. He was far too sensitive and modest a man, and perhaps too tired as well, to attempt any parental domination and there was a lot of solid good sense mingled with his folly. I remember, for instance, one occasion when he was talking about how grand his family had been in past generations. This displeased me and I asked him, rather rudely, why he was such a snob. His reply was disarming:

'When I was young I had good looks, a good brain and was well born. I've lost my looks, I never used my brain and now only my family is left. Why shouldn't I talk about it?'

That was later. Now, in the Café Royal, the outbreak of another war had in some measure rejuvenated him. (He had served at one time as an officer in the French Foreign Legion. He was about to rejoin it. Alas, the Legion checked on his record with the British authorities and his final military career was soon over.) He expressed his pleasure that I was to serve in the Royal Navy, as he had done. Grinning through my horse-collar I told him that they would not have me: they were not taking Americans.

'What nonsense!' he said. 'You're my son. You wish to join the Navy, I take it?'

'Of course I do,' I lied. 'But I can't.'

'We'll see about that,' he said, and left the table.

He was soon back. He had made an appointment for me to see Admiral Ramsay, the Fifth Sea Lord, who was then in charge of the Fleet Air Arm, that very afternoon, at a quarter to three. Indeed he himself would take me along to the Admiralty. 'Black' Ramsay was an old friend: they had been in *Britannia* together. 'Black' Ramsay was a formidable fellow who could arrange almost anything. His wife, who was a princess, had had a whole Canadian regiment named after her. I felt that my destiny was being taken out of my hands, and my grin began to vanish. Margaret and I would have to catch a later train to Battle, where we planned to spend a brief honeymoon before she returned to Oxford.

The old sea-dog was delighted to meet my father again after all these years, and they exchanged reminiscences while I glanced about his large office and wished, with growing misery, that I were back in the Café Royal where Margaret was waiting. At last he turned his piercing eyes on me. So I wished to join the Fleet Air Arm? Splendid. I realised, of course, that my life there would be not only very uncomfortable but also extremely dangerous? Good. And that by American law I would automatically forfeit my United States citizenship? Not that I was likely to have much use for that or any other passport after the war. It was most refreshing, the Admiral told me, to meet so keen a volunteer in these decadent days. It was, of course, only what he would expect of my father's son. And I would receive my calling up papers in due course.

Our honeymoon was not a success. Margaret did her best, and even attempted to cheer me up by reading 'Saki' aloud to me, but this only confirmed me in my opinion that he was a totally unfunny and essentially nasty writer. And then I returned to Hurley, and she to Oxford. We visited one another when we could, which was not as often as I should have wished. I asked her to leave Oxford, but this she refused to do: it would upset her father, far away in Burma. I trailed about Hurley wondering whether her term would end before I received my call-up papers. I tried to write my novel, but it was sour stuff. Such periods of indecision, of waiting in limbo, have always caused me profound emotional unease. In an attempt to expedite my fate I even volunteered for the Finnish Army when the Russians invaded that country in December. At the Finnish Legation they were most courteous, but since I neither knew their language nor had any military experience, they declined my offer.

The phoneyness of our marriage, in that winter of phoney war, became unmistakably apparent during Margaret's Christmas vacation, which we spent in a furnished flat in Queen Street, Mayfair. I was too young and did not know how to look after a wife whom I did not understand. (My attempts to excuse my failure by muttering to myself about the mysteries of the Orient did not even convince me, let alone her.) I did no work, but just hung about the place, drinking rather too much and feeling vaguely unhappy. Still tinged with Oxford snobbery, I imagined that a good way to please Margaret would be to spend money, more money than I had got. Almost every evening we dressed up in evening clothes and went to an expensive nightclub in Leicester Square where we passed many penumbrous hours in the company of friends whom we scarcely knew or liked.

I had tricked and bullied poor Margaret into an essentially loveless marriage. I failed to make her love me, though she tried her best. We never quarrelled, but it was clearly a failure. I could hardly blame her, when she returned to Oxford and there decided that she preferred someone else. I was unhappy, of course, but it was the selfish unhappiness of failure and not the cruel misery of love betrayed. Indeed I have little doubt that I was secretly, though unconsciously, relieved. We remained good friends and met occasionally, though we never again lived together. Eventually we committed the English crime of collusion (legalised hypocrisy, highly profitable to the members of the legal profession) and obtained a divorce. She married a sensible musician, who did not waste his time in the Four Hundred and they have, I sincerely hope, lived happily ever after.

By the time my first marriage petered out, my career as a pilot had also become a non-happening. I had been summoned to Gosport, which is a place near Southampton where the Fleet Air Arm had their depot, and had failed to pass their medical examination. My right eye was too weak for me to be entrusted with a naval plane, and I trailed rather disconsolately back to Church House, Hurley. This must have been late February, or maybe early March, of 1940. The war remained as phoney as ever and I had no great regrets that there was, apparently, no part in it for me to play. I reconciled myself to civilian life.

But not to civilian life 'for the duration' at Hurley. There was a most agreeable and obliging Greek ship-owner who used to frequent the Old Bell there, and I asked him if he could help me find a job. He could and did, immediately, with a firm of marine insurance brokers. I rented an underground room in Sidney Street, Chelsea, and moved to London at once.

It would be incorrect to say that I enjoyed my time in the insurance game—the only 'proper' job I have ever held—but I found it interesting and even intriguing in a macabre sort of way. Except for banking on the highest level, marine insurance is perhaps the most esoteric manifestation of capitalism in action and surely among the least productive. True, I was only a sort of office boy and it may well be that the florid men for whom I worked, and whom I glimpsed from time to time in the lift or walking along corridors as they returned from their lunch at 3.30, were in fact drawing huge salaries for making decisions of primary importance to their firm, Lloyd's, the shipping industry, the nation and indeed the whole Allied war effort. At the time, though, I doubted this.

My job, my humble job, was the actual writing of the insurance policies. If the firm of Polecat and Slowworm wished to send, each month, a consignment of calico underpants worth £85,000 from Manchester to Pernambuco, this consignment was insured against loss by war damage, fire, shipwreck and so on. In the event of the Germans stealing or destroying the underpants, the British government paid Lord Polecat for his loss. In the event of the ship foundering a whole host of insurance companies and Lloyd's underwriters reimbursed the noble company director. (One of my jobs was to write their names in a fair hand upon the back of the policy.) However, the real essence of my job was to prepare these policies in such a way as to obviate the necessity of payment. I had as my principal weapon a rubber stamp which, when pressed against the policy form, left behind the words AS PER SPECIFICATION ATTACHED. I then attached the specifications, small pieces of printed paper, sometimes consisting of little more than a single line (*Damage by lightermen notwithstanding*), at others several square inches of legal jargon which stated, shall we say, that all those people whose names appeared on the reverse of the policy were not to blame if the ship's captain got drunk and confused New Guinea with British Guiana, or if a plague of locusts suddenly descended upon the vessel, maybe a motor vessel AS PER SPECIFICATION ATTACHED, while it was ploughing its way across the North Sea. Some of these little bits of printed paper had a single gummed edge: for others I employed a pot of glue with a rather cumbersome brush. It all seemed a lot of senseless drivel to me. I suspected, and still suspect, that most people employed in that great financial powerhouse called the City of London are engaged in equally pointless, formalistic, Byzantine activities. On the other hand the city of Byzantium has long fascinated me, as it did Yeats and so many others. In those days the fascination was very close. In 1940 the Nazis were outside our walls even as the Turks had ululated around theirs, but the specifications, licked or glued, had still to be attached, damage by lightermen notwithstanding.

I did not receive much in the way of a salary from the marine insurance brokers. Indeed it did little more than pay my busfares, the carnation that in those days I fancied for my buttonhole and the modest lunches I ate in City pubs. However my mother still gave me the allowance she had promised to make me until I was twenty-one, and I made out all right.

I ate my lunches alone, usually with a book, though once the war began to hot up with the invasions of Norway in April the midday papers became more interesting. The other workers in my office were not good company. I had one male colleague of about my own age who was fractionally my superior and never forgot this. He was a member of that extreme Calvinist sect called Plymouth Brethren. This meant that besides being a teetotaller and non-smoker he was also a pacifist and exempt from military service on religious grounds. He wore clothes as sober as himself and cast glances of disapproval at my carnation. I remember thinking at the time that such persons, enjoying very favoured treatment from the authorities and escaping the most obvious forms of indirect taxation, should be taxed directly, a Faith Tax. Indeed I am somewhat surprised that none of our latter-day atheistical politicians has so far introduced one.

231

In any event there could be no question of going to the pub with him, and the other young men in my part of the office had been called up.

They had been replaced by young women. Something curious has happened to the City of London's young women in the quarter-century that has passed since I worked there. It is said that the middle-aged male eye is comparatively unappreciative, that to a man in his forties the girls are never as pretty as they used to be, not individual women of course, but the flow of girls in their summer dresses who pass one in the streets. Well, so far as I myself am concerned with the girls in City offices—and I must say that my concern is slight these days—precisely the reverse has occurred with the passage of the years. On the rare occasions when some scuffle with the Inland Revenue or some wheedle about a mortgage takes me nowadays to Leadenhall Street or Poultry I am astonished, sometimes rendered almost speechless, by the prettiness and even beauty of the secretaries, receptionists, typists and telephonists whom I there encounter. The businessmen with whom I have to deal appear, nowadays, to enjoy the ministrations of nymphettes, houris, model girls, *sportives*, and international beauty queens, all dressed in the height of fashion, perfectly made up, with a frank and open or secret and seductive smile for all. How the sturdy businessmen manage to keep their minds on their sums when swimming in this veritable Olympic pool of delicious femininity I do not know.

In the spring of 1940, the last spring of the old City of London doomed to go up in flames before that year was out, there was no such distraction, at least not in the office where I worked. There was nothing there to lead the mind away from the specifications to be attached or even from the gluepot with which to attach them. The girls were, without exception, pallid, flaccid, unhealthy creatures, bulging in the wrong places, washing down a steady diet of aspirin with cups of dusty tea, as ill-dressed as they were ill-favoured and clearly uninterested in an opposite sex which could not conceivably have the slightest interest in them. So I went for my bread and cheese in the Tiger on Tower Hill alone. I

232

found female companionship in the evening, further west. The pretty girls I flirted and danced with and kissed and made love to in Chelsea and Kensington and Mayfair— people still lived in Mayfair in those days—must now have grown-up daughters. Maybe those daughters all work in the City and in the offices of the new Mayfair where nobody lives any more.

Sometimes I and my friends would spend our evenings in the doomed City. It is a curious place, when the offices are closed and empty, more curious then than now, its tangle of narrow, mediaeval streets deserted, its pubs quite empty and only the river still alive. As dusk fell no lights came on in the blacked-out heart of Britain nor on the darkened boats. On moonlit nights the old buildings assumed strange and often surprising shapes against the spring sky, and voices would soften as we made our way past the bloody-historied Tower towards the Thames and the pubs which preserved a marine, riparian liveliness of their own when behind them all the City was asleep. There was a unique beauty to those quiet City walks, heavy with a premonition of nostalgia which became more conscious once the Germans had invaded France and the Low Countries on May 10th.

By then I was living in a flat in Draycott Avenue, with the girl whom I shall call Charlotte and of whom I shall have more to say in the next chapter. We had a fine, tumbledown flat which I have described in one of my novels. (One large room combined the functions of bathroom, kitchen and dining-room. There was a tub at one end, in which I soaped myself while Charlotte fried breakfast bacon at the other. We then ate it, at the plain table in the middle.) There was almost no furniture, though there were mattresses in some of the rooms on which friends slept. (On one occasion the landlord, to whom I owed rent, walked into such a room where Michael Wharton was asleep. The landlord asked: 'Are you Mr FitzGibbon?' Michael replied: 'No. Are you?' The landlord went away, shaking his head, and never bothered me again.) It was a good place for giving parties in, and we gave many. We had lots of friends who did not go to the Four Hundred, and we were gay and happy, as we should have been at our age, and also immensely sad, as we had to be in that age. Guderian's tanks rolled towards the Channel and the British press published obvious and optimistic lies. We knew it could not last, yet from day to day I postponed taking the decisive step I had been so anxious to take six months before. I could not postpone it for long.

The decision was forced on me by pride and by one of my bosses in the marine insurance brokers'. This florid gentleman sent for me and for the Plymouth Brother. He told us he was pleased with our work. He announced that we were to receive a minute increase in pay. He said, with friendly bonhomie, that he realised we were, even so, grossly underpaid, but he hoped that we in turn realised we were on to a very good thing. Now that the war had started in earnest, he said, all the young men who worked in his firm would soon be called up. Except us, the Plymouth Brother because of his religious exemption, I because of my United States Citizenship. We could therefore expect very rapid promotion and by the time the war was over, he laughingly added, one or other of us might actually be seated behind the very desk at which he was seated now.

This was a morning of late May. I did not lunch at the Tiger that day, but caught a tube to Acton (I had seen an advertisement for an army recruiting station there) and volunteered for the British Army as a private. They did not ask me if I were an American, nor did I offer the information. I was to report at a depot in Surrey in three days' time.

I returned to the City and told my florid boss of my decision. He took it quite well and even gave me a ten-pound bonus. I was, he said, the first employee of the firm ever to *volunteer* for military service. Charlotte and I spent the ten pounds that evening. We walked home on a fine summer's night and sang *Oh, Johnny* all the way down Piccadilly.

14

AT THE RECRUITING station I was put through a very simple medical examination and pronounced A1, or fit for active service in His Majesty's Army. I was then asked what regiment I would care to join, and was faced with an immediate poser, for I knew the names of none. This may sound strange in view of my pseudo-military education at Wellington College and the fact that many of my contemporaries and friends were then joining the Army. I suspect that my total ignorance of all military matters was in part a subconscious rejection of my public school and all it stood for. To this rejection may be added the fact that I had never felt any sort of identification with British soldiers. I had quite easily, ever since early childhood, identified myself with the officers of Miss Wright's, and my father's, Royal Navy: the extreme individualism of First World War fighter pilots as portrayed in the movies and in novels also offered a specious appeal to my own individualism: but for the undifferentiated mass of men in khaki I had only a vague and equally undifferentiated sympathy. They manned trenches, or attacked across no man's land in their tens and hundreds of thousands. What did the names of their regiments matter? I had heard of Uhlans and Spahis and Hussars, but had reason to believe that these were foreign units. I said I did not care which regiment they put me in.

'You're a tall fellow,' said the recruiting sergeant. 'You'd better join the Guards.'

'All right,' I said, rather miserably. It was all the same to me.

'Which regiment of Guards would you care to join?'

So here we were again, but I could not persevere with my ignorant passivity.

'Which regiments of Guards have you got?' I asked.

The sergeant gave me a curious glance and said:

'Grenadiers, Coldstream, Scots, Irish and Welsh.'

The first two sounded fanciful to me. The Scots led me to

235

think, quite inappropriately, of Giselle's smoke-enveloped father. The Welsh meant nothing to me.

'Put me down for the Irish ones,' I said.

The sergeant gave me another curious glance.

'Right,' he said. 'Report at Caterham in three days' time. Here's your travel warrant.'

When I returned that evening to our delicious, tumble-down, half-furnished Chelsea flat, Charlotte was not particularly surprised to hear what I had done. No doubt we had discussed the ultimate inevitability of this step, and if she was therefore not downcast, no more was she elated, though her patriotism was simple and unaffected.

Charlotte was a very beautiful girl, a year or so older than myself, with lovely corn-coloured hair and a peachy-and-creamy complexion. It gave her appearance, but nothing of her character, to the heroine of my war novel, *The Fair Game*. Lola, in that novel, was an extremely forceful and determined young woman. Charlotte was the very opposite, reserved, gentle, extremely shy and the victim in those days of a nervous asthma. She had been an art student, but was no sort of bohemian or intellectual. Her loyalties were quiet, simple and straightforward: to the man she loved, to her friends, to her family, and to her country. She had a very sweet smile and no vices. If she inclined to any one of the seven deadly sins it was, perhaps, sloth. Even this she did her best to overcome, cooking and cleaning, though she disliked domestic work, and taking admirable, ill-paid, worth-while jobs. At the time in question she was working in a home for disabled soldiers, showing them how to make toys and such. She looked utterly honest: she was.

I had met her through her brother, now a well-known figure in the word of the arts. He was a pacifist and from the very beginning had announced his intention of registering as a conscientious objector, which he did. Since his grounds were not religious, the tribunal refused to exempt him from military service, but compromised by compelling him to pass the war doing various humiliating, disagreeable and on occasion disgusting jobs. Charlotte shared his pacifist views and fully sympathised with him in his misfortunes. However she had another brother, of whom she was equally fond, and who was a pilot in the R.A.F. It was for her a great personal tragedy when he failed to return from a mission, quite early in the war. These two brothers represented, in tangible, human terms, a paradox within herself which she never fully resolved. And in this she was in some ways a living microcosm of her and my generation, or at least of our circle, for pacifism and patriotism—which in this context meant anti-fascism—are clearly incompatible in time of war.

Thus, though a pacifist, she herself volunteered for the Women's Auxiliary Air Force in late 1940 and served throughout the following winter as the equivalent of a private at Biggin Hill airfield, which was steadily and heavily bombed. Later she volunteered for war work of another sort. It was almost as though the duality of her attitude forced her to make decisions which many other girls could have let go by default, particularly since her asthma made her exempt. This attitude of hers clearly caused her great strain during the war years and was not unconnected, I imagine, with her asthma, for she was far too honest to cheat herself by trying to reconcile the irreconcilable.

Charlotte, in the years when I knew and loved her, was repeatedly the victim of society. Her own honesty was so transparently obvious that in this world, where most of us become conditioned to its dirty devices, she was an object of suspicion. Many believed that only confidence tricksters can appear, in looks and action, as honest as did she. In that same summer of 1940, Charlotte organised a small fête for her disabled Servicemen at which toys which she had taught them to make were sold. There was some small discrepancy in the final accounts, and she was accused of having stolen the few shillings that had vanished. She was innocent, of course, but she felt she must resign. When she volunteered for the W.A.A.F. the best that they could do for this intelligent girl was to make her a batwoman to a female officer. Naturally she felt that her patriotic impulse was being abused; she hated both the work and the life: her asthma got worse: and in the spring of 1941 she resigned. Her commanding officer gave her a sour little lecture about patriotism. I was

237

selfishly delighted, because her resignation meant that she could join me, but she was unhappy about the whole business. She felt that somehow she had failed.

Dylan Thomas once told me of leaving a nightclub on crutches, having broken a leg. Some youths in the street saw him and shouted:

'A cripple! Let's beat him up!'

Charlotte was so utterly honest and so patently patriotic that many people, to justify their own dishonesty, felt compelled somehow to 'prove' the opposite. This unpleasant reaction is of course far from rare in other aspects of human life: thus many unhappily married people will go to great lengths in order to disrupt a happy marriage. Luckily Charlotte survived their buffetings to marry a man as good and as honest as herself and to have his children. They, too, are doubtless in for some difficult passages with the devil's disciples. On June 3rd, 1940, when she saw me off at Clapham Junction where I caught my train to the Guards' Depot at Caterham, honest tears were flowing down her peachy-and-creamy cheeks. I have never since set foot on the platforms of that most grimy station, but whenever my train passes through them I see her tears again.

I suppose that I feared lest the Guards' Depot be a mere brutal version of Wellington College and had I gone there as a potential 'officer'—there were special squads for upper- and middle-class recruits—I might have found an echo of that distasteful public-school ethos which I was to encounter, once again, at Sandhurst a few months later. As it was, the young men with whom I shared a Nissen hut, drilled on the barrack squares and drank stout in the Naafi were all of impeccable working-class origin. Furthermore, since they were Irishmen (about one third from the Republic, one third from the North and one third from Liverpool, Glasgow or London) they quite lacked the specifically English types of class-consciousness. They neither resented the fact that I was educated, nor did they mimic my accent. They too were timid in these new and alien surroundings and they made no attempt to disguise the fact by bluster or bravado. At first one big homesick boy from Sligo cried himself to sleep every night. None of us thought any the worse of him for this. I celebrated my twenty-first birthday a few days after arriving at Caterham. I had no money at all, for my allowance from my mother automatically ceased on that day and most of my minute pay as a recruit was deducted at source and sent to Margaret. She sent it back to me, but this took time and on June 8th, 1940, no coins jingled in the pockets of my ill-fitting battle-dress trousers. My new friends, however, were not going to let me die of thirst on so important a day in my life and Frank Timlin and Dan Dogherty and Paddy Walsh and Seamus O'Connor and heaven knows who else bought me pints of rich draught Guinness in the huge, bleak canteen and we sang songs and it was a fine birthday party.

They often sang, after lights out, in the barrack hut. What they sang, however, were not the ballads of Ould Oireland but last year's pop hits, *The Lambeth Walk* or *Deep in the Heart of Texas*. When they did sing Irish songs these were either the corniest possible, *When Irish Eyes are Smiling* or *In Dublin's Fair City* or maudlin modern fakes: I recall one of which the opening line was: 'When the Rose of Tralee met Danny Boy. . . .' They sang these quite tunefully, with immense sentimental gusto and total unselfconsciousness. We all thoroughly enjoyed these concerts of ours.

All day long we drilled or did P.T. or were otherwise out in the fresh air beneath the June sun that blazed down from dawn, when we rose, to dusk, when we went to sleep. We became tremendously healthy and brown. Indeed I do not remember ever having felt quite so healthy, or so hungry, or so tired at the end of the day. It was all very simple and easy, the drilling and that, and above all every decision was made for us. We were not even allowed out for the first month or so. The war seemed infinitely remote, far remoter here than it had done in London, since none of my comrades ever discussed it or even read a newspaper. Paris fell and France surrendered while we were fully occupied learning how to slow march and to present arms. We polished our brasses and blancoed our webbing and our boots became black glass; we sang about the Blarney Stone and spent our pennies on Naafi stodge, with never a thought for the

German Sixteenth Army preparing our destruction just across the Channel. I missed Charlotte, but when the evening came I was too exhausted and sun-drenched even for that to worry me. It was a fine life, and a magnificent rest cure. And, like all rest cures, all retreats from the world, too good to last, both for objective and subjective reasons.

Objectively, 'they' discovered me. I had got into the wrong slot. My uncle-by-marriage had been an officer in the Irish Guards, one of my closest Oxford friends was now an ensign in the regiment: it therefore followed that I should not be drinking stout with Dan Dogherty but should be myself on the way to a commission. Since it had never occurred to me that I could possibly be an army officer, I was flattered. Subjectively I was becoming somewhat bored by the conversation of my fellow recruits. Philip Toynbee, whom I had known slightly at Oxford and in London before the war, was also at Caterham. Philip, with his impeccable social connections and his infallible instinct to conform to the changing tastes of the English Establishments and anti-Establishments, was of course a 'potential officer' in a special squad of hand-picked aristocrats. I have always enjoyed his company and appreciated his wit, while usually dismissing the conventional nature of his liberal opinions. I found myself, now, spending more and more of my limited spare time in his company and that of the other potential officers. Sentimental though I may have been, and indeed still am, about Paddy Walsh and the others of my squad, I have always prized very highly the company of people who say amusing things, and if they are prepared to laugh at my jokes too, so much the better. Thus did my brief romance with the proletariat end and I slide into Sandhurst, there to be trained as an officer in His Majesty's Irish Guards.

In order that I be not further contaminated by familiarity with the guardsmen I was destined to command, the Irish Guards sent me on a long leave between Caterham and Sandhurst. They were not allowed to do this, but managed to circumvent army regulations by attaching me to the band. In wartime there was no band, and thus I was, in the words of the Regimental Sergeant-Major, entitled to go home 'or any place else you fancy'. Being in the band, I drew bandsman's pay, and since I was technically on leave I drew subsistence allowance, billeting allowance, travel allowance and heaven knows what else. Margaret by now was sending me back my wife allowance, so, by private soldier standards, I was quite rich. Charlotte and I went to Westmorland and spent several weeks with Michael Wharton and his wife. In my Irish Guards uniform I expected to be treated as something of a hero in the pubs, but in fact was regarded with the deepest suspicion, for they all knew from previous visits that I was an American and could not understand what I was doing spending week after week, in Irish bandsman's garb, in Hoff. No more, really, could I. This was the period of spy and fifth column mania and at last a detective was sent to interview me. He was profoundly apologetic.

In late September I went to the Royal Military College and the worst six months of all my long army career began. In the first place I suffered a severe economic slump, in that I lost my bandsman's pay and all the other emoluments. My pay was now that of a simple guardsman unsupported by any private means whatsoever. While this had just been tolerable at Caterham, where I was surrounded by men most of whom were identically situated, at Sandhurst almost all the other cadets were rich. Furthermore we were expected to 'live like gentlemen', which in this context means travelling first-class, frequenting bars rather than pubs, and paying porters to carry one's bags. A great gloom descended on me. Sandhurst is only a mile or so away from Wellington College and even the scrubby, sandy landscape depressed me utterly. Charlotte had joined the W.A.A.F. and we could almost never meet. I found the company of most of my fellow officer-cadets quite intolerable.

In one of my novels I described, quite briefly, my feelings about Sandhurst, and I cannot improve on that description save by altering a few words so as to make fiction into autobiography:

Sandhurst was very boring and snobbish. The cadet who had the room next to mine put a new blade in his razor every day.

The servant we shared used to bring me his old ones, so I never had to buy any, and indeed had quite a stock when I left. This was a great saving.

We sat in classrooms and listened to lectures about Organisation and Tactics. We dug trenches, sometimes, and went for night exercises, stumbling about in the darkness with little compasses from which almost all the luminous paint had been rubbed off.

Each platoon dined at one table, with its officer at the head. Our officer was a cool young man who drank half a bottle of Krug with every meal.

He reprimanded me once on an exercise, because he had seen me nip the burning end off a cigarette which I then put back in the packet. He said it was unbecoming.

They bombed London pretty well every night. When they bombed Reading instead, we could see the flames in the sky and one cadet, who had been there, said that there was a tremendous smell of burned biscuits.

I was glad that Charlotte was not in London, but I wished that she was better at writing letters.

At weekends almost all the cadets jumped into fast cars and sped away to their homes or places like the Hind's Head. The weekends were depressing, because you can't get far from Camberley on a bicycle.

I was not merely unhappy at Sandhurst, and bored, but mutinous as well. The whole atmosphere of the place repelled me and I found the work totally uninteresting. I had no wish to become an army officer and made no attempt to fit in or to study as I should. At any other period of the war, and at any other Officer Cadet Training Unit even at that period, I would undoubtedly have been relegated to the ranks. But in the autumn of 1940 the British were desperately short of officers and the Guards were also remarkably tolerant and easy-going. In fact during my time only one cadet actually failed the course. He was an extremely vulgar fellow who was for ever boasting about how rich he was. I suspect that that was why they fired him.

I myself did not go into the Irish Guards. Whether or not they would have had me in my idle and perhaps boorish behaviour at Sandhurst I cannot say. The question did not arise, for I had realised that I could not possibly afford a commission in that regiment. I could not even afford the uniforms. So I joined the Intelligence Corps instead. I was kept back at Sandhurst for a few weeks for idleness—I spent all the time in the sanatorium with flu—and in late January was commissioned a 2nd Lieutenant in Intelligence. I was almost immediately sent on another interminable course, the basic intelligence course, at Matlock in Derbyshire.

First, though, a small and disagreeable incident had occurred at Oxford, where the I Corps had taken over Pembroke College, to which I was sent en route to Matlock. It will be recalled that a couple of years before, in what now seemed almost a previous incarnation, I had departed from Oxford leaving various debts behind me. No sooner did I return to that city than a whole wasp's nest of tradesmen, lawyers and bailiffs descended upon me with bills, threats and writs. Had I been a civilian I could have told them to wait or even to go to hell. The debts had been incurred when I was a minor and, as Dr Marett had assured me, I was neither legally nor in his opinion morally bound to pay them. But I was not a civilian. I was an army officer and for my first three months as such was more or less on appro. They could take away my commission at any time and for any cause. And I was assured by the adjutant that it would be taken away if I were sued for debt. But the pay I received from the Army—if I remember correctly I then got as a 2nd Lieutenant some £3 10s. a week, out of which I had to pay mess fees and so on—was scarcely enough to live on, let alone to liquidate old bills with.

The adjutant, an elderly one-eyed Irishman with a purplish complexion who still wore the buttons of an Irish regiment disbanded in 1921, was sympathetic and helpful. He approached the various tradesmen, explained my predicament and asked them not to press me for immediate payment. Some, in particular Basil Blackwell's bookshop, were decent enough to agree. (They have all been paid long since, I hasten to add.) I needed £250 at once. The Irish adjutant, doubtless recalling his own Edwardian past, suggested a firm of money-lenders, but since I had no security to offer of any sort they were of no use either. Eventually my friend Ozzy Darrel lent me enough to stave my creditors off—I paid him back a little every month, for what seemed years and years—and on this gloomy note I departed for Matlock.

(And here I must say in parenthesis that throughout the two years in which I held a commission in the British Army there was not a single day when I was not bedevilled by money worries, usually acute. I was not, I think, extravagant. I smoked, it is true, and I drank a certain amount of beer, but then I was not supposed to be a Plymouth Brother or I would not have been in the Army at all. I did not gamble, nor spend money on women, for Charlotte always paid her own way. I had no car and the minimum number of uniforms. But I simply could not manage on the pay. I say this not out of self-pity, for there were thousands of others in a similar situation during these years when the greater part of the British Army was training in the British Isles, but I cannot believe that it is a very good idea to instil financial *angst* into a country's officer corps in time of war, while in time of peace, of course, they simply resign their commissions and get jobs with Shell or Metal Box. Presumably it is all part of the long and accelerating process of national self-destruction which is most successfully achieved by the destruction of the governing class and which the 'liberals' glorify as egalitarianism. Certainly there could be no financial explanation for the Government's meanness. To have paid their officers a decent salary, equivalent say to that of the Canadians, would have meant a negligible increase in the cost of fighting the war and would certainly have more than paid for itself in improved morale and therefore greater initiative. But almost nobody, except the officers themselves, appeared to see this. I recall, towards the end of the war, when I was an American officer and decently paid, being told by a divorced wife of England's richest duke that American officers were overpaid. I was rendered speechless: this seldom happens to me.)

The course at Matlock was held in an institution called

Smedley's Hydro. Designed, I believe, as a clinic for arthritis, it was very hot and stuffy with double windows that could not be, or at least were not, opened. We took little exercise and spent most of the day attending classes in small rooms filled with cigarette smoke. Headaches prevailed, in my case aggravated by the nature of our studies. We were there to learn about the German Army, and it was assumed, first, that we understood the organisation and tactics of the British Army—which I did not, having paid no attention at Sandhurst—and secondly that we read and spoke German with moderate fluency—which again I did not, having forgotten most of my knowledge of that unattractive tongue. I thus found the lectures, study groups and so on almost incomprehensible. We were given large quantities of roneoed papers to read, often in German, each evening. Had I performed this portion of my duties I would, no doubt, have done better during the map exercises, and so on. But so moody and depressed was I by the Hydro, money worries, loneliness, my failure to understand German, army life and the prospect of a war that then seemed likely to last for ever that I simply did not try. Instead I spent my evenings playing billiards with Ozzy. It is hardly surprising that I failed the course with ignominy. My report described me as 'not only idle but stupid'. I, and the Colonel, agreed instantly that I would be far better off in the infantry. I asked that I be sent to the Oxford and Buckinghamshire Light Infantry, a regiment with which I had unearthed a family connexion. I was therefore sent home, with subsistence allowance, billeting allowance and the rest of it, though without bandsman's pay, while waiting to see whether or not the Ox. and Bucks would have me. I went to Church House, Hurley. This was April of 1941, and the worst of my war was over. Thus, as can be seen, mine was one of the less bad wars.

And now a truly sylvan intermezzo blotted out, for me, the cacophony of war and the discords of personal failure and frustration. I have written in an earlier chapter that my memories of wartime Hurley are in general unhappy ones. The late spring and early summer of 1941 are the exception. Charlotte resigned from the W.A.A.F. and she joined me at

Church House. 'They' had failed her, too, in the cruel and absurd tests to which we were subjected in those days. Neither she nor I was bitter, for she knew that she was not unpatriotic just as I knew that I was not stupid, and we both accepted the need of eventually submitting to 'their' rules and whims once again: after all, brutal and unjust as 'they' might be, they were still infinitely superior to their Nazi peers. But meanwhile, for some inscrutable reason of their own—their reasons in those days always seemed inscrutable: only later did I understand that they were simply unreasonable—they had granted us a reprieve. Nor did we know how long this gift would endure before 'they' snatched us back for further courses of boredom, insult and humiliation.

In fact it lasted for some two months, months which Charlotte and I spent as foresters in a small and deserted wood for a *Freischütz* with only short-range silver bullets. We were paid by an official from the Forestry Commission on Fridays (my pay as a forester exceeded my pay as a 2nd Lieutenant and I was well aware that I was committing a crime by accepting both): otherwise nobody ever visited our sylvan domain. The trees that were to be timber had been felled before our time. Our job was to strip them and burn the small branches on bonfires which we built in the glades and rides between the standing timber, which was both hard wood and soft.

We took sandwiches with us, and a bottle of beer, for our lunch. We wore shorts and shirts and gym-shoes. As the days got warmer we took off the shirts, sometimes the shorts too, and if the ride in which we were swinging our billhooks or building our fires was mossy and soft underfoot we would abandon our gym-shoes as well, and play at Adam and Eve, amid birdsong in our little wood, for nobody else ever came there. Once, seated on a fallen tree, we watched a mole slowly dig his way out of the ground, walk a yard or two in his distasteful sunlight, and dig his way back into his own dark safety again. Charlotte was very beautiful and blonde, in her lovely sunlight that filtered through the trees and poured into the rides.

I have always been fortunate in that my powers of recuperation are quick and good. After only a week or so of forestry, of Charlotte, of drinking beer in the evenings in the garden of the Old Bell and of reading, my nerves were back to normal and my judgment, such as it was, restored. The Army, and the war, could then be seen in a more reasonable perspective, or at least in one that seemed more reasonable to me. Thus I recall, one morning, walking to the wood after breakfast and the morning papers, meditating upon the words 'Fighter Command' and 'Bomber Command', phrases of great power, almost traumatic power in those days, and thus not without a certain romantic beauty reminiscent of 'Grand Army' or 'High Seas Fleet'. But what, I asked myself, did this juxtaposition of terms actually mean? (I knew, of course, about the Air Force organisations to which they referred.) What was in the mind of the man who had first joined the concepts together to form what was semantically a meaningless unit? I forget what conclusion, if any, I reached, but I remember my pleasure that I could speculate upon such matters at all. It seemed to me a return to sanity after the near insanity of Sandhurst, Oxford II and Matlock.

We spent over two months at Hurley and resolved to do our best never to let 'them' separate us for long again. Then I was ordered to report to the 2nd Battalion, the Oxford and Buckinghamshire Light Infantry, a battalion always referred to as the 52nd, which had been its number in the last century before the British infantry was given territorial affiliations. It was currently stationed at Ross-on-Wye, where Charlotte soon joined me for weekends.

This was a regular battalion, recently returned from sixteen years in India. Almost all the other ranks were leathery long-term regulars and so was a large proportion of the officers. A high standard of professionalism prevailed. They knew their jobs and thus made it comparatively easy for me to learn mine. I was taught more about soldiering in one week by my platoon sergeant in the 52nd than I had learned from all the instructors at Sandhurst and Matlock in six months. We lived under canvas, marched all over the Welsh mountains at light infantry pace, and were taking part in highly realistic day and night exercises almost continually. The independent brigade of which the 52nd formed part was said at the time to be the best trained infantry formation in the British Isles. I began to realise that soldiering need not be quite so stupid and miserable a business as I had come to believe.

The officers were, on the whole, quiet and reserved, sure of themselves both as soldiers and as people. Thus their relationship with the men was easy and frank: with one another they were like the members of a very good club who would not dream of enquiring about another member's private life or being in any other way snobbish or impertinent. If one were an officer in the 52nd that, for the other officers of the regiment, was enough. One might be—I frequently was—severely reprimanded for making mistakes when on duty: off duty there was no nonsense about anybody calling anyone else 'sir' in our officers' mess, for there we were all equals. I would have been quite happy to spend the rest of my war with them, though in that case it would seem improbable that I should be writing this book now. But it was not to be. It was decided that the 52nd should become airborne troops, which of course entailed considerable reorganisation and retraining as well as a more strict medical examination. My weak right eye, which had already saved my life by preventing me from flying with the Fleet Air Arm, attracted the doctors' attention. Had I been an officer of outstanding ability and experience I have no doubt that this mild physical handicap would have been overlooked, but I was not and so, with polite expression of regret on the behalf of my commanding officer, I was transferred to the 70th ('Young Soldiers') Battalion of the Ox. and Bucks late in 1941. As a special gesture of friendliness I was allowed to take my soldier servant with me, a wizened Durham coalminer by the name of Carter, the father of ten children. It was strictly against army regulations to transfer soldier servants with their officers in this fashion, but the 52nd attached little importance to army regulations of this sort and the colonel of my new battalion was also an old 52nd man who fully

248

sympathised. He would never have dreamed of leaving his servant behind when transferred from one unit to another.

Not that Carter was a particularly good servant: I imagine few coalminers are. Once he dropped my valise beneath the wheels of a train, which sliced it in two. But he was most willing, and also very entertaining company. He felt somewhat out of place among the 'Young Soldiers', all of whom were young enough to be members of his enormous family. However he was a first-class footballer and captained the battalion soccer team. When I transferred to the United States Army I tried once again to take him with me, but in this I failed. I do not believe that anyone in the United States Army apart from myself had ever served in the 52nd.

As for the regiment, it was dropped in Sicily, in Normandy and again, I think, at Arnhem. Few if any of the officers with whom I had marched over the Welsh mountains and who had remained in the 52nd survived the war. Thus my weak eye probably saved my life a second time. It may have saved it yet again, when I volunteered for the Commandos in the summer of 1942 and again failed a medical for the usual reason.

The Young Soldiers' battalions of the Second World War were, like so much else to do with the Army, fairly pointless institutions. There was a regulation, it may even have been an Act of Parliament, whereby soldiers below a certain age— I think it was nineteen—could not be sent abroad. The political sentimentality of this ukase is self-evident, though one would have thought that the suitability of these youths for active service overseas was a matter better decided by the officers who knew them than by dates on birth certificates. Militarily it meant that no regular battalion could have them on its strength, since it could not leave a percentage of its soldiers behind were it suddenly ordered abroad. Thus they were all put together in these battalions, where they could not learn from one another since none of them knew anything, and where they were supposed to be instructed in military matters by N.C.O.s and officers who usually, like myself, found the assignment boring and unprofitable, for once the young soldiers reached the minimum age limit for service overseas they were transferred elsewhere. We thus had a constant stream of untrained, and on occasion untrainable, recruits passing through our hands. As they were not allowed to be proper soldiers, most of them would have been far better employed elsewhere than in the Army.

Some of the young soldiers were middle-class boys who thought, quite correctly, that service of this sort would hasten their entrance to an Officer Cadet Training Unit and a commission. They were usually promoted corporal rapidly. There was one in my platoon, whom I shall call Corporal Cooper, an amiable young man whom I encountered twenty and more years later on the platform of the Gard du Nord while waiting for the Paris-London train. We were delighted to meet after so long a time and since I had spent all my money in Paris the previous evening I had no hesitation in asking him to cash me a cheque for ten pounds, so that I might buy my share of the champagne on train and boat. As we pulled in to Victoria Corporal Cooper remarked, most amicably:

'I do think I should tell you that I am not a corporal any more. I remained in the Army and am at present a major-general.'

Others were stolid, working-class young men who had simply volunteered for the Army because that was the career of their choice. Many of them, I imagine, ended up as non-commissioned or warrant officers. They should not have been asked to waste their time in this unit, but sent to a proper battalion straight away.

Finally there was also—as in all bodies of volunteer soldiers—a criminal element. Youths who had been had up for assaulting their little sisters, or slashing cinema seats, or coshing tobacconists, would mutter, in the dock, to the magistrate:

'I wanna join the Army.'

The magistrate would then beam with pleasure, tell them they were splendid, patriotic fellows, and we would get them.

They were in the minority, but still constituted a sufficiently numerous minority to give the 70th Battalion something of the nature of a perambulating Borstal. Many of them were near-cretins, which did not make squad instruction any easier, nor did it prevent them from stealing from the other soldiers, flogging their equipment, attempting to rape land girls and on at least one occasion shooting a cow. Some of them were quite funny in a Royal Court Theatre sort of way, but the humour palled almost as rapidly as does that of Osborne's or Wesker's plays, since their anti-social messiness made life so boring and monotonous for everyone else, with constant kit inspections, endless route marches to wear them out, interminable extra disciplinary parades which consumed the spare time of the officers and N.C.O.s. Most depressing of all, the juvenile delinquents clearly derived no pleasure from their dirt and malice.

The officers were not quite so miscellaneous a collection, though they, too, varied from men of the 52nd type to battle-weary Commandos (one of whom once got so angry with an impertinent delinquent that he pinked him with a bayonet) to mild nonentities who vegetated quietly with pipes. All this took place in Northern Ireland, itself a province not designed to dispel depression.

After a brief glance at this new setting into which I had been posted—and the posting gave every evidence of being fairly permanent by army standards, for a 'Young Soldiers' ' battalion in Ulster was in many respects the end of the line—I decided that my first intention, to use military parlance, must be to have Charlotte with me; my second, to get out. By this time, as my experience with Carter had shown, I was becoming moderately good at working the military machine in my own interests and I then thought I was better than I actually was. Any scruples I might once have had about honesty or integrity towards that machine, as opposed to units such as the 52nd, had been totally dispelled. Therefore, though still only a very junior infantry officer, I applied staff officer's technique to seeing how this particular problem might be most expeditiously solved in my own and Charlotte's interest.

It turned out at first glance to be absurdly simple. Officers attached to units such as mine, when stationed in Northern Ireland, were allowed to live in billets with their wives. I had a wife and nobody in the 70th Battalion, or so far as I was aware in Northern Ireland, knew that Charlotte was not she. It all seemed as easy as that. I applied for permission to live in conjugal bliss: granted. I looked for rooms where I was stationed (Donaghadee), found and rented them. I telephoned Charlotte: she bought a ticket to Belfast. This was early December of 1941 and I looked forward to a happy winter of domesticity after dull days with the delinquents and the other Young Soldiers, slippers by the fire, tea-kettle on the hob, books off the shelves, nights in one another's arms, even perhaps writing from time to time. I felt very clever, a sure sign with me, as I now realise, that some dangerous storm is rapidly gathering out of sight and soon to be overhead.

She telephoned me from Liverpool. She was in the office of some port control or emigration official who would not allow her on board the Belfast boat as she was unmarried and had no authorisation to visit Northern Ireland. I told her to inform the official that she was on her way over to marry me. After some time he came on the line himself. He said he needed proof of this statement. I treated him with utter civility and spoke with complete self-confidence. Proof would be forthcoming at once. Meanwhile would he allow her to board the midnight boat? No, not before he had proof from the authorities that she was in fact coming over to marry me. Again I assured him that this would be in his hands, or at least over the telephone, within a matter of hours. Rather reluctantly he agreed to accept telephonic confirmation of the intended marriage and I knew that I had gained a major point. I also realised that I was getting perilously close to committing bigamy, that most English of offences which, as somebody once remarked, is only respectability carried to criminal lengths.

Now I clearly could not go to the military authorities and ask them to commit perjury. I thought of getting a friend to ring up the Liverpool official and pretend to be my battalion adjutant, but then I feared lest that official ring back and thus involve my friend in serious trouble for misrepresentation. So I mounted my motorcycle and drove to a town some twenty miles away where I located the local registrar. By now it was evening and he, fortunately, had had a very good dinner. I, I may say, had had none. Charlotte had now been waiting in Liverpool for many hours. My anxiety on her behalf doubtless enthused my oratory.

I did not tell the red-faced registrar the truth, but I threw myself upon his mercy. I had, I said, made a fool of myself. I had not realised that the banns should have been published before my fiancée might sail across. The poor girl was desperate, as was I. Could he publish the banns at once, this very evening? With an unsteady hand the registrar poured himself a mahogany-coloured whisky and, as an afterthought, one for me as well. Yes, he said, he was always prepared to help star-crossed lovers. Shertainly he'd (hiccup) publish the banns that very minute. He laid a fatherly hand on my shoulder, and now I came to the second part of my complicated and mendacious plan. Shyly, tentatively, I asked him if he could ring the Liverpool official. Shertainly. He got through at once and gave the poor man a thorough dressing down. ('Were you never young yourself (hiccup)? That poor little girlie in your bloody office. Of course I'm gonna marry 'em, just as shoon as you bloody Englishmen shtop interfering with the course of true love.') I was given one for the road and in a cloud of whisky and good wishes drove back like the wind to Donaghadee. I had clearly taken several steps nearer to the abominable crime of bigamy, but Charlotte was on the night boat that would be sailing in a couple of hours.

Back at my battalion headquarters I found the adjutant moodily playing backgammon with the quartermaster, a man for whom he had, as I knew, a marked distaste. I extracted him from his game, gave him a very strong drink, told him that my wife was arriving at dawn next day and asked for an immediate week's leave. He blinked a bit, but steamroller tactics do sometimes work, and after he had had another very large drink—alcohol, whether consumed by myself or others, does not always work to advantage, but this evening it proved a useful and even a powerful ally—he led me to his office, signed my leave papers, gave me travel vouchers, explained that I must wear only civilian clothes in Dublin and, so help us, wished me the best of luck.

The immediate end of this tale of duplicity is simple, the aftermath more complicated. I met Charlotte's boat; we caught the Dublin train and spent a week in that lovely city which neither of us had ever visited before: while there I telephoned the boozy registrar and informed him that we had, in fact, been married in the Republic. (So I never did commit bigamy or indeed any other serious crime.) We returned to Donaghadee, and on the evening of our return the colonel asked us to dinner. His wife asked us:

'And where were you two married?'

Charlotte replied:

'Caxton Hall.'

I replied simultaneously:

'Chelsea Registry Office.'

The subject was changed, and never referred to, either by the colonel or his wife, again.

Now all this may make an amusing tale in retrospect. I do not, and did not, regard my dishonesty as anything but fully justified. Charlotte and I were hurting no one, and were simply outwitting one of 'their' more pointless wartime regulations. (She could have joined me quite legally had my battalion been stationed in Scotland or Wales. Why not, therefore, in Northern Ireland?) What is more, so far as I was concerned it was good practice in that art of internal manoeuvring which one has to acquire if one is to live satisfactorily imbedded in any large and impersonal organisation.

What I did not then realise was that for Charlotte this piece of legerdemain had certain grave disadvantages. In the first place she could not go back to England if she wished ever to return to Ireland, since the operation clearly did not bear repetition. This was not particularly serious, since she was quite happy to remain in Ireland so long as I was stationed there, which, as it happened, was for nearly a further year. Nevertheless she was, in some measure, trapped by duplicity. Furthermore, in an age of dockets and permits, it was impossible for her to get a job in Ireland without revealing her true identity. This was a much more serious matter. As I have said earlier, she was not only a girl who forced herself to overcome a slight natural tendency to sloth but was also and for the most complex reasons intensely patriotic. I was away all day long, wearing out the Young Soldiers. Since we had no children and lived in very modest furnished digs, she was condemned to almost total inactivity, and this bored and worried her. Finally the basic dishonesty of her situation gradually began to get her down. She knew that this was in no way my fault. By English law I could not begin to get a divorce from Margaret—which was what both Margaret and I wished—until October of 1942 and the divorce courts were then so blocked with cases that a further eighteen months must elapse before I could offer Charlotte marriage. In 1941, 1944 seemed an almost impossible distance away. As a young infantry officer I would probably have been posted abroad by then: I might well be dead. Charlotte recognised all this, and since she loved me and knew I loved her, she was prepared to live with me, though to do so was in truth opposed to her basic principles. The result was that tensions were slowly built up within our relationship which ultimately killed it, though I do not believe that either of us was aware of this at the time.

What happened at last was this. When we returned to England in late 1942 Charlotte immediately got herself a job connected with the war. She was asked to work a great deal of overtime, particularly at night, and this she did, though she could have refused. I thus saw less and less of her and began to resent my lonely evenings. So they did not remain lonely for long. Then I was due to get leave and she arranged for a holiday from her job to coincide with my leave. My leave was postponed, but the people for whom she worked refused to give her a similar postponement. I told her she ought to insist and to threaten resignation. This she refused to do and we had our first, last and only real row. She went on her holiday alone. She came back earlier than expected and found me in bed with somebody else. And that was that. I do not feel proud of the way I treated Charlotte, nor have I any excuses to make. She deserved much better than she got from me. I am glad to say she has now got it from her husband, who was for many years one of my very closest friends and for whom I have nothing but admiration and affection.

It was when Charlotte and I were first in Dublin that the Japanese bombed Pearl Harbor and America entered the war. I immediately went to the United States Embassy, which was then located in Phoenix Park, and asked for the military attaché. My reaction was largely instinctive: now that the Americans were also at war, I felt that I belonged with them. Needless to say, the American Embassy, Dublin, was in a state of very considerable turmoil on December 8th, 1941 and the military attaché did not know what to make of my suggestion that I be granted an immediate commission in his army. He referred me to another diplomatist, after having first made a note of my name, unit and address, and this second cooky-pusher informed me coldly and categorically that I had forfeited my American citizenship by joining the British forces. So, my leave over, I made my way back to Ulster and set about escaping from the juvenile delinquents by volunteering for anything available. I have already mentioned the Commandos, who sent me on a rather tough battle course before discovering about my weak eye. Then the Intelligence people turned up again. I was interviewed with the prospect of being turned into an interrogator of captured Germans. (The interview, like all such interviews, was fairly farcical. My friend Auberon Herbert claims that when he was similarly interviewed by Mil. Int. he was asked: 'If two men can sing a song in fifteen minutes, how many songs can eight men sing in twenty-five minutes?') I was accepted for the interrogation course, which took place at Cambridge in the autumn of 1942.

Just before leaving Ireland I received an official communication which informed me, to my very considerable astonishment, that I was to report to American Army headquarters in London with a view to transfer. Charlotte and I therefore packed up all our few possessions: I completed the course at Cambridge, which this time I managed to pass with moderate distinction, and I was given a brief attachment to M.I.3b,

German Order of Battle, in the War Office. The adjutant of the 70th Bn, Ox. and Bucks, was meanwhile sending me angry telegrams telling me to return at once. But these I ignored, for I knew it would be only a matter of days before I was in another army altogether. I was commissioned 1st Lieutenant in the Army of the United States one cold December day of 1942. My pay was immediately increased by precisely threefold.

15

ONE AUGUST EVENING of 1944 I was seated in the G 2 (Intelligence) caravan of General Bradley's tactical head-quarters, in France. The main wall of this caravan was covered by a large map of the Western Front where General Bradley's Twelfth Army Group and Field-Marshal Mont-gomery's Twenty-first Army Group were in the process of defeating and, as we hoped, annihilating the German armies in France. A few days before the United States First Army had broken through the German front in Normandy and Bradley had pushed Patton's Third Army through the gap thus created. Then the Americans had, in part, swung north, to link up with the British and Canadians who were advancing southwards. It seemed possible that we would encircle and capture the whole of the German Seventh Army as well as all the German panzer divisions that still existed in the West. This would have been a victory comparable to the great German victories in France in 1940 and in Russia in 1941 and 1942.

It was my job to keep the G 2 map up to date by marking the position of the German units and formations. Twice a day at least I briefed General Bradley, his principal staff officers and any visiting generals on the latest situation

R

reports. Bradley, being a very good general indeed, did a great deal of his planning in front of the intelligence map: he already knew where his own divisions had got to. Thus, though only a captain, I was privileged to hear a number of most important decisions made and to gain an insight, at the age of twenty-five, into how such decisions are reached.

On the evening in question he arrived, with his staff officers, in excellent spirits. He was a most equably tempered man, very fair and very polite to his subordinates, and never, so far as I could see, ruffled or harassed. This evening he was positively beaming.

'Gentlemen,' he said, 'I have very good news for you indeed. I have just spoken to the Field-marshal on the phone. The Canadians have reached Trun. This means that the German Seventh Army is in the bag. And this, in turn, means that the war will be over this year, maybe this month. With the Russians still in Russia.'

I moved the German pins back behind Trun. No large enemy formation had yet moved out of the pocket which was now, for all intents and purposes, closed. Our victory appeared complete. I began my briefing. And then the telephone rang.

It was Montgomery's Chief of Staff, asking for General Allen, who held the same job at our headquarters. After a moment General Allen said:

'I think you had better speak directly to General Bradley.'

Bradley took the telephone. He grunted once or twice, said:

'I see. Thank you.'

Then he put the telephone down and thought deeply for perhaps as long as half a minute. He walked across to the map. Needless to say, none of the dozen or so officers in the caravan spoke. Then he returned to the telephone, picked it up, and asked to be connected with General Patton at Third Army. He got through at once.

'George—' he began. Then he was cut off. His self-control was icy, his voice as always soft and well modulated. He said:

'I am well aware I've been cut off. This is General Bradley speaking. Can I or can I not speak to General Patton on an American army telephone?'

He was immediately reconnected.

'George,' he began again, 'the Field-Marshal was misinformed again. The Canadians are still twelve miles north of Trun. Don't go north. Go and take Paris.'

He replaced the telephone in its cradle, resumed his seat, turned to me, and said:

'And now please continue with the briefing.'

My first three years in the armies of Britain and the United States had taught me very little. Indeed intellectually this had been, for me, a period of retrogression. What did I read in those days? I have only the haziest recollection of sporadic history and biography—Prescott's *Conquest of Mexico* is a book that remains in my memory from Irish days—and I suspect that in fact I read very little. I wrote a certain amount, again in Ireland, but it is thin, derivative stuff which I have never attempted to have published and never shall. No, intellectually these were barren years, but towards the end of 1943 this took a turn for the better, and in two respects.

The Americans had attached me to an organisation called ETOUSA, which means European Theatre of Operation United States Army. It was located at 20 Grosvenor Square and I was in the G 2 (military intelligence) section concerned with German order of battle. Since ETOUSA was not an operational headquarters this was, for a long time, mere play-acting, but it was also training, for I wrote papers on various subjects and was thus in fairly constant touch with other headquarters, British and American, which had a greater operational reality. I began to see something of what the war was about and how it was being fought.

Then, late in 1943, I was transferred to a new American headquarters. Originally concerned with planning the cross-Channel operation for the following year, it was always intended to become the staff for the commander of American troops in that, the greatest operation of the war. At first we were told that this would be General Marshall, later General Bradley. I was now given access to the most secret forms of intelligence and also to the plans for Operation Neptune (the invasion of Normandy) and Operation Overlord (the campaign to follow). Although the really constructive intelligence work was done at the War Office and elsewhere, I represented the future American army group on certain comparatively high-level intelligence committees. In fact I was in the know, entrusted with secrets of very great importance indeed, and this at the age of twenty-four. I think the reader will agree that had my superiors been able then to read this volume of autobiography they would hardly have shown such confidence either in my discretion or in my military ability. However, and without any pretence at modesty, I can say that I do not believe I let them down in any way, for at last I had been given a job the importance of which I realised and which I found of absorbing interest.

As anyone who has ever been connected with intelligence knows, such work is almost never a matter of making spectacular discoveries but of collating a mass of fragmentary information—some of which has been incorrectly reported, some deliberately created by the enemy in order to mislead—and making of this a mosaic, a meaningful pattern. Pieces of the mosaic will always be missing, but the nature of these can often be deduced from the neighbouring stones and from the nature of the pattern as a whole. Thus scholars, and perhaps particularly archaeologists, are very good at evaluating intelligence. So are artists, whose job is the creation of patterns, the detection of meaning. In my sort of intelligence work, German order of battle, which dealt in great measure with numbered units, a feeling for numbers and the connections between them is also important, since an astonishing amount of information can be deduced, by an educated mind, from what appears the scantiest facts. Although I made only one or two very minor original contributions to the Allied intelligence picture of the German forces before D-day, I derived considerable pleasure, intellectual and even aesthetic, from this work.

Then, both before and after the invasion, I was most interested to see how command is in fact exercised, how power actually functions. Military power in action is probably power at its simplest and most naked, involving little more than the appreciation of a situation, the taking of decisions and the issuing of orders. The higher the head-quarters, of course, the more complex the appreciation and the more important the decision. And I did learn how few are the men who are capable, swiftly and correctly, of both. I daresay my point of view is biased by loyalty to General Bradley, whom I admired immensely both as a man and a general, and so I should like to tell one other anecdote about him which would seem to me to exemplify his courage as a general.

When the United States First Army broke the German front in Normandy, a single bridge was captured intact, at Avranches. That evening, after the intelligence briefing, General Bradley asked his supply chief, a certain General Moses:

'General, how many armoured divisions can you keep supplied over one bridge?'

General Moses replied:

'Two, maybe three. At the most four.'

General Bradley said:

'You'll have to do better than that. I'm putting the whole of Patton's Third Army over that bridge at once.'

And he did, the tanks and trucks carrying gasoline instead of ammunition or food, and they advanced four hundred miles while Field-Marshal Montgomery's armour moved forty, and they would have gone straight into Germany had Eisenhower not cut off their gas in order to allow the leisurely British to catch up.

Eisenhower seldom made decisions. He was a committee man whose primary interest, so far as we could see, was to offend no one, or at least no one in British uniform, and particularly not Winston Churchill. Montgomery made decisions, but we felt at Twelfth Army Group that he lacked intellectual flexibility. It was lucky, we thought, that he was still fighting his old enemy-friend Erwin Rommel in an imaginary Africa. 'They've both got sand in their shoes,' somebody said at the time. 'They don't understand about war in Europe.' And his envy of the great American victories, which showed itself both in rudeness to the American generals and in the mounting of pointless or disastrous 'competitive' campaigns such as Arnhem or his Rhine crossing, certainly did not hasten the Allied victory. Unfortunately in all this Montgomery had the active support of Winston Churchill, with his romantic nineteenth-century ideas of British grandeur, and, at second hand, the passive support of Franklin Roosevelt who, in military matters at least, seems to have been bedazzled by his friend the Former Naval Person and who, from a very different viewpoint, also always regarded the war as running second to his own political ambitions. Bradley did not give a damn for politics. He merely wished to win the war, fast, and his personal ambition was minimal. In my judgments of public men I have always, though usually not consciously, used my opinion of General Bradley's attitude and behaviour as a standard. It is admittedly a very high one.

It was also part of my job to try and gauge the minds, motives and probable reactions of the German commanders and of their political leaders. Later in the war, when I had left General Bradley's staff, I worked in a War Office/War Department organisation where I was entrusted with a study of the German General Staff, its organisation and methods. Originally this was to help our authorities decide whether the German General Staff should be indicted as a criminal organisation. I was glad when that nonsensical piece of vengeful injustice was dropped and I hope that my work may have contributed in some small measure to this decision. Later still, after the war was over, I edited a book on the German General Staff, written by staff officer prisoners of war at Camp Ritchie, in Maryland. This book was not intended for publication but was supposed to be of help in training and re-organising the British and American general staffs. Whether it did so or not I cannot say, for I had left the Army before it was printed. However these studies of the German General Staff and of the German military mind gave me some of the background knowledge which later enabled me to write my history of the German resistance to Hitler.

With the French I only came into contact twice (save that I absented myself without leave for one day and attached myself to General Leclerc's Deuxième Blindée in the hope of entering Paris; alas, we got no further than the Porte d'Orléans that day. But at least I did see a few naked girls dancing on top of tanks, and was given a glass of *porto* by a French middle-class couple whose son was a prisoner in Germany. They had hung out a home-made American flag and they had promised themselves that they would give the *porto* to the first American soldier they saw, who happened to be me. The *porto* was delicious. So was the flag, which consisted of forty-eight stripes and thirteen stars).

My two contacts with French generals were occasions of folly, one of my doing and one General de Gaulle's.

The first occasion was in August of 1944. The Vichy regime disposed of a small military force known as the Premier Régiment de France, which was anxious to surrender to us. Its colonel, together with a Vichy general and his adjutant, would be arriving at Bradley's headquarters at 10.30 a.m. for the small surrender ceremony. Unfortunately Bradley would be out, as would my intelligence general and my colonel. I was told to treat the French with courtesy but nothing more, to remember that they were traitors, to lock them up in a tent with a sentry outside, to give them no food or drink, to answer no questions or grant any requests, and to leave them there until my superiors returned. They duly arrived and I did as I had been told. They stood about in the unfurnished tent all day. It was a very hot day too. Unfortunately, though, they were not from the Premier Régiment de France. They were General Noiret, who was then de Gaulle's Chief of Staff, and two other Free French officers. When I apologised to General Noiret he roared with laughter and was good enough to say that had he been me he would have made exactly the same mistake and have behaved precisely as I had done.

A little later General de Gaulle came to see General Bradley. General de Gaulle cannot, or at least will not, speak English. General Bradley cannot, or could not in those days, speak French. The French officer-interpreter had somehow been mislaid en route and at General Bradley's very small tactical headquarters I was the only officer available really fluent in both languages. So I was produced. De Gaulle took one look at me, a captain, and announced that he could not have as interpreter an officer of less than field rank. Instead of promoting me on the spot, an American colonel was sent for who, as I knew, could really speak no French at all. (He had once asked me what was the French for cognac.) How the two great men got on, and what ideas were exchanged with him as medium, I do not know. But then they had presumably almost nothing to say to one another.

Two final military reminiscences. While I was in France that autumn, my second wife, Theodora, was in London, though she often visited my mother at Church House, Hurley, The V-1s, pilotless planes or flying bombs, had been falling on London since June, but these did not worry her. Now the V-2s, or rockets, were added, and these did worry me, because I knew something about atomic energy and our scientific intelligence people then believed that the Germans were far closer to making an atom bomb than in fact they were. Furthermore the V-2 was regarded by our scientists as so expensive to produce and to fuel that it made little military sense unless it were intended to carry a nuclear warhead. Therefore the logical conclusion was that they were merely ranging with H.E., merely getting the bugs out of the beastly rockets, and that once this had been done they would put something very much livelier into them, and London would be destroyed.

Now at this time the atom bomb was the war's number one secret. I could not write to Theo why I wished her to stay out of London: I could only say that her being there frightened me. I could not even hint at a possible, more appalling weapon. And she replied airily that neither the bombs nor the rockets frightened her in the slightest—which I knew was the case—and that though she appreciated my concern she really saw no need for me to worry. Thus there are times, such as this, when the possession of knowledge is not power at all.

The other incident took place many months later, when

I was once again stationed in London, working on my study of the German General Staff. When I read of the dropping of the first atomic bomb on Hiroshima this seemed to me an act of such wanton brutality and political folly that I wrote a letter to the President of the United States asking that I be allowed to resign my commission. I sent this through channels, and have not yet received a reply.

Much earlier in this chapter I said that in the autumn of 1943 my life—my intellectual life for lack of a better word—took a turn for the better in two ways. The United States Army gave me an interesting job to do and paid me a living wage for doing it. And my private life, by which I mean everything that was not directly concerned with the Army, was taken over—again I cannot think of a better phrase—by Theodora.

When I met her she was known as Tony, though like most English girls her name was really Joan, which, for reasons which will not escape connoisseurs of middle-class English girlhood, she preferred to spell Joanne. I did not care for any of these names, none of which was remotely suited to her strong, bohemian personality, her blonde and classical beauty or her efficient and yet easy-going attitude. I therefore decided that henceforth she would be called Theodora, or Theo for short, and so she has been ever since, though we have now been divorced for seven years.

In those distant days she was living with a photographer of my acquaintance named Peter Rose Pulham—he had been a very good photographer indeed, and my sister Mimi had modelled for him before the war—who had decided that photography was vulgar and that he ought to be a painter. Unfortunately he was not nearly as good a painter as he had been a photographer and therefore made no money. Lots of painters in those days who objected to military service were in the fire service, and he was too. He was a charming man, extremely well read, highly entertaining company, and I think just about the most snobbish person I have ever met. In order to support them in their Chelsea flat, Theo, who had once aspired to be an actress and who, to prove this,

265

used occasionally to produce a dog-eared playbill for a play called *Gentlemen's Relish* in which she said she had appeared under yet another name, Karen Petersen, had obtained work in a dress-shop run by two German gentlemen named Herr Treitel and Herr Meyer. She decided that she would rather live with me, in my Chelsea flat, which was far less grand than Peter's of course, but we remained good friends of his both then and later. Alas, he died of hunger—in France, of course, in a château, of course, in the middle 1950s—though snobbery was the real cause of his premature death.

As for Herrn Treitel and Meyer, I had no trouble at all in persuading her to sever her connection with them. We then acquired, on a lease, a pretty little house in Godfrey Street where we lived a happy life with a large poodle called Mouche, occasionally harbouring a girl-friend of Theo's named Sophie (real name also Joan) who was usually in a state of desertion from the Royal Artillery. While I was away in Grosvenor Square Theo scrubbed our little house with something called Gumption and prepared delicious and by wartime standards enormous meals. (She was and is a superb cook: her cookery books, all written many years later, are proof of this, and do not need my commendation.) In the evenings we went to the pubs, and so did our friends. Not only did we like going to pubs, but also, in these end-of-war years, there was no way of taking drink home. In the wartime Chelsea pubs I picked up again, largely through Theo, those contacts with the world of painting and writing which I had lost during my last few grim years in the British Army.

I have attempted to describe that Chelsea pub life during the years between 1943 and 1946 in my *Life of Dylan Thomas* and also, in some measure, in my first novel *The Arabian Bird*. In essence, however, it defies description. I and my friends were not linked by any mutual philosophy or even view of the world as 'Bloomsbury' seems to have been in earlier years or the Communist intellectuals were in the 1930s. We were, I think, all interested in the arts, which we probably regarded as more important than any other form of human activity, and some of us were interested in ideas as well, but these interests were utterly disparate. What was there in common between, say, Norman Douglas and Vernon Watkins other than a passionate concern for the best use of the English language? What between Sir Francis Rose and Robert Newton, save that each was totally dedicated to his own art?

Many years later, when yet another marriage of mine was on the rocks and I was writing my biography of Dylan, I telephoned Theo to whom I had then not spoken for several years. I wished to ask her about myself and my own character, but hesitated to do so. Instead I asked her about Dylan and our other friends. What had happened to us all? I said, Why were so many of us dead or alcoholics or old before our time? With characteristic largesse she replied at once:

'When I first met you, Constantine, in Chelsea during the war, you and your friends wanted to drink all the drinks, sleep with all the girls, paint all the pictures, act in all the plays, write all the poems, *and* beat the Germans. And you did. Are you really surprised?'

And that must be the epitaph to this book and to the life of the young man I once was. Before even I had left the Army I had begun to write my first novel. I have been writing ever since. And, as is the case with most other writers, if there is anything that is of interest to others in my post-war life, then it can only be what is written in those books.

Ros-Cairbre, 1966